The Machine Learning Solutions Architect Handbook

Create machine learning platforms to run solutions in an enterprise setting

David Ping

BIRMINGHAM—MUMBAI

The Machine Learning Solutions Architect Handbook

Publishing Product Manager: Reshma Raman
Senior Editor: Mohammed Yusuf Imaratwale
Content Development Editor: Sean Lobo
Technical Editor: Devanshi Ayare
Copy Editor: Safis Editing
Project Coordinator: Aparna Ravikumar Nair
Proofreader: Safis Editing
Indexer: Pratik Shirodkar
Production Designer: Shankar Kalbhor

First published: January 2022

Production reference: 3090322

Published by Packt Publishing Ltd.
Livery Place
35 Livery Street
Birmingham
B3 2PB, UK.

ISBN 978-1-80107-216-8

www.packt.com

Contributors

About the author

David Ping is a senior technology leader with over 25 years of experience in the technology and financial services industry. His technology focus areas include cloud architecture, enterprise ML platform design, large-scale model training, intelligent document processing, intelligent media processing, intelligent search, and data platforms. He currently leads an AI/ML solutions architecture team at AWS, where he helps global companies design and build AI/ML solutions in the AWS cloud. Before joining AWS, David held various senior technology leadership roles at Credit Suisse and JPMorgan. He started his career as a software engineer at Intel. David has an engineering degree from Cornell University.

About the reviewers

Kamesh Ganesan is a cloud evangelist, a seasoned technology professional, an author, and a leader with over 24 years of IT experience in all major cloud technologies, including AWS, Azure, GCP, Oracle, and Alibaba Cloud. He has over 50 IT certifications, including many cloud certifications. He has played many roles and architected and delivered mission-critical and innovative technology solutions that helped his enterprise, commercial, and government clients to be very successful. He has authored AWS and Azure books and has reviewed many IT/cloud technology books and courses.

A special thanks to my wife, Hemalatha, for her constant support, and thanks to my kids, Sachin and Arjun, for their love. Also, my parents for their unwavering encouragement throughout my life.

Simon Zamarin is an AI/ML specialist solution architect at AWS. He has over 5 years of experience in data science, engineering, and analytics. His main focus as a specialist solutions architect is on helping customers get the most value out of their data assets.

Giuseppe Angelo Porcelli is a principal machine learning specialist solutions architect at Amazon Web Services. With multiple years of experience in software engineering, software and system architecture, and machine learning, Giuseppe helps businesses of any size and industry design solutions that use ML to solve the most challenging problems. Currently, his areas of specialization are ML architecture, ML industrialization, and MLOps; he is also passionate about product development and SaaS. Giuseppe holds several AWS certifications, including AWS Machine Learning Specialty and AWS Solution Architect Professional. In his spare time, he enjoys skiing and playing football with friends, and taking care of his two lovely young boys.

Vishakha Gupta is a data scientist at one of the world's largest healthcare organizations, a Fortune 5 company. She has postgraduate degree (B.Tech. and M.Tech.) from IIIT Gwalior in information technology with majors in data science. She has previously been part of organizations such as Nasdaq and BNY Mellon. She is a multi-skilled learner and has excelled in various domains of data science and web technology. Her work involves the research and development of enterprise-level solutions based on machine learning, deep learning, and natural language processing for healthcare - and insurance-related use cases. Her latest published IEEE research work is on speech prediction through mute videos.

Table of Contents

Section 2: The Science, Tools, and Infrastructure Platform for Machine Learning

3
Machine Learning Algorithms

4
Data Management for Machine Learning

5
Open Source Machine Learning Libraries

6

Kubernetes Container Orchestration Infrastructure Management

Section 3: Technical Architecture Design and Regulatory Considerations for Enterprise ML Platforms

7

Open Source Machine Learning Platforms

8

Building a Data Science Environment Using AWS ML Services

9

Building an Enterprise ML Architecture with AWS ML Services

12
Building ML Solutions with AWS AI Services

Index

Other Books You May Enjoy

Preface

As artificial intelligence and **machine learning (ML)** become increasingly prevalent in many industries, there is an increasing demand for ML solutions architects who can translate business needs into ML solutions and design ML technology platforms. This book is designed to help people learn ML concepts, algorithms, system architecture patterns, and ML tools to solve business and technical challenges, with an emphasis on large-scale ML systems architecture and operations in an enterprise setting.

The book first introduces ML and business fundamentals, such as the types of ML, business use cases, and ML algorithms. It then dives deep into data management for ML and the various AWS services for building a data management architecture for ML.

After the data management deep dive, the book focuses on two technical approaches to building ML platforms: using open source technologies such as Kubernetes, Kubeflow, MLflow, and Seldon Core, and the use of managed ML services such as Amazon SageMaker, Step Functions, and CodePipeline.

The book then gets into advanced ML engineering topics, including distributed model training and low-latency model serving to meet large-scale model training and high-performance model serving requirements.

Governance and privacy are important considerations for running models in production. In this book, I also cover ML governance requirements and how an ML platform can support ML governance in areas such as documentation, model inventory, bias detection, model explainability, and model privacy.

Building ML-powered solutions do not always require building ML models or infrastructure from scratch. In the book's last chapter, I will introduce AWS AI services and the problems that AI services can help solve. You will learn the core capabilities of some AI services and where you can use them for building ML-powered business applications.

By the end of this book, you will understand the various business, data science, and technology domains of ML solutions and infrastructure. You will be able to articulate the architecture patterns and considerations for building enterprise ML platforms and develop hands-on skills with various open source and AWS technologies. This book can also help you prepare for ML architecture-related job interviews.

Who this book is for

This book is designed for two primary audiences: developers and cloud architects who are looking for guidance and hands-on learning materials to become ML solutions architects, and experienced ML architecture practitioners and data scientists who are looking to develop a broader understanding of industry ML use cases, enterprise data and ML architecture patterns, data management and ML tools, ML governance, and advanced ML engineering techniques.

This book can also benefit data engineers and cloud system administrators looking to understand how data management and cloud system architecture fit into the overall ML platform architecture.

This book assumes you have some Python programming knowledge and are familiar with AWS services. Some of the chapters are designed for ML beginners to learn the core ML fundamentals, and they might overlap with the knowledge already possessed by experienced ML practitioners.

What this book covers

Chapter 1, *Machine Learning and Machine Learning Solutions Architecture*, introduces the core concepts of ML and the ML solutions architecture function.

Chapter 2, *Business Use Cases for Machine Learning*, talks about the core business fundamentals, workflows, and common ML use cases in financial services, media entertainment, health care, manufacturing, and retail.

Chapter 3, *Machine Learning Algorithms*, introduces common ML and deep learning algorithms for classification, regression, clustering, time series, recommendations, computer vision, natural language processing, and data generation. You will get hands-on experience of setting up a Jupyter server and building ML models on your local machine.

Chapter 4, *Data Management for Machine Learning*, covers platform capabilities, system architecture, and AWS tools for building data management capabilities for ML. You will develop hands-on skills with AWS services for building data management pipelines for ML.

Chapter 5, Open Source Machine Learning Libraries, covers the core features of scikit-learn, Spark ML, and TensorFlow, and how to use these ML libraries for data preparation, model training, and model serving. You will practice building deep learning models using TensorFlow and PyTorch.

Chapter 6, Kubernetes Container Orchestration Infrastructure Management, introduces containers, Kubernetes concepts, Kubernetes networking, and Kubernetes security. Kubernetes is a core open source infrastructure for building open source ML solutions. You will also practice setting up the Kubernetes platform on AWS EKS and deploying an ML workload in Kubernetes.

Chapter 7, Open Source Machine Learning Platform, talks about the core concepts and the technical details of various open source ML platform technologies, such as Kubeflow, MLflow, AirFlow, and Seldon Core. The chapter also covers how to use these technologies to build a data science environment and ML automation pipeline, and provides you with instructions to develop hands-on experience with these open source technologies.

Chapter 8, Building a Data Science Environment Using AWS Services, introduces various AWS managed services for building data science environments, including Amazon SageMaker, Amazon ECR, and Amazon CodeCommit. You will also get hands-on experience with these services to configure a data science environment for experimentation and model training.

Chapter 9, Building an Enterprise ML Architecture with AWS ML Services, talks about the core requirements for an enterprise ML platform, discusses the architecture patterns for building an enterprise ML platform on AWS, and dives deep into the various core ML capabilities of SageMaker and other AWS services. You will also learn MLOps and monitoring architecture with a hands-on exercise using sample ML pipelines for model training and model deployment.

Chapter 10, Advanced ML Engineering, covers core concepts and technologies for large-scale distributed model training, such as data parallel and model parallel model training using DeepSpeed and PyTorch DistributeDataParallel. It also dives deep into the technical approaches for low-latency model inference, such as using hardware acceleration, model optimization, and graph and operator optimization. You will also get hands on with distributed data parallel models training using a SageMaker training cluster.

Chapter 11, ML Governance, Bias, Explainability, and Privacy, discusses the ML governance, bias, explainability, and privacy requirements and capabilities for production model deployment. You will also learn techniques for bias detection, explainability, and ML privacy with hands-on exercises using SageMaker Clarify and PyTorch Opacus.

Chapter 12, Building ML Solutions with AWS AI Services, introduces AWS AI services and architecture patterns for incorporating these AI services into ML-powered business applications.

To get the most out of this book

Here is a list of the hardware/software requirements for the book:

Software/hardware covered in the book	Operating system requirements
Angular 9	Windows, macOS, or Linux
TypeScript 3.7	
ECMAScript 11	

If you are using the digital version of this book, we advise you to type the code yourself or access the code from the book's GitHub repository (a link is available in the next section). Doing so will help you avoid any potential errors related to the copying and pasting of code.

Download the example code files

You can download the example code files for this book from GitHub at `https://github.com/PacktPublishing/The-Machine-Learning-Solutions-Architect-Handbook`. If there's an update to the code, it will be updated in the GitHub repository.

We also have other code bundles from our rich catalog of books and videos available at `https://github.com/PacktPublishing/`. Check them out!

Download the color images

We also provide a PDF file that has color images of the screenshots and diagrams used in this book. You can download it here: `https://static.packt-cdn.com/downloads/9781801072168_ColorImages.pdf`.

Conventions used

There are a number of text conventions used throughout this book.

`Code in text`: Indicates code words in text, database table names, folder names, filenames, file extensions, pathnames, dummy URLs, user input, and Twitter handles. Here is an example: "Mount the downloaded `WebStorm-10*.dmg` disk image file as another disk in your system."

A block of code is set as follows:

```
import pandas as pd
churn_data = pd.read_csv("churn.csv")
churn_data.head()
```

When we wish to draw your attention to a particular part of a code block, the relevant lines or items are set in bold:

```
# The following command calculates the various statistics
for the features.
churn_data.describe()
# The following command displays the histograms for the
different features.
# You can replace the column names to plot the histograms
for other features
churn_data.hist(['CreditScore', 'Age', 'Balance'])
# The following command calculate the correlations among
features
churn_data.corr()
```

Any command-line input or output is written as follows:

```
! pip3 install --upgrade tensorflow
```

Bold: Indicates a new term, an important word, or words that you see on screen. For instance, words in menus or dialog boxes appear in **bold**. Here is an example: An example of a deep learning-based solution is the **Amazon Echo virtual assistant**.

> **Tips or Important Notes**
> Appear like this.

Get in touch

Feedback from our readers is always welcome.

General feedback: If you have questions about any aspect of this book, email us at customercare@packtpub.com and mention the book title in the subject of your message.

Errata: Although we have taken every care to ensure the accuracy of our content, mistakes do happen. If you have found a mistake in this book, we would be grateful if you would report this to us. Please visit www.packtpub.com/support/errata and fill in the form.

Piracy: If you come across any illegal copies of our works in any form on the internet, we would be grateful if you would provide us with the location address or website name. Please contact us at copyright@packt.com with a link to the material.

If you are interested in becoming an author: If there is a topic that you have expertise in and you are interested in either writing or contributing to a book, please visit authors.packtpub.com.

Share Your Thoughts

Once you've read *The Machine Learning Solutions Architect Handbook*, we'd love to hear your thoughts! Scan the QR code below to go straight to the Amazon review page for this book and share your feedback.

https://packt.link/r/1-801-07216-7

Your review is important to us and the tech community and will help us make sure we're delivering excellent quality content.

Section 1: Solving Business Challenges with Machine Learning Solution Architecture

In *Section 1*, you will learn about some of the core machine learning fundamentals, its challenges, and how machine learning can be applied to real-world business problems, to set the context for the rest of the book.

This section comprises the following chapters:

- *Chapter 1, Machine Learning and Machine Learning Solutions Architecture*
- *Chapter 2, Business Use Cases for Machine Learning*

1
Machine Learning and Machine Learning Solutions Architecture

The field of **artificial intelligence** (**AI**) and **machine learning** (**ML**) has had a long history. Over the last 70+ years, ML has evolved from checker game-playing computer programs in the 1950s to advanced AI capable of beating the human world champion in the game of *Go*. Along the way, the technology infrastructure for ML has also evolved from a single machine/server for small experiments and models to highly complex end-to-end ML platforms capable of training, managing, and deploying tens of thousands of ML models. The hyper-growth in the AI/ML field has resulted in the creation of many new professional roles, such as **MLOps engineering**, **ML product management**, and **ML software engineering** across a range of industries.

Machine learning solutions architecture (**ML solutions architecture**) is another relatively new discipline that is playing an increasingly critical role in the full end-to-end ML life cycle as ML projects become increasingly complex in terms of *business impact*, *science sophistication*, and the *technology landscape*.

This chapter talks about the basic concepts of ML and where ML solutions architecture fits in the full data science life cycle. You will learn the three main types of ML, including **supervised**, **unsupervised**, and **reinforcement** learning. We will discuss the different steps it will take to get an ML project from the ideas stage to production and the challenges faced by organizations when implementing an ML initiative. Finally, we will finish the chapter by briefly discussing the core focus areas of ML solutions architecture, including system architecture, workflow automation, and security and compliance.

Upon completing this chapter, you should be able to identify the three main ML types and what type of problems they are designed to solve. You will understand the role of an ML solutions architect and what business and technology areas you need to focus on to support end-to-end ML initiatives.

In this chapter, we are going to cover the following main topics:

- What is ML, and how does it work?
- The ML life cycle and its key challenges
- What is ML solutions architecture, and where does it fit in the overall life cycle?

What are AI and ML?

AI can be defined as a machine demonstrating intelligence similar to that of human natural intelligence, such as distinguishing different types of flowers through vision, understanding languages, or driving cars. Having AI capability does not necessarily mean a system has to be powered only by ML. An AI system can also be powered by other techniques, such as rule-based engines. ML is a form of AI that learns how to perform a task using different learning techniques, such as learning from examples using historical data or learning by trial and error. An example of ML would be making credit decisions using an ML algorithm with access to historical credit decision data.

Deep learning (**DL**) is a subset of ML that uses a large number of artificial neurons (known as an **artificial neural network**) to learn, which is similar to how a human brain learns. An example of a deep learning-based solution is the **Amazon Echo virtual assistant**. To better understand how ML works, let's first talk about the different approaches taken by machines to learn. They are as follows:

- **Supervised ML**
- **Unsupervised machine learning**
- **Reinforcement learning**

Let's have a look at each one of them in detail.

Supervised ML

Supervised ML is a type of ML where, when training an ML model, an ML algorithm is provided with the input data features (for example, the size and zip code of houses) and the answers, also known as **labels** (for example, the prices of the houses). A dataset with labels is called a **labeled dataset**. You can think of supervised ML as learning by example. To understand what this means, let's use an example of how we humans learn to distinguish different objects. Say you are first provided with a number of pictures of different flowers and their names. You are then told to study the characteristics of the flowers, such as the shape, size, and color for each provided flower name. After you have gone through a number of different pictures for each flower, you are then given flower pictures without the names and asked to distinguish them. Based on what you have learned previously, you should be able to tell the names of flowers if they have the characteristics of the known flowers.

In general, the more training pictures with variations you have looked at during the learning time, the more accurate you will likely be when you try to name flowers in the new pictures. Conceptually, this is how supervised ML works. The following figure (*Figure 1.1*) shows a labeled dataset being fed into a computer vision algorithm to train an ML model:

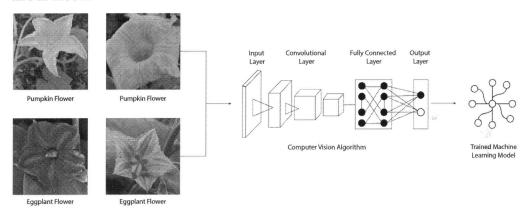

Figure 1.1 – Supervised ML

Supervised ML is mainly used for classification tasks that assign a label from a discrete set of categories to an example (for example, telling the names of different objects) and regression tasks that predict a continuous value (for example, estimating the value of something given supporting information). In the real world, the majority of ML solutions are based on supervised ML techniques. The following are some examples of ML solutions that use supervised ML:

- Classifying documents into different document types automatically, as part of a document management workflow. The typical business benefits of ML-based document processing are the reduction of manual effort, which reduces costs, faster processing time, and higher processing quality.

- Assessing the sentiment of news articles to help understand the market perception of a brand or product or facilitate investment decisions.

- Automating the objects or faces detection in images as part of a media image processing workflow. The business benefits this delivers are cost-saving from the reduction of human labor, faster processing, and higher accuracy.

- Predicting the probability that someone will default on a bank loan. The business benefits this delivers are faster decision-making on loan application reviews and approvals, lower processing costs, and a reduced impact on a company's financial statement due to loan defaults.

Unsupervised ML

Unsupervised ML is a type of ML where an ML algorithm is provided with input data features without labels. Let's continue with the flower example, however in this case, you are now only provided with the pictures of the flowers and not their names. In this scenario, you will not be able to figure out the names of the flowers, regardless of how much time you spend looking at the pictures. However, through visual inspection, you should be able to identify the common characteristics (for example, color, size, and shape) of different types of flowers across the pictures, and group flowers with common characteristics in the same group.

This is similar to how unsupervised ML works. Specifically, in this particular case, you have performed the **clustering** task in unsupervised ML:

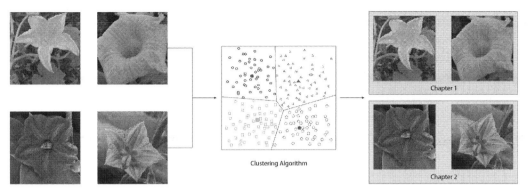

Figure 1.2 – Unsupervised ML

In addition to the clustering technique, there are many other techniques in unsupervised ML. Another common and useful unsupervised ML technique is **dimensionality reduction**, where a smaller number of transformed features represent the original set of features while maintaining the critical information from the original features so that they can be largely reproduced in the number of data dimensions and size. To understand this more intuitively, let's take a look at *Figure 1.3*:

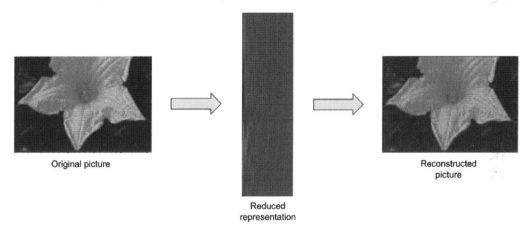

Figure 1.3 – Reconstruction of an image from reduced features

In this figure, the original picture on the left is transformed to the reduced representation in the middle. While the reduced representation does not look like the original picture at all, it still maintains the critical information about the original picture, so that when the picture on the right is reconstructed using the reduced representation, the reconstructed image looks almost the same as the original picture. The process that transforms the original picture to the reduced representation is called dimensionality reduction.

The main benefits of dimensionality reduction are reduction of the training dataset and that it helps speed up the model training. Dimensionality reduction also helps visualize high dimensional datasets in lower dimensions (for example, reducing the dataset to three dimensions to be plotted and visually inspected).

Unsupervised ML is mainly used for recognizing underlying patterns within a dataset. Since unsupervised learning is not provided with actual labels to learn from, its predictions have greater uncertainties than predictions using the supervised ML approach. The following are some real-life examples of unsupervised ML solutions:

- **Customer segmentation for target marketing**: This is done by using customer attributes such as demographics and historical engagement data. The data-driven customer segmentation approach is usually more accurate than human judgment, which can be biased and subjective.

- **Computer network intrusion detection**: This is done by detecting outlier patterns that are different from normal network traffic patterns. Detecting anomalies in network traffic manually and rule-based processing is extremely challenging due to the high volume and changing dynamics of traffic patterns.

- **Reducing the dimensions of datasets**: This is done to visualize them in a 2D or 3D environment to help understand the data better and more easily.

Reinforcement learning

Reinforcement learning is a type of ML where an ML model learns by trying out different actions and adjusts its future behaviors sequentially based on the received response from the action. For example, suppose you are playing a space invader video game for the first time without knowing the game's rules. In that case, you will initially try out different actions randomly using the controls, such as moving left and right or shooting the canon. As different moves are made, you will see responses to your moves, such as getting killed or killing the invader, and you will also see your score increase or decrease. Through these responses, you will know what a good move is versus a bad move in order to stay alive and increase your score. After much trial and error, you will eventually be a very good player of the game. This is basically how reinforcement learning works.

A very popular example of reinforcement learning is the AlphaGo computer program, which uses mainly reinforcement learning to learn how to play the game of Go. Figure 1.4 shows the flow of reinforcement learning where an agent (for example, the player of a space invader game) takes actions (for example, moving the left/right control) in the environment (for example, the current state of the game) and receives rewards or penalties (score increase/decrease). As a result, the agent will adjust its future moves to maximize the rewards in the future states of the environment. This cycle continues for a very large number of rounds, and the agent will improve and become better over time:

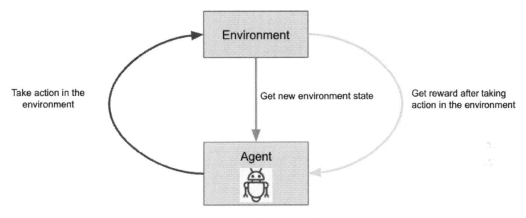

Figure 1.4 – Reinforcement learning

There are many practical use cases for reinforcement learning in the real world. The following are some examples for reinforcement learning:

- Robots or self-driving cars learn how to walk or navigate in unknown environments by trying out different moves and responding to the received results.

- A recommendation engine optimizes product recommendations through adjustments based on the feedback of the customers to different product recommendations.

- A truck delivery company optimizes the delivery route of its fleet to determine the delivery sequence required to achieve the best rewards, such as the lowest cost or shortest time.

ML versus traditional software

Before I started working in the field of AI/ML, I spent many years building computer software platforms for large financial services institutions. Some of the business problems I worked on had complex rules, such as identifying companies for comparable analysis for investment banking deals, or creating a master database for all the different companies' identifiers from the different data providers. We had to implement hardcoded rules in database stored procedures and application server backends to solve these problems. We often debated if certain rules made sense or not for the business problems we tried to solve. As rules changed, we had to reimplement the rules and make sure the changes did not break anything. To test for new releases or changes, we often replied to human experts to exhaustively test and validate all the business logic implemented before the production release. It was a very time-consuming and error-prone process and required a significant amount of engineering, testing against the documented specification, and rigorous change management for deployment every time new rules were introduced, or existing rules needed to be changed. We often relied to users to report business logic issues in production, and when an issue was reported in production, we sometimes had to open up the source code to troubleshoot or explain the logic of how it worked. I remember I often asked myself if there were better ways to do this.

After I started working in the field of AI/ML, I started to solve many similar challenges using ML techniques. With ML, I did not need to come up with complex rules that often require deep data and domain expertise to create or maintain the complex rules for decision making. Instead, I focused on collecting high-quality data and used ML algorithms to learn the rules and patterns from the data directly. This new approach eliminated many of the challenging aspects of creating new rules (for example, a deep domain expertise requirement, or avoiding human bias) and maintaining existing rules. To validate the model before the production release, we could examine model performance metrics such as **accuracy**. While it still required data science expertise to interpret the model metrics against the nature of the business problems and dataset, it did not require exhaustive manual testing of all the different scenarios. When a model was deployed into production, we would monitor if the model performed as expected by monitoring any significant changes in production data versus the data we have collected for model training. We would collect new labels for production data and test the model performance periodically to ensure its predictive power had not degraded. To explain why a model made a decision the way it did, we did not need to open up source code to re-examine the hardcoded logic. Instead, we would rely on ML techniques to help explain the relative importance of different input features to understand what factors were most influential in the decision-making by the ML models.

The following figure (*Figure 1.5*) shows a graphical view of the process differences between developing a piece of software and training an ML model:

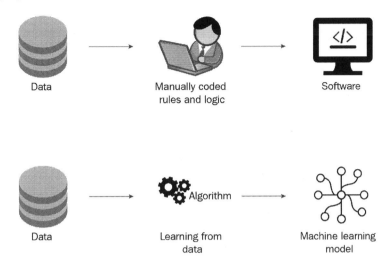

Figure 1.5 – ML and computer software

Now that you know the difference between ML and traditional software, it is time to dive deep into understanding the different stages in an ML life cycle.

ML life cycle

One of the first ML projects that I worked on was a sport predictive analytics problem for a major sports league brand. I was given a list of predictive analytics outcomes to think about to see if there were ML solutions for the problems. I was a casual viewer of the sports; I didn't know anything about the analytics to be generated, nor the rules of the games in detail. I was given some sample data, but I had no idea what to do with it.

The first thing I started to work on was to learn the sport. I studied things like how the games were played, the different player positions, and how to determine and identify certain events. Only after acquiring the relevant domain knowledge did the data start to make sense to me. I then discussed the impact of the different analytics outcomes with the stakeholders and assessed the modeling feasibility based on the data we had. We came up with a couple of top ML analytics with the most business impact to work on, decided how they would be integrated into the existing business workflow, and how they would be measured on their impacts.

I then started to inspect and explore the data in closer detail to understand what information was available and what was missing. I processed and prepared the dataset based on a couple of ML algorithms I was thinking about using and carried out different experiments. I did not have a tool to track the different experiment results, so I had to track what I have done manually. After some initial rounds of experimentation, I felt the existing data was not enough to train a high-performance model, and I needed to build a custom deep learning model to incorporate data of different modalities. The data owner was able to provide additional datasets I looked for, and after more experiments with custom algorithms and significant data preparations and feature engineering, I was able to train a model that met the business needs.

After that, the hard part came – to deploy and operationalize the model in production and integrate it into the existing business workflow and system architecture. We went through many architecture and engineering discussions and eventually built out a deployment architecture for the model.

As you can see from my personal experience, there are many different steps in taking a business idea or expected business outcome from ideation to production deployment. Now, let's formally review a typical life cycle of an ML project. A formal ML life cycle includes steps such as business understanding, data acquisition and understanding, data preparation, model building, model evaluation, and model deployment. Since a big component of the life cycle is experimentation with different datasets, features, and algorithms, the whole process can be highly iterative. In addition, there is no guarantee that a working model can be created at the end of the process. Factors such as the availability and quality of data, feature engineering techniques (the process of using domain knowledge to extract useful features from raw data), and the capability of the learning algorithms, among others, can all prevent a successful outcome.

The following figure shows the key steps in ML projects:

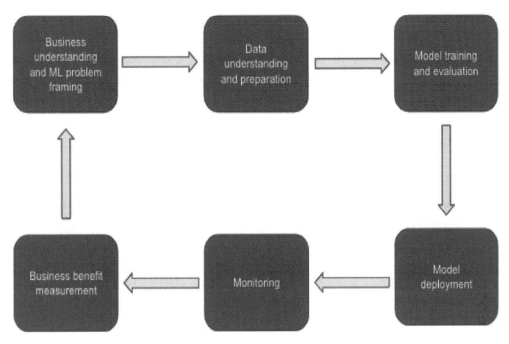

Figure 1.6 – ML life cycle

In the next few sections, we will discuss each of these steps in greater detail.

Business understanding and ML problem framing

The first step in the life cycle is the **business understanding** step. In this step, you would need to develop a clear understanding of the business goals and define the business performance metrics that can be used to measure the success of the ML project. The following are some examples of business goals:

- Cost reduction for operational processes, such as document processing.

- Mitigation of business or operational risks, such as fraud and compliance.

- Product or service revenue improvements, such as better target marketing, new insight generation for better decision making, and increased customer satisfaction

Specific examples of business metrics for measurement could be the number of hours reduced in a business process, an increased number of true positive fraud instances detected, a conversion rate improvement from target marketing, or the extent of churn rate reductions. This is a very important step to get right to ensure there is sufficient justification for an ML project and that the outcome of the project can be successfully measured.

After the business goals and business metrics are defined, you then need to determine if the business problem can be solved using an ML solution. While ML has a wide scope of applications, it does not mean it can solve all business problems.

Data understanding and data preparation

There is a saying that data is the new oil, and this is especially true for ML. Without the required data, you cannot move forward with an ML project. That's why the next step in the ML life cycle is **data acquisition**, **understanding**, and **preparation**.

Based on the business problems and ML approach, you will need to gather and understand the available data to determine if you have the right data and data volume to solve the ML problem. For example, suppose the business problem to address is credit card fraud detection. In that case, you will need datasets such as historical credit card transaction data, customer demographics, account data, device usage data, and networking access data. Detailed data analysis is then needed to determine if the dataset features and quality are sufficient for the modeling tasks. You also need to decide if the data needs labeling, such as `fraud` or `not-fraud`. During this step, depending on the data quality, a significant amount of data wrangling might be performed to prepare and clean the data and to generate the dataset for model training and model evaluation.

Model training and evaluation

Using the training and validation datasets created, a data scientist will need to run a number of experiments using different ML algorithms and dataset features for feature selection and model development. This is a highly iterative process and could require a large number of data processing and model development runs to find the right algorithm and dataset combination for optimal model performance. In addition to model performance, you might also need to consider data bias and model explainability to meet regulatory requirements.

After the model is trained and before it is deployed into production, the model quality needs to be validated using the relevant technical metrics, such as the **accuracy score**. This is usually done using a **holdout dataset**, also known as a **test dataset**, to gauge how the model performs on unseen data. It is very important to understand what metrics to use for model validation, as it varies depending on the ML problems and the dataset used. For example, model accuracy would be a good validation metric for a document classification use case if the number of document types is relatively balanced. Model accuracy will not be a good metric to evaluate the model performance for a fraud detection use case – this is because if the number of frauds is small and the model predicts `not-fraud` all the time, the model accuracy could still be very high.

Model deployment

Once the model is fully trained and validated to meet the expected performance metric, it can be deployed into production and the business workflow. There are two main deployment concepts here. The first is the deployment of the model itself to be used by a client application to generate predictions. The second concept is to integrate this prediction workflow into a business workflow application. For example, deploying the credit fraud model would either host the model behind an API for real-time prediction or as a package that can be loaded dynamically to support batch predictions. Additionally, this prediction workflow also needs to be integrated into business workflow applications for fraud detection that might include the fraud detection of real-time transactions, decision automation based on prediction output, and fraud detection analytics for detailed fraud analysis.

Model monitoring

Model deployment is not the end of the ML life cycle. Unlike software, whose behavior is highly deterministic since developers explicitly code its logic, an ML model could behave differently in production from its behavior in model training and validation. This could be caused by changes in the production data characteristics, data distribution, or the potential manipulation of request data. Therefore, model monitoring is an important post-deployment step for detecting model drift or data drift.

Business metric tracking

The actual business impact should be tracked and measured as an ongoing process to ensure the model delivers the expected business benefits by comparing the business metrics before and after the model deployment, or A/B testing where a business metric is compared between workflows with or without the ML model. If the model does not deliver the expected benefits, it should be re-evaluated for improvement opportunities. This could also mean framing the business problem as a different ML problem. For example, if churn prediction does not help improve customer satisfaction, then consider a personalized product/service offering to solve the problem.

Now that we have talked about what is involved in an end-to-end ML life cycle, let's look at the ML challenges in the next section.

ML challenges

Over the years, I have worked on many real-world problems using ML solutions and encountered different challenges faced by the different industries during ML adoptions.

I often get this question when working on ML projects: *We have a lot of data – can you help us figure out what insights we can generate using ML?* This is called the business use case challenge. Not being able to identify business use cases for ML is a very big hurdle for many companies. Without a properly identified business problem and its value proposition and benefit, it would be challenging to get an ML project off the ground.

When I have conversations with different companies across their industries, I normally ask them what the top challenge for ML is. One of the most frequent answers I always get is about data – that is, data quality, data inventory, data accessibility, data governance, and data availability. This problem affects both data-poor and data-rich companies and is often exacerbated by data silos, data security, and industry regulations.

The shortage of data science and ML talent is another major challenge I have heard from many companies. Companies, in general, are having a tough time attracting and retaining top ML talent, which is a common problem across all industries. As the ML platform becomes more complex and the scope of ML projects increases, the need for other ML-related functions starts to surface. Nowadays, in addition to just data scientists, an organization would also need function roles for ML product management, ML infrastructure engineering, and ML operations management.

Through my experiences, another key challenge that many companies have shared is gaining cultural acceptance of ML-based solutions. Many people treat ML as a threat to their job functions. Their lack of knowledge of ML makes them uncomfortable in adopting these new methods in their business workflow.

The practice of ML solutions architecture aims to help solve some of the challenges in ML. Next, let's take a closer look at ML solutions architecture and its place in the ML life cycle.

ML solutions architecture

When I initially worked as an ML solutions architect with companies on ML projects, the focus was mainly on data science and modeling. Both the problem scope and the number of models were small. Most of the problems could be solved using simple ML techniques. The dataset was also small and did not require a large infrastructure for model training. The scope of the ML initiative at these companies was limited to a few data scientists or teams. As an ML architect back then, I mostly needed data science skills and general cloud architecture knowledge to work on those projects.

Over the last several years, the ML initiatives at different companies have become a lot more complex and started to involve a lot more functions and people at the companies. I've found myself talking to business executives more about ML strategies and organizational design to enable broad adoption across their enterprise. I have been asked to help design more complex ML platforms using a wide range of technologies for large enterprises across many business units that met stringent security and compliance needs. There have been more architecture and process discussions around ML workflow orchestration and operations in recent years than ever before. And more and more companies are looking to train ML models of enormous size with terabytes of training data. The number of ML models trained and deployed by some companies has gone up to tens of thousands from a few dozen models just a couple of years ago. Sophisticated and security-sensitive customers have also been looking for guidance on ML privacy, model explainability, and data and model bias. As a practitioner in ML solutions architecture, I've found the skills and knowledge required to be effective in this function have changed drastically.

So, where does ML solutions architecture fit in this complex business, data, science, and technology Venn diagram? Based on my years of experience working with companies of different sizes and in different industries, I see ML solutions architecture as an overarching discipline that helps connect the various pieces of an ML initiative covering everything from the business requirements to the technology. An ML solutions architect interacts with different business and technology partners, comes up with ML solutions for the business problems, and designs the technology platforms to run the ML solutions.

From a specific function perspective, ML solutions architecture covers the following areas:

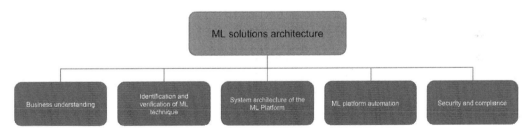

Figure 1.7 – ML solutions architecture coverage

Let's take a look at each of these elements:

- **Business understanding**: Business problem understanding and transformation using AI and ML

- **Identification and verification of ML techniques**: Identification and verification of ML techniques for solving specific ML problems

- **System architecture of the ML technology platform**: System architecture design and implementation of the ML technology platforms

- **ML platform automation**: ML platform automation technical design

- **Security and compliance**: Security, compliance, and audit considerations for the ML platform and ML models

Business understanding and ML transformation

The goal of the business workflow analysis is to identify inefficiencies in the workflows and determine if ML can be applied to help eliminate pain points, improve efficiency, or even create new revenue opportunities.

For example, when you conduct analysis for a call center operation, you want to identify pain points such as long customer waiting times, knowledge gaps among customer service agents, the inability to extract customer insights from call recordings, and the lack of ability to target customers for incremental services and products. After you have identified these pain points, you want to find out what data is available and what business metrics to improve. Based on the pain points and the availability of data, you can come up with some hypotheses on potential ML solutions, such as a virtual assistant to handle common customer inquiries, audio to text transcription to allow the text analysis of transcribed text, and intent detection for product cross-sell and up-sell.

Sometimes, a business process modification is required to adopt ML solutions for the established business goals. Using the same call center example, if there is a business need to do more product cross-sell or up-sell based on the insights generated from the call recording analytics, but there is no business process that would act on the insights to target the customers for cross-sell/up-sell, then an automated target marketing process or proactive out-reach process by the sales professionals should be introduced.

Identification and verification of ML techniques

Once a list of ML options is identified, determine the need for validating the ML assumption. This could involve simple **Proof of Concept** (**POC**) modeling to validate the available dataset and modeling approach, or technology POC using pre-built AI services, or testing of ML frameworks. For example, you might want to test the feasibility of text transcription from audio files using an existing text transcription service or build a custom propensity model for a new product conversion from a marketing campaign. ML solutions architecture does not focus on the research and development of new machine algorithms, which is usually the job of the applied data scientists and research data scientists.

Instead, ML solutions architecture focuses on identifying and applying ML algorithms to solve different ML problems such as predictive analytics, computer vision, and/or natural language processing. Also, the goal of any modeling task here is not to build production-quality models, but rather to validate the approach for further experimentations, which is usually the responsibility of full-time applied data scientists.

System architecture design and implementation

The most important aspect of ML solutions architecture coverage is the technical architecture design of the ML platform. The platform will need to provide the technical capability to support the different phases of the ML cycle and personas, such as data scientists and ops engineers. Specifically, an ML platform needs to have the following core functions:

- **Data explorations and experimentation**: Data scientists use the ML platform for data exploration, experimentation, model building, and model evaluation. The ML platform needs to provide capabilities such as data science development tools for model authoring and experimentation, data wrangling tools for data exploration and wrangling, source code control for code management, and a package repository for library package management.

- **Data management and large-scale data processing**: Data scientists or data engineers will need the technical capability to store, access, and process large amounts of data for cleansing, transformation, and feature engineering.

- **Model training infrastructure management**: The ML platform will need to provide model training infrastructure for different modeling training using different types of computing resources, storage, and networking configurations. It also needs to support different types of ML libraries or frameworks, such as **scikit-learn**, **TensorFlow**, and **PyTorch**.

- **Model hosting/serving**: The ML platform will need to provide the technical capability to host and serve the model for prediction generations, either for real-time, batch, or both.

- **Model management**: Trained ML models will need to be managed and tracked for easy access and lookup, with relevant metadata.

- **Feature management**: Common and reusable features will need to be managed and served for model training and model serving purposes.

ML platform workflow automation

A key aspect of ML platform design is **workflow automation** and **continuous integration/continuous deployment (CI/CD)**. ML is a multi-step workflow – it needs to be automated, which includes data processing, model training, model validation, and model hosting. Infrastructure provisioning automation and self-service is another aspect of automation design. Key components of workflow automation include the following:

- **Pipeline design and management**: The ability to create different automation pipelines for various tasks, such as model training and model hosting.

- **Pipeline execution and monitoring**: The ability to run different pipelines and monitor the pipeline execution status for the entire pipeline and each of the steps.

- **Model monitoring configuration**: The ability to monitor the model in production for various metrics, such as data drift (where the distribution of data used in production deviates from the distribution of data used for model training), model drift (where the performance of the model degrades in the production compared with training results), and bias detection (the ML model replicating or amplifying bias towards certain individuals).

Security and compliance

Another important aspect of ML solutions architecture is the security and compliance consideration in a sensitive or enterprise setting:

- **Authentication and authorization**: The ML platform needs to provide authentication and authorization mechanisms to manage the access to the platform and different resources and services.

- **Network security**: The ML platform needs to be configure for different network security to prevent unauthorized access.

- **Data encryption**: For security-sensitive organizations, data encryption is another important aspect of the design consideration for the ML platform.

- **Audit and compliance**: Audit and compliance staff need the information to help them understand how decisions are made by the predictive models if required, the lineage of a model from data to model artifacts, and any bias exhibited in the data and model. The ML platform will need to provide model explainability, bias detection, and model traceability across the various datastore and service components, among other capabilities.

Testing your knowledge

Alright! You have just completed this chapter. Let's see if you have understood and retained the knowledge you have just acquired.

Take a look at the list of the following scenarios and determine which of the three ML types can be applied (*supervised*, *unsupervised*, or *reinforcement*):

1. There is a list of online feedback on products. Each comment has been labeled with a `sentiment` class (for example, `positive`, `negative`, or `neutral`). You have been asked to build an ML model to predict the sentiment of new feedback.

2. You have historical house pricing information and details about the house, such as zip code, number of bedrooms, house size, and house condition. You have been asked to build an ML model to predict the price of a house.

3. You have been asked to identify potentially fraudulent transactions on your company's e-commerce site. You have data such as historical transaction data, user information, credit history, devices, and network access data. However, you don't know which transactions are fraudulent.

Take a look at the following questions on the ML life cycle and ML solutions architecture to see how you would answer them:

1. There is a business workflow that processes a request with a set of well-defined decision rules, and there is no tolerance to deviate from the decision rules when making decisions. Should you consider ML to automate the business workflow?

2. You have deployed an ML model into production. However, you do not see the expected improvement in the business KPIs. What should you do?

3. There is a manual process that's currently handled by a small number of people. You found an ML solution that can automate this process, however, the cost of building and running the ML solution is higher than the cost saved from automation. Should you proceed with the ML project?

4. As an ML solutions architect, you have been asked to validate an ML approach for solving a business problem. What steps would you take to validate the approach?

Summary

In this chapter, we covered several topics, including what AI and ML are, the key steps in an end-to-end ML life cycle, and the core functions of ML solutions architecture. Now, you should be able to identify the key differences between the three main types of ML and the kind of business problems they can solve. You have also learned that business and data understanding is critical to the successful outcome of an ML project, in addition to modeling and engineering. Lastly, you now have an understanding of how ML solutions architecture fits into the ML life cycle.

In the next chapter, we will go over some ML use cases across a number of industries, such as financial services and media and entertainment.

2
Business Use Cases for Machine Learning

As a **machine learning** (**ML**) practitioner, I often need to develop a deep understanding of different businesses to have effective conversations with the business and technology leaders. This should not come as a surprise since the ultimate goal for any **machine learning solution architecture** (**ML solution architecture**) is to solve practical business problems with science and technology solutions. As such, one of the main ML solution architecture focus areas is to develop a broad understanding of different business domains, business workflows, and relevant data. Without this understanding, it would be challenging to make sense of the data and design and develop practical ML solutions for business problems.

In this chapter, you will learn about some real-world ML use cases across several industry verticals. You will develop an understanding of key business workflows and challenges in industries such as financial services and retail, and where ML technologies can help solve these challenges. The learning goal is not for you to become an expert in an industry or its ML use case and techniques, but to make you aware of real-world ML use cases in the context of business requirements and workflows. After reading this chapter, you will be able to apply similar thinking in your line of business and be able to identify ML solutions.

In this chapter, we will cover the following topics:

- ML use cases in financial services
- ML use cases in media and entertainment
- ML use cases in healthcare and life sciences
- ML use cases in manufacturing
- ML use cases in retail
- ML use case identification exercis

ML use cases in financial services

The **Financial Services Industry** (**FSI**), one of the most technologically savvy industries, is a front-runner in ML investment and adoption. Over the last several years, I have seen a wide range of ML solutions being adopted across different business functions within financial services. In capital markets, ML is being used in front, middle, and back offices to support investment decisions, trade optimization, risk management, and transaction settlement processing. In insurance, carriers are using ML to streamline underwriting, prevent fraud, and automate claim management. And banks are using ML to improve customer experience, combat fraud, and make loan approval decisions. Next, we will discuss several core business areas within financial services and how ML can be used to solve some of these business challenges.

Capital markets front office

In finance, the front office is the business area that directly generates revenue and mainly consists of customer-facing roles such as sales, traders, investment bankers, and financial advisors. Front office departments engage their customers with products and services such as **Merger and Acquisition** (**M&A**) and IPO advisory, wealth management, and the trading of financial assets such as equity (for example, stocks), fixed income (for example, bonds), commodities (for example, oil), and currency products. Now, let's look at some specific business functions in the front office area.

Sales trading and research

In sales trading, a firm's sales staff monitors investment news such as earnings reports or M&A activities and looks for investment opportunities to pitch to their institutional clients. The trading staff then execute the trades for their clients, also known as agency trading. Trading staff can also execute trades for the firm they work for, also known as **prop trading**. Trading staff often need to trade large quantities of securities. So, it is crucial to optimize the trading strategy to acquire the shares at favorable prices without driving up prices. Sales and trading staff are supported by research teams who focus on researching and analyzing equities and fixed income assets and provide their recommendations to sales and trading staff.

Another type of trading is algorithmic trading, where a computer is used for trading securities automatically based on predefined logic and market conditions. Some of the core challenges in sales trading and research are as follows:

- A tight timeline is faced by research analysts to deliver a research report.
- Gathering a large amount of market information to collect and analyze to develop trading strategies and make an informed trading decision.
- The markets need to be constantly monitored to adjust the trading strategy.
- Achieving the optimal trading at the preferred price without driving the market up or down. The following diagram shows the business flow of a sales trading desk and how different players interact to complete a trading activity:

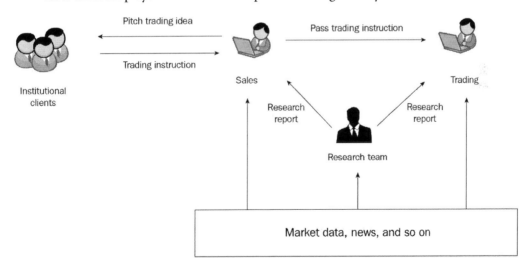

Figure 2.1 – Sales, trading, and research

There are many opportunities for ML in sales trading and research. **Natural language processing (NLP)** models can automatically extract key entities such as people, events, organizations, and places from data sources such as SEC filing, news announcements, and earnings call transcripts. NLP can also discover relationships among discovered entities and help understand market sentiments toward a company and its stock by analyzing large amounts of news, research reports, and earning calls to inform trading decisions.

Natural language generation (NLG) can assist with narrative writing and report generation. Computer vision has been used to help identify market signals from alternative data sources such as satellite images to understand business patterns such as retail traffic. In trading, ML models can sift through large amounts of data to discover patterns such as stock similarity using data points such as company fundamentals, trading patterns, and technical indicators to inform trading strategies such as pair trading. And in trade execution, ML models can help estimate trading cost and identify optimal trading execution strategies to minimize costs and optimize profits. There is a massive amount of time series data in financial services, such as prices of different financial instruments, that can be used to discover market signals and estimate market trends. ML has been adopted for use cases such as financial time series classification and forecasting financial instruments and economic indicators.

Investment banking

When corporations, governments, and institutions need access to capital to fund business operations and growth, they engage investment bankers for capital raising (selling of stocks or bonds) services. The following diagram shows the relationship between investment bankers and investors. In addition to capital raising, the investment banking department also engages in M&A advisory to assist their clients in negotiating and structuring merger and acquisition deals from start to finish. Investment banking staff take on many activities such as financial modeling, business valuation, pitch book generation, and transaction document preparation to complete and execute an investment banking deal. They are also responsible for general relationship management and business development management activities.

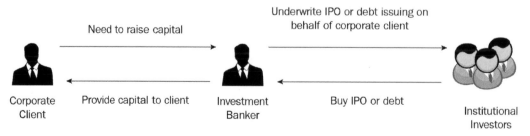

Figure 2.2 – Investment banking workflow

One of the main challenges in an investment banking workflow is searching for and analyzing large amounts of **structured** (financial statements) and **unstructured** data (annual reports, filing, news, and internal documents). Typical junior bankers spend many hours searching for documents that might contain useful information and manually extract information from the documents to prepare pitch books or perform financial modeling. Investment banks have been experimenting and adopting ML to help with this labor-intensive process. They are using NLP to extract structured tabular data automatically from large amounts of PDF documents. Specifically, **named entity recognition (NER)** techniques can help with automatic entity extraction from documents. ML-based reading comprehension technology can assist bankers in finding relevant information from large volumes of text quickly and accurately using natural human questions instead of simple text string matching. Documents can also be automatically tagged with metadata and classified using the ML technique to improve document management and information retrievals. Other common challenges in the investment banking workflow that can be solved with ML include linking company identifiers from different data sources and the name resolution of different variations of company names.

Wealth management

In the **wealth management (WM)** business, WM firms advise their clients with wealth planning and structuring services to grow and preserve their clients' wealth. These institutions differentiate themselves from more investment advisory-focused brokerage firms in that WM firms bring together tax planning, wealth preserving, and estate planning to meet their client's more complex financial planning goals. WM firms engage clients to understand their life goals and spending patterns and design customized financial planning solutions for their clients. Some of the challenges that are faced by WM firms are as follows:

- WM clients are demanding more holistic and personalized financial planning strategies for their WM needs.

- WM clients are becoming increasingly tech-savvy, and many are demanding new channels of engagement in addition to direct client-advisor interactions.

- WM advisors need to cover increasingly more clients while maintaining the same personalized services and planning.

To offer more personalized services, WM firms are adopting ML-based solutions to understand client behaviors and needs. For example, WM firms use their clients' transaction history, portfolio details, conversation logs, investment preferences, and life goals to build ML models that can make personalized recommendations on investment products and services. These models recommend the next best action by combining both the clients' propensity to take an offer and other business metrics such as the expected medium- or long-term value of the action.

The following diagram shows the concept of the **Next Best Action** method:

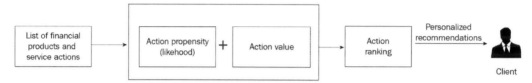

Figure 2.3 – Next Best Action recommendation

To improve client engagement and experience, WM firms build virtual assistants that can provide personalized answers to clients' inquiries without human intervention and automatically fulfill client demands. WM firms are equipping **Financial Advisors (FAs)** with AI-based solutions that can automate tasks such as transcribing audio conversations to text for text analysis. ML models are also being used to help assess clients' sentiment and alert FAs of potential customer churn.

Capital markets back office operations

The back office is the part of financial services companies that handles non-client facing and support activities. Their main functions include trade settlement and clearance, record keeping, regulatory compliance, accounting, and technology services. It is one of the areas for early ML adoption due to the financial benefits and cost-saving it could bring from ML-based automation and its improved ability to meet regulatory (for example, anti-money laundering) and internal controls requirements (for example, trade surveillance). Next, let's take a look at some back office business processes and where ML can be applied.

Net Asset Value review

Financial services companies that offer Mutual Funds and ETFs need to accurately reflect the values of the funds for trading and reporting purposes. They use a **Net Asset Value (NAV)** calculation, which is the value of an entity's assets minus its liability, to represent the value of the fund. NAV is the price at which an investor can buy and sell the fund. Every day, after the market closes, fund administrators must calculate the NAV price with 100% accuracy, and the process consists of five core steps:

1. Stock reconciliation

2. Reflection of any corporate actions

3. Pricing the instrument

4. Booking, calculating, and reconciling fees and interest accruals, as well as cash reconciliation

5. NAV/price validation

The following diagram shows the core steps in the NAV review process:

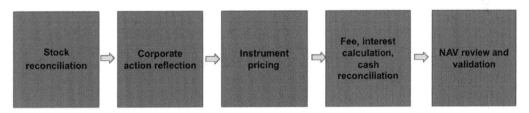

Figure 2.4 – Net Asset Value review process

Step 5 is the most vital because if it is done incorrectly, the fund administrator could be liable, which can result in monetary compensations to investors. Traditional methods use fixed thresholds to flag exceptions, such as incorrectly valued stock or corporation actions not being correctly processed for analysts for review, which could result in large volumes of false positives and wasted time. Large volumes of data need to be used for investigation and reviews such as the prices of the instruments, fees and interest, assets (for example, equities, bonds, and futures), cash positions, and corporate actions data.

The main objective of the NAV validation step is to identify pricing exceptions, which can be treated as an anomaly detection problem. ML-based anomaly detection solutions have been adopted to identify potential pricing irregularities and flag these irregularities for further human investigation. The ML approach has proven to significantly reduce false positives and save significant amounts of time for human reviewers.

Post-trade settlement failure prediction

After the front office executes a trade, several post-trade processes are involved to complete the trade, such as settlement and clearance. **Post-trade settlement** is the process where buyers and sellers compare trade details, approve the transaction, change records of ownership and arrange for securities and cash to be transferred. Trade settlements are handled automatically using **straight-through processing**. However, some trade settlements fail due to various reasons, such as sellers failing to deliver securities, and brokers will need to use their reserves to complete the transaction. To ensure the stockpile is set at the correct level so that valuable capital can be used elsewhere, predicting settlement failure is critical.

The following diagram shows the workflow for the trade where buyers and sellers buy and sell their securities at exchange through their respective brokerage firms:

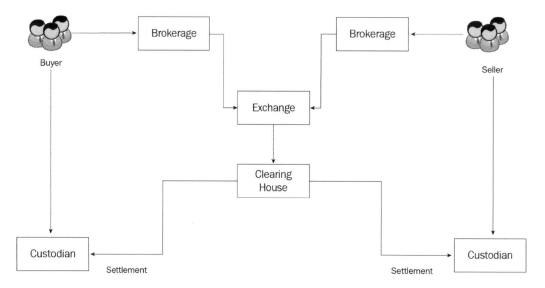

Figure 2.5 – Trading workflow

After the trade is executed, a clearing house such as DTCC would handle the clearance and settlement of the trades with the respective custodians for the buyer and sellers.

To ensure the right amount of stockpile reserve is maintained to reduce capital expenditure cost and optimize the buyer and sellers' transaction rates, brokerage houses have been using ML models to predict trade failure early in the process. This allows the broker to take preventive or corrective actions.

Risk management and fraud

Risk management and fraud are part of the middle office operations of financial services firms, including investment banks and commercial banks, and they are one of the top areas for ML adoption in financial services due to their large financial and regulatory impact.

There are many kinds of fraud and risk management use cases for ML, such as anti-money laundering, trade surveillance, credit card transaction fraud, and insurance claim fraud. Let's take a look at a few of them.

Anti-money laundering

Anti-money laundering (AML) is a set of laws and regulations that have been established to prevent criminals from legitimizing illegally obtained funds legally through complex financial transactions. Under these laws and regulations, financial institutions are required to help detect activities that aid illegal money laundering. Financial services companies devote substantial amounts of financial, technical, and people resources to combat AML activities. Traditionally, companies have been using rule-based systems to detect AML activities. However, rule-based systems usually have a limited view as it is challenging to include a large number of features to be evaluated in a rule-based system. Also, it is hard to keep the rules up to date with new changes; a rule-based solution can only detect well-known frauds that have happened in the past.

Machine learning-based solutions have been used in multiple areas of AML, such as the following:

- Network link analysis to reveal the complex social and business relationships among different entities and jurisdictions.

- Clustering analysis to find similar and dissimilar entities to spot trends in criminal activity patterns.

- Deep learning-based predictive analytics to identify criminal activity.

- NLP to gather as much information as possible for the vast number of entities from unstructured data sources.

The following diagram shows the data flow for AML analysis, the reporting requirements for regulators, and internal risk management and audit functions:

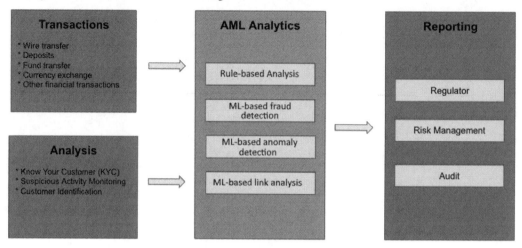

Figure 2.6 – Anti-money laundering detection flow

An AML platform takes data from many different sources, including transactions data and internal analysis data such as **Know Your Customer (KYC)** and **Suspicious Activity** data. This data is processed and fed into different rule and ML-based analytics engines to monitor fraudulent activities. The findings can be sent to internal risk management and auditing, as well as regulators.

Trade surveillance

Traders at financial firms are intermediaries who buy and sell securities and other financial instruments on behalf of their clients. They execute orders and advise clients on entering and existing financial positions. **Trade surveillance** is the process of identifying and investigating potential market abuse by traders or financial organizations. Examples of market abuse include market manipulation, such as the dissemination of false and misleading information, manipulating trading volumes through large amounts of wash trading, and insider trading through the disclosure of non-public information. Financial institutions are required to comply with market abuse regulations such as **Market Abuse Regulation (MAR)**, **Markets in Financial Instruments Directive II (MiFID II)**, and internal compliance to protect themselves, such as damage to their reputations and financial performance. The challenges in enforcing trade surveillance include the lack of a proactive approach to abuse detection such as large noise/signal ratios resulting in many false positives, which increases the cost of case processing and investigations. One typical approach to abuse detection is to build complex rule-based systems with different fixed thresholds for decision making.

There are multiple ways to frame trade surveillance problems as ML problems, including the following:

- Framing the abuse detection of activities as a classification problem to replace rule-based systems

- Framing data extraction information such as entities (for example, restricted stocks) from unstructured data sources (for example, emails and chats) as NLP entity extraction problems

- Transforming entity relationship analysis (for example, trader-trader collaborations in market abuse) as machine learning-based network analysis problems

- Treating abusive behaviors as anomalies and using unsupervised ML techniques for anomaly detection

Many different datasets can be useful for building ML models for trade surveillance such as **P and L** information, positions, order book details, e-communications, linkage information among traders and their trades, market data, trading history, and details such as counterparty details, trade price, order type, and exchanges.

The following diagram shows the typical data flow and business workflow for trade surveillance management within a financial services company:

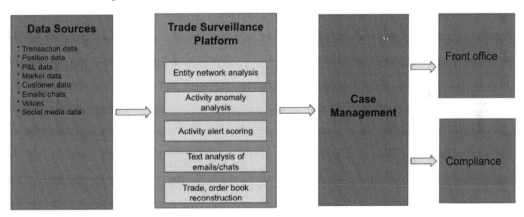

Figure 2.7 – Trade surveillance workflow

A trade surveillance system monitors many different data sources, and it feeds its findings to both the front office and compliance department for further investigation and enforcement.

Credit risk

When banks issue loans to businesses and individuals, there is the potential risk that the borrower might not be able to pay the required payment. As a result, banks suffer financial loss in both principal and interest from financial activities such as making loans for mortgages and credit cards. To minimize this default risk, banks go through credit risk modeling to assess the risk of making a loan by focusing on two main aspects:

- The probability that the borrower will default on the loan

- The impact on the lender's financial situation

Traditional human-based reviews of loan applications are slow and error-prone, resulting in high loan processing costs and lost opportunities due to incorrect and slow loan approval processing.

The following diagram shows a typical business workflow for credit risk assessment and its various decision points within the process:

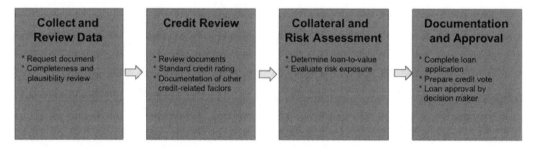

Figure 2.8 – Credit risk approval workflow

To reduce credit risk associated with loans, many banks have widely adopted ML techniques to predict loan default and associated risk scores more accurately and quickly. The credit risk management modeling process requires the collection of financial information from borrowers, such as income, cash flow, debt, assets and collaterals, the utilization of credits, and other information such as loan type and loan payment behaviors. Since this process involves large amounts of information being extracted from unstructured data sources (financial statements) and then analyzed, machine learning-based solutions such as **Optical Character Recognition (OCR)** and NLP information extraction and understanding have been widely adopted for automated intelligence document processing.

Insurance

The insurance industry consists of several sub-sectors based on the insurance product types offered by the different insurance companies, such as accident and health insurance, property and casualty insurance, and life insurance. In addition to the insurance companies that provide coverage through insurance policies, insurance technology providers are also key players in the insurance industry.

There are two main business processes in most insurance companies: the insurance underwriting process and the insurance claim management process.

Insurance underwriting

Insurance underwriting is the process of assessing the risk of providing insurance coverage for people and assets. Through this process, an insurance company establishes the insurance premium for the risks that it is willing to take on. Insurance companies normally use insurance software and actuarial data to assess the magnitude of the risk. The underwriting processes vary, depending on the insurance products. For example, the steps for property insurance are normally as follows:

1. The customer files an insurance application through an agent or insurance company directly.

2. The underwriter at the insurance company assesses the application by considering different factors such as the applicant's loss and insurance history, actuarial factors to determine whether the insurance company should take on the risk, and what the price and premium should be for the risk. Then, they make an additional adjustment to the policy, such as coverage amount and deductibles.

3. If the application is accepted, then an insurance policy is issued.

During the underwriting process, an underwriter has to collect and review a large amount of data, estimate the risk of a claim based on the data and underwriter's personal experience, and come up with a premium that can be justified. Human underwriters would only be able to review a subset of data and could introduce personal bias into the decision-making process. ML models would be able to act on a lot more data to make more accurate data-driven decisions on risk factors such as the probability of claims and the claim's outcome, and it would make decisions much faster than what a human underwriter can do. To come up with the premium for the policy, an underwriter would spend a lot of time assessing the different risk factors. ML models can help generate recommended premiums by using large amounts of historical data and risk factors.

Insurance claim management

Insurance claim management is the process where an insurance company assesses the insured's claims and reimburses the person who's insured for the damage and loss that they incurred according to the agreement in the policy. The claim processes for the different insurances are different. The steps for a property insurance claim are normally as follows:

1. The person who is insured files a claim and supplies evidence for the claim, such as pictures of the damage and a police report for automobiles.

2. The insurance company assigns an adjuster to assess the damage.

3. The adjuster determines the damage, performs fraud assessment, and sends the claim for payment approval.

Some of the main challenges that are faced in the insurance claim management process are as follows:

- Time-consuming manual effort is needed for the damaged/lost item inventory process and data entry.

- The need for speedy claim damage assessment and adjustment.

- Insurance fraud.

Insurance companies collect a lot of data during the insurance claim process, such as property details, items damage data and photos, the insurance policy, the claims history, and historical fraud data.

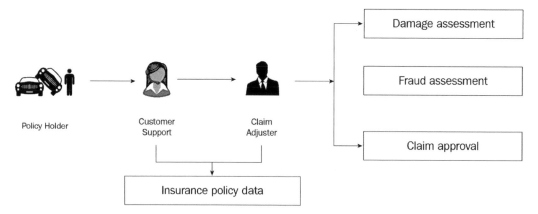

Figure 2.9 – Insurance claim management workflow

ML can automate manual processes such as extracting data from documents and identifying insured objects from pictures to reduce manual effort in data collection. In damage assessment, ML can help assess different damages and the estimated cost for repair and replacement to speed up claim processing. In the fight for insurance fraud, ML can help detect exceptions in insurance claims and predict potential fraud for further investigation.

ML use cases in media and entertainment

The **media and entertainment** (**M&E**) industry consists of businesses that engage in the production and distribution of films, television, streaming content, music, games, and publishing. The current M&E landscape has been shaped by the increasing adoption of streaming and **over-the-top** (**OTT**) content delivery versus traditional broadcasting. M&E customers, faced with ever-increasing media content choices, are shifting their consumption habits and demanding more personalized and enhanced experiences across different devices, anytime, anywhere. M&E companies are also faced with fierce competition in the industry, and to stay competitive, M&E companies need to identify new monetization channels, improve user experience, and improve operational efficiency. The following diagram shows the main steps in the media production and distribution workflow:

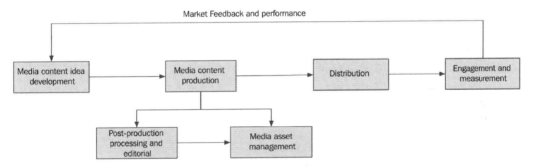

Figure 2.10 – Media production and distribution workflow

Over the last several years, I have seen M&E companies increasingly adopting ML in the different stages of the media life cycle, such as content generation and content distribution, to improve efficiency and spur business growth. For example, ML has been used to enable better content management and search, new content development, monetization optimization, and compliance and quality control.

Content development and production

In the early planning phase of the film production life cycle, content producers need to make decisions on the next content based on factors such as estimated performance, revenue, and profitability. Filmmakers adopt ML-based predictive analytics models to help predict the popularity and profitability of new ideas by analyzing factors such as casts, scripts, the past performance of different films, and target audience. This allows producers to quickly eliminate ideas with small market potential to focus their effort on developing more promising and profitable ideas.

To support personalized content viewing needs, content producers often segment long video content into smaller micro-segments around certain events, scenes, or actors, so that they can be distributed individually or repackaged into something more personalized to individual preferences. This ML-based approach can be used for creating video clips by detecting elements such as scenes, actors, and events for the different target audiences with different tastes and preferences.

Content management and discovery

M&E companies with large digital content assets need to curate their content to create new content for new monetization opportunities. To do that, these companies need rich metadata for the digital assets to enable different content to be searched and discovered. Consumers also need to search for content easily and accurately for different usages, such as for personal entertainment or research. Without metadata tagging or the ability to understand the content, it is quite challenging to discover relevant content. Many companies hire humans to review and tag this content with meaningful metadata for discovery as part of the digital asset management workflow. Since manual tagging is very costly and time-consuming, most content is not tagged with sufficient metadata to support effective content management and discovery.

Computer vision models can automatically tag image and video content for items such as objects, genres, people, places, or themes. ML models can also interpret the meaning of textual content such as topics, sentiment, entities, and sometimes video. Audio content also needs to be transcribed into text for additional text analysis, such as summarization. Machine learning-based text summarization can help you summarize long text as part of the content metadata generation. The following diagram shows where ML-based analysis solutions fit into the media asset management flow:

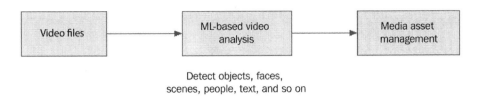

Figure 2.11 – ML-based media analysis workflow

Machine learning-based content processing is being increasingly adopted by M&E companies to streamline media asset management workflows, and it has resulted in meaningful cost savings and enhanced content discovery.

Content distribution and customer engagement

Nowadays, media content such as films and music are increasingly being distributed through digital **video on demand** (**VOD**) and live streaming on different devices, bypassing traditional media such as DVDs and broadcasting. Consumers nowadays have a lot of options when it comes to media provider choices. Customer acquisition and retention are also a challenge for many media providers. M&E companies are increasingly focusing on customer needs and preferences to improve user experience and increase retention. They have turned to highly personalized product features and content to keep users engaged and stay on the platform. One effective way for highly personalized engagement is the content recommendation engine, and this has become the primary method to get consumers to consume content and keep them engaged. Content delivery platform providers use viewing and engagement behavior data and other profile data to train highly personalized recommendation ML models. And they use these recommendation models to target individuals based on their preference and viewing pattern, along with a combination of diverse media content, including videos, music, and games.

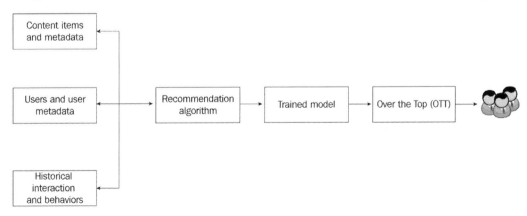

Figure 2.12 – Recommendation ML model training

Recommendation technologies have been around for many years and have improved greatly over the years. Nowadays, recommendation engines can learn patterns using multiple data inputs, such as those historical interactions users have with content and watching behaviors, different sequential patterns of the interactions, and the metadata associated with the users and content. Modern recommendation engines can also learn from the user's real-time behaviors/decisions and make dynamic recommendation decisions based on real-time user behaviors.

ML use cases in healthcare and life sciences

Healthcare and life science is one of the largest and most complex industries. Within this industry, there are several sectors, including the following:

- **Drugs**: These are the drug manufacturers, such as biotechnology firms, pharmaceutical firms, and the makers of genetics drugs.

- **Medical equipment**: These are the companies that manufacture both standard products as well as hi-tech equipment.

- **Managed healthcare**: These are the companies that provide health insurance policies.

- **Health facilities**: These are the hospitals, clinics, and labs.

- Government agencies such as CDC and FDA.

The industry has adopted ML for a wide range of use cases, such as medical diagnosis and imaging, drug discovery, medical data analysis and management, and disease prediction and treatment.

Medical imaging analysis

Medical imaging is the process and technique of creating a visual representation of the human body for medical analysis. Medical professionals, such as radiologists and pathologists, use medical imaging to assist with medical condition assessments and prescribe medical treatments. However, the industry is facing a shortage of qualified medical professionals, and sometimes, these professionals have to spend a lot of time reviewing a large number of medical images to determine whether a patient has a medical condition.

One ML-based solution is to treat medical imaging analysis as a computer vision object detection problem. In the case of cancer cell detection, cancerous tissues can be identified and labeled in the existing medical images as training data for computer vision algorithms. Once the model has been trained, and its accuracy has been validated to be acceptable, it can be used to automate the screening of a large number of X-ray images to highlight the ones that are important for the pathologists to review. The following diagram shows the process of training a computer vision model using labeled image data:

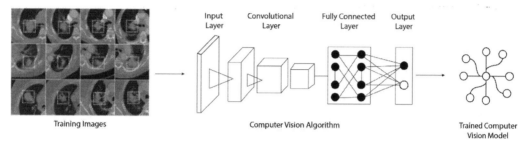

Figure 2.13 – Using computer vision for cancer detection

To enable more accurate prediction, image data can be combined with non-image data, such as clinical diagnosis data, to train a joint model to make the prediction.

Drug discovery

Drug discovery and development is a long, complex, and costly process. It consists of key stages such as the following:

- **Discovery and development**, where the goal is to find a lead compound targeting a particular protein or gene as a drug candidate through basic research
- **Preclinical research**, where the goal is to determine the efficacy and safety of the drug
- **Clinical development**, which involves clinical trials and volunteer studies to fine-tune the drug
- **FDA review**, where the drug is reviewed holistically to either approve or reject it
- **Post-market monitoring**, to ensure the safety of the drug

During the drug discovery phase, the main goal is to develop a molecule compound that can have a positive biological effect on a protein target to treat a disease without negative effects such as toxicity issues. One area that ML can help with is the process of compound design, where we can model the molecule compound as a sequence vector and use the advancements in natural language processing to learn about these patterns. We can do this using the existing molecule compounds with a variety of molecular structures. Once the model has been trained, it can be used to generate new compound suggestions for discovery purposes instead of having these molecules be created by humans manually to save time. The suggested compounds can be tested and validated with a target protein for interaction. The following diagram shows the flow of converting molecule compounds into SMILES representations and training a model that generates new compound sequences:

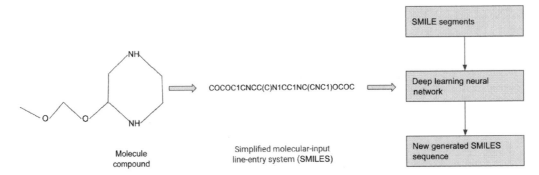

Figure 2.14 – Molecule compound generation

In addition to compound design, ML-based approaches have also been adopted in other stages of the drug discovery life cycle, such as identifying cohorts for clinical trials.

Healthcare data management

Large amounts of patient healthcare data is collected and generated in the healthcare industry every day. It comes in various formats, such as insurance claim data, doctor's handwritten notes, recorded medical conversations, and images such as X-rays. Medical companies need to extract useful information from these data sources to develop comprehensive views about patients or to support medical coding for medical billing processes. A significant amount of manual processing, often by people with health domain expertise, goes into organizing this data and extracting information from these data sources. This process is both expensive and error-prone. As a result, large amounts of patient healthcare data remain in its original form and is not comprehensively utilized.

In recent years, deep learning-based solutions have been adopted to help with health data management, especially with medical information extraction from unstructured data such as doctor's notes, recorded medical conversations, and medical images. These deep learning solutions can not only extract text from handwritten notes, images, and audio files, but they can also identify medical terms and conditions, drug names, prescription instructions, and the relationship among those different entities and terms. The following diagram shows the flow of extracting information from unstructured data sources using ML and using the results for different tasks, such as medical coding and clinical decision support:

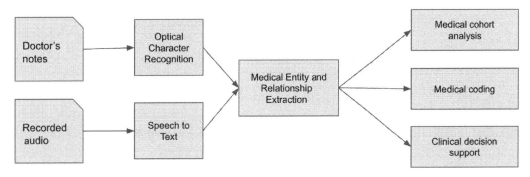

Figure 2.15 – Medical data management

Almost 80% of healthcare data is unstructured data, and advances in ML are helping to unlock useful insights that are otherwise hidden in text and images.

ML use cases in manufacturing

Manufacturing is an industry sector that produces tangible finished products. It includes many sub-sectors such as consumer goods, electronics goods, industrial equipment, automobiles, furniture, building materials, sporting goods, clothing, and toys. There are multiple stages in a typical product manufacturing life cycle, including product design, prototyping, manufacturing and assembling, and post-manufacturing service and support. The following diagram shows the typical business functions and flow in the manufacturing sector:

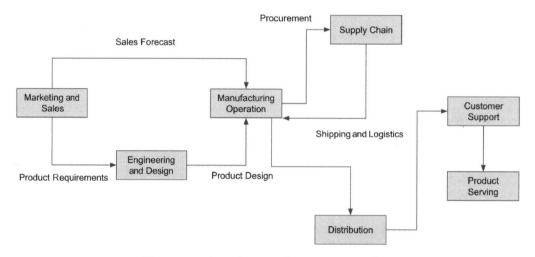

Figure 2.16 – Manufacturing business process flow

AI and ML have played an essential role in the manufacturing process, such as sales forecasting, predictive machine maintenance, quality control and robotic automation for manufacturing quality and yield, and process and supply chain optimization to improve overall operational efficiency.

Engineering and product design

Product design is the process where a product designer combines their creative power, the practical needs of market/consumers, and constraints to develop a product that will be successful once it has been launched. Designers often need to create many different variations of a new product concept during the design phase that will meet different needs and constraints. For example, in the apparel industry, fashion designers would analyze the needs and preferences of customers, such as color, texture, and styles, and develop these designs and generate the graphics for the apparel.

The manufacturing industry has been leveraging generative design ML technology to assist with new product concept design. For example, ML techniques such as **Generative Adversarial Networks (GANs)** have been used to generate new graphics for logo design and 3D industrial components such as machinery gears. The following diagram shows the basic concept of a GAN, where a generator model is trained to create fake images that can fool a discriminator. After the generator becomes good enough to fool the discriminator, it can be used to generate new images for items such as clothing.

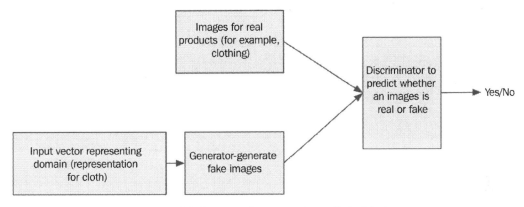

Figure 2.17 – GAN concept for generating realistic fake images

In addition to generative design, ML techniques have also been used to analyze market requirements and estimate new products' market potentials.

Manufacturing operations – product quality and yield

Quality control is an important step in the manufacturing process to ensure a product's quality before it is shipped. Many manufactures rely on humans to inspect the manufactured products, which is highly time-consuming and costly. For example, factory workers would visually inspect the products for surface scratches, missing parts, color differences, and deformations.

Computer vision-based technology has been used to automate many aspects of the manufacturing lines' quality control process. For example, a computer object detection model can be trained using labeled image data to help identify the objects to be inspected from the captured images, and then a computer vision-based defective model can be trained using images labeled with good parts and bad parts to help inspect detected objects and classify them as either defective or not defective.

Manufacturing operations – machine maintenance

Industrial manufacturing equipment and machinery need regular maintenance to ensure smooth operations. Any unplanned outages due to equipment failures would not only result in high repair or replacement costs, but they would also disrupt production schedules, impacting delivering schedules to downstream tasks or customers. While following a regular maintenance schedule would alleviate this problem to a certain extent, having the ability to forecast potential problems in advance would further reduce the risk of any unforeseen failures.

Machine learning-based predictive maintenance analytics help reduce the risk of potential failures by predicting whether a piece of equipment will likely fail within a time window using a variety of data, such as telemetry data collected by **Internet of Things (IoT)** sensors. The maintenance crew can use the prediction results and take proactive maintenance actions to prevent disruptive failure.

ML use cases in retail

Retail businesses sell consumer products directly to customers through retail stores or e-commerce channels. They get supplies through wholesale distributors or from manufacturers directly. The industry has been going through some significant transformations. While e-commerce is growing much faster than traditional retail business, traditional brick-and-mortar stores are also transforming in-store shopping experiences to stay competitive. Retailers are looking for new ways to improve the overall shopping experience through both online and physical channels. New trends such as social commerce, augmented reality, virtual assistant shopping, smart stores, and 1:1 personalization are becoming some of the key differentiators among retail businesses.

AI and ML are a key driving force behind the retail industry's transformation, from inventory optimization and demand forecasting to highly personalized and immersive shopping experiences such as personalized product recommendations, virtual reality shopping, and cashier-less store shopping. In addition, AI and ML are also helping retailers fight crimes such as fraud and shoplifting.

Product search and discovery

When consumers shop online and need to search for a particular product, they rely on search engines to find the product on various e-commerce websites. This greatly simplifies the shopping experience when you know the name or certain attributes of the products to search for. However, sometimes, you only have a picture of the product and do not know what correct terms to search for.

Deep learning-powered visual search is a technology that can help you quickly identify and return similar-looking products from a picture of an item. Visual search technology works by creating a digital representation (also known as encoding/embedding) of the item's pictures and stores them in a high-performance item index. When a shopper needs to find a similar-looking item using a picture, the new picture is encoded into a digital representation, and the digital representation is searched against the item index using efficient distance-based comparison. The items that are the closest to the target items are returned. The following diagram shows an architecture for building an ML-based image search capability:

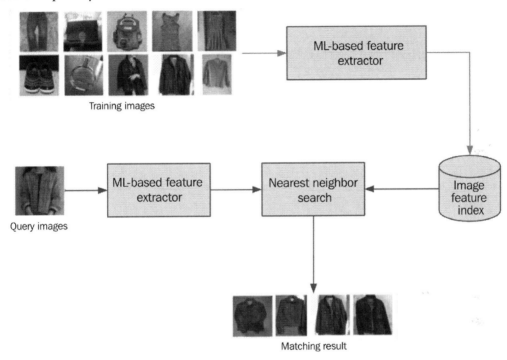

Figure 2.18 – Image search architecture

Visual search-based recommendations have been adopted by many large e-commerce sites such as Amazon.com to enhance the shopping experience.

Target marketing

Retailers use different marketing campaigns and advertising techniques, such as direct marketing email or digital advertisements, to target prospective shoppers with incentives or discounts based on the shopper's segments. These campaigns' effectiveness heavily depends on the right customer targeting to achieve a high conversion rate, all while reducing the campaign's cost or advertising and generating less end user disturbance.

Segmentation is one traditional way to understand the different customer segments to help improve marketing campaigns' effectiveness. There are different ways to do segmentations with machine learning, such as unsupervised clustering of customers based on data such as basic demographic data. This allows you to group customers into several segments and create unique marketing campaigns for each segment.

A more effective target marketing approach is to use highly personalized **user-centric marketing campaigns**. They work by creating accurate individual profiles using large amounts of individual behavior data such as historical transaction data, responses data to historical campaigns, and alternative textual data such as social media data. Highly personalized campaigns with customized marketing messages can be generated using these personal profiles for a higher conversion rate. The ML approach to user-centric target marketing predicts the conversion rate, such as the **click-through rate (CTR)**, for different users and sends ads to users with a high conversion rate. This can be a classification or regression problem by learning the relationship between the user features and the probability of conversion.

Contextual advertising is another way to reach the target audience by placing advertisements such as display ads or video ads on web pages that match the advertisement's content. An example of contextual advertising is to place cooking product advertisements on cooking recipe sites. Because the ads are highly relevant to the content, they will likely resonate with the websites' readers and result in a much higher click-through rate. ML can help with detecting ads from a context so that the ads are placed correctly. For example, computer vision models can detect objects, people, and themes in video ads to extract contextual information and match them to the website's content.

Sentiment analysis

Retail businesses often need to understand the perception of their brand from their consumers' point of view. Positive and negative sentiments toward a retailer could greatly improve or damage a retail business. As more online platforms are becoming available, it is easier than ever for consumers to voice their feelings toward a product or business from their real-life experiences. Retail businesses are adopting different techniques to assess their customer's feelings and emotions toward their product and brand by analyzing feedback solicited from their shoppers or monitoring and analyzing their social media channels. Effective sentiment analysis can help identify areas for improvement, such as operational and product improvement, as well as for gathering intelligence in relation to potentially malicious brand reputation attacks.

Sentiment analysis is mainly a text classification problem that uses labeled text data (for example, a product review is labeled either positive or negative). Many different ML classifier algorithms, including deep learning-based algorithms, can be used to train a model to detect sentiment in a piece of text.

Product demand forecasting

Retail businesses need to do inventory planning and demand forecasting to optimize retail revenue and manage inventory costs. This helps them avoid out-of-stock situations while reducing the cost of stocking inventory. Traditionally, retailers have been using different demand forecasting techniques such as buyer surveys, collective opinions from multiple inputs, projections based on past demands, or expert opinions.

Statistical and ML techniques such as regression analysis and deep learning-based approaches can help produce more accurate and data-driven demand forecasting. In addition to using historical demand and sales data to model future forecasts, deep learning-based algorithms can also incorporate other related data such as price, holidays, special events, and product attributes to train an ML model that's capable of producing more accurate forecasts. The following diagram shows the concept of building a deep learning model using multiple data sources to generate forecasting models:

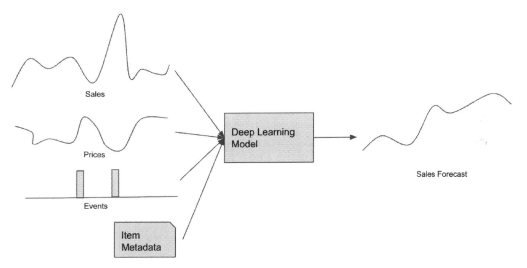

Figure 2.19 – Deep learning-based forecasting model

ML-based forecasting models can generate point forecasts (a number) of probabilistic forecasts (a forecast with a confidence score). Many retail businesses use ML to generate baseline forecasts, and professional forecasters review them and make adjustments based on human expertise and other factors.

ML use case identification exercise

In this exercise, you are going to apply what you have learned in this chapter to your line of business. The goal is to go through a thinking process to business problems that can potentially be solved with machine learning:

1. Think about a business operation in your line of business. Create a workflow of the operation and identify any known issues, such as a lack of automation, human errors, and long processing cycles in the workflow.

2. List the business impact of these issues in terms of lost revenue, increased cost, poor customer and employee satisfaction, and potential regulatory and compliance risk exposure. Try to quantify the business impact as much as possible.

3. Pick one or two problems with the most significant impact if the problems can be solved. Think about ML approaches (supervised machine learning, unsupervised machine learning, or reinforcement machine learning) to solve the problem.

4. List the data that could be helpful for building ML solutions.

5. Write a proposal for your idea that includes the problem statement, identified opportunities and business value, data availability, and implementation and adoption challenges.

6. List the business and technology stakeholders that you will need to work with to bring your idea to life.

Summary

In this chapter, we covered several ML use cases across multiple industries. You now should have a basic understanding of some top industries and some of the core business workflows in those industries. You have learned about some of the relevant use cases, the business impact that those use cases have, and the ML approaches for solving them.

The next chapter will cover how machines learn and some of the most commonly used ML algorithms.

Section 2: The Science, Tools, and Infrastructure Platform for Machine Learning

In *Section 2*, you will learn about the core sciences and technologies for data science experimentations and ML data science platforms for data scientists.

This section comprises the following chapters:

- *Chapter 3, Machine Learning Algorithms*
- *Chapter 4, Data Management for Machine Learning*
- *Chapter 5, Open Source Machine Learning Libraries*
- *Chapter 6, Kubernetes Container Orchestration Infrastructure Management*

3
Machine Learning Algorithms

Machine learning (**ML**) algorithm design is usually not the main focus for a practitioner of ML solutions architecture. However, ML solutions architects still need to develop a solid understanding of the common real-world ML algorithms and how those algorithms solve real business problems. Without this understanding, you will find it difficult to identify the right data science solutions for the problem at hand and design the appropriate technology infrastructure to run these algorithms.

In this chapter, you will develop a deeper understanding of how ML works first. We will then cover some common ML and deep learning algorithms for the different ML tasks, such as **classification**, **regression**, **object detection**, **recommendation**, **forecasting**, and **natural language generation**. You will learn the core concepts behind these algorithms, their advantages and disadvantages, and where to apply them in the real world. Specifically, we are going to cover the following topics:

- How machines learn
- Overview of ML algorithms
- Hands-on exercise

Technical requirements

You need a personal computer (**Mac** or **Windows**) to complete the hands-on exercise portion of this chapter.

You need to download the dataset from `https://www.kaggle.com/mathchi/churn-for-bank-customers`. Additional instructions will be provided in the *Hands-on exercise* section.

How machines learn

In *Chapter 1, Machine Learning and Machine Learning Solutions Architecture*, we briefly talked about how ML algorithms can improve themselves by processing data and updating model parameters to generate models (analogous to traditional compiled binary from computer source code). So, how does an algorithm actually learn? In short, ML algorithms learn by optimizing (for example, minimizing or maximizing) an **objective function** (also known as a **loss function**). You can think of an objective function as a business metric, such as the difference between the projected sales of a product and the actual sales, and the goal of optimizing this objective would be to reduce the difference between the actual sales number and the projected sales number. To optimize this objective, an ML algorithm would iterate and process through large amounts of historical sales data (training data) and adjust its internal model parameters until it can minimize the differences between the projected values and the actual values. This process of finding the optimal model parameters is called **optimization**, and the mathematical routines for performing the optimization are called **optimizers**.

To illustrate what optimization means, let's use a simple example of training an ML model to predict the sales of a product using its price as the input variable. Here, we use a linear function as the ML algorithm, shown as follows:

$$sales = W * price + B$$

In this example, we want to minimize the difference between the actual sales and predicted sales, and we use the following **mean square error** (**MSE**) as the loss function to optimize. The specific optimization task is to find the optimal values for the W and B model parameters that produce the minimal MSE. In this example, W and B are also known as *weight* and *bias*, respectively. The value of a weight indicates the relative importance of an input variable and the bias represents the mean value for the output:

$$Error = \frac{1}{n} \sum_{i=1}^{n} (predicted_i - actual_i)^2$$

There are many techniques for solving ML optimization problems. One of the preferred optimization techniques is **gradient descent** and its various variants, which are commonly used for the optimization of neural networks and many other ML algorithms. Gradient descent is iterative and works by calculating the rate of error change (gradient) contributed to the total error by each input variable and updating the model parameters (*W* and *B* in this example) accordingly at each step to reduce error gradually over many steps. Gradient descent also controls how much change to make to the model parameters at each step by using a parameter called **learning rate**. The learning rate is also known as a **hyperparameter** of the ML algorithm. The following figure shows how the *W* value can be optimized using gradient descent:

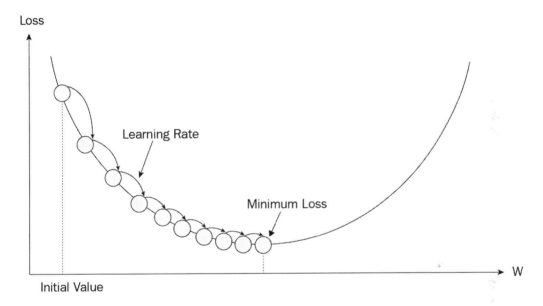

Figure 3.1 – Gradient descent

The main steps in gradient descent optimization include:

1. Assigning a random value to *W* initially.

2. Calculating the error (loss) with the assigned *W* value.

3. Calculating the gradient (rate of change) of the error for the loss function. The value of the gradient can be positive, zero, or negative.

4. If the gradient is either positive or negative, updating the *W* value in the direction that will reduce the error in the next step. In this example, we move *W* to the right to make it bigger.

5.   Repeat *Steps 2 to 4* until the gradient is *0*, which indicates the optimal value of *W* is found as the loss is at a minimal. Finding the optimal value is also called **convergence**.

Besides gradient descent, there are other alternative optimization techniques, such as **normal equation**, for finding the optimal parameters for ML algorithms such as linear regression. Instead of the iterative approach used by gradient descent, normal equation uses a one-step analytical approach for computing the coefficients of linear regression models. Some other algorithms also have algorithm-specific solutions for model training optimization, which we will cover in the next section.

Now, we have briefly talked about the fundamentals of how a machine learns. Next, let's dive into the individual ML algorithms.

Overview of ML algorithms

A large number of ML algorithms have been developed to date, and more are being researched and invented at an accelerated pace by academia and industry alike. This section will review some popular traditional and deep learning algorithms and how these algorithms can be applied to different kinds of ML problems. But first, let's quickly discuss the considerations when choosing an ML algorithm for the task.

Consideration for choosing ML algorithms

There are a number of considerations when it comes to choosing ML algorithms for different tasks:

- **Training data size**: Some ML algorithms, such as deep learning algorithms, can work very well and produce highly accurate models, but they require large amounts of the training data. Traditional ML algorithms, such as **linear models**, can work effectively when the dataset is small but cannot take advantage of large datasets as effectively as **deep learning neural network algorithms**. Traditional ML algorithms require humans to extract and engineer useful input features from the training data to train the model. When the size of the training data becomes large, it becomes more difficult to extract and engineer useful features to improve model performance. This is one of the reasons that traditional ML algorithms cannot take advantage of large datasets. On the other hand, deep learning algorithms can extract features automatically from the training data.

- **Accuracy and interpretability**: Some ML algorithms, such as deep learning algorithms, can produce highly accurate models, such as **computer vision** or **natural language processing** (**NLP**) models. However, these can be highly complex and harder to explain. Some simpler algorithms, such as **linear regression** (to be covered later), can be easily interpreted even though the accuracy might not be as high as deep learning models.

- **Training time**: Different algorithms have different training speeds against the same dataset. Simple models, such as linear models, are faster to train, while deep learning models would take longer to train.

  There are a couple of quantitative measures for algorithm complexity. **Time complexity** describes the compute time/operations needed to run an ML algorithm, and **space complexity** is the amount of computing memory needed to run the algorithm. **Big O** is a notation for describing time and space complexity, which defines the estimated upper bound of an algorithm. For example, the time complexity for linear search is $0(N)$, and the time complexity for binary search would be represented by $0(log (N))$, where N is the number of data samples in the target list.

- **Data linearity**: For data with linear relationships between the input data and output data, linear models can work quite well. However, for a dataset with non-linear relationships (that is, the input variable and output variable do not change proportionally), linear models may not always be able to capture deeper intrinsic relationships, and we normally need algorithms such as deep learning neural networks and decision trees to handle complex datasets.

- **Number of features**: A training dataset can contain a large number of features, and not all of them are relevant for model training. Some ML algorithms can handle irrelevant or noisy features well, and some others may get negatively impacted in training speed or model performance with a lot of irrelevant or noisy features during training. Different algorithms have different approaches for reducing the influence of noisy or uninformative features through a technique called **regularization**. Some regularization techniques work by adding additional error terms to the training loss function to reduce the influences of noisy data. Other methods, such as **dropout**, randomly remove nodes in neural networks to achieve regularization.

Now, we have reviewed some key considerations for ML algorithms. Next, let's deep dive into the different types of algorithms by the problems they solve.

Algorithms for classification and regression problems

The vast majority of the ML problems the world currently solves are **classification** and **regression** problems. In the following section, we will take a look at some of the common classification and regression algorithms.

Linear regression algorithm

Linear regression algorithms are designed for solving regression problems and predict a continuous value given a set of independent inputs. This kind of algorithm is used extensively in practical applications, such as estimating the product sales as a function of the product price or understanding the yield of a crop as a function of rainfall and fertilizer.

Linear regression uses a linear function of a set of coefficients and input variables to predict a scalar output. The formula for the linear regression is written as follows:

$$f(x) = W_1 * X_1 + W_2 * X_2 + \cdots + W_n * X_n + \varepsilon$$

Here, the Xs are the input variables, Ws are the coefficients, and ε is the error term. The motivation behind linear regression is that for a dataset where the output has a linear relationship with its inputs, its output value can be estimated by the weighted sum of the inputs. The intuition behind linear regression is to find a line or hyperplane that can estimate the value for a set of input values. Linear regression can work efficiently with small datasets. It is also highly interpretable, meaning that you can use the coefficient to understand the strength of the relationship between the input variable and the output response. However, as it is a linear model, it does not work well when the dataset is complex, with non-linear relationships. Linear regression also assumes input features to be mutually independent (no co-linearity), meaning the value of one feature does not influence the value of another feature. When there is co-linearity among the input features, it makes it hard to trust the significance of correlated features.

Logistic regression algorithm

A **logistic regression** algorithm is often used for binary classification tasks. Real-world examples of using logistic regression include *predicting the probability of someone clicking on an advertisement* or *whether someone could qualify for a loan.*

Logistic regression models the probability of a set of input data belonging to a class or event, such as transaction fraud or passing/failing an exam. It is also a linear model as the linear regression and its output is a linear combination of various inputs. However, since linear regression does not always produce a number between 0 and 1 (as needed for probability), logistic regression is used to return a value between 0 and 1 to represent probability. The intuition behind logistic regression is to find a line or plane/hyperplane that can cleanly separate two sets of data points as much as possible. The following formula is the function for the logistic regression, where X is a linear combination of input variables ($B+W1X$). Here, the W is the regression coefficient:

$$f(x) = \frac{1}{1 + e^{-X}}$$

Similar to linear regression, logistic regression's advantage is its fast training speed and its interpretability. Logistic regression is a linear model, so it cannot be used for solving problems with complex non-linear relationships.

Decision tree algorithm

A **decision tree** is used extensively in many real-world ML use cases, such as *heart disease prediction*, *target marketing*, and *loan default prediction*. They can be used for both classification and regression problems.

The motivation behind a decision tree is that data can be split using rules in a hierarchical manner, so similar data points will follow a similar decision path. Specifically, it works by splitting the input data using different features at different branches of the tree. For example, if age is a feature used for splitting at a branch, then use a conditional check (such as *age > 50*) to split the data at a branch. It makes decisions on which feature and where to split by using various algorithms, such as the **Gini purity index** (the **Gini index** measures the probability of a variable being classified incorrectly) and **information gain** (information gain calculates the reduction in entropy before and after the split).

We are not going to get into the details of specific algorithms in this book, but the main idea is to try out different tree split options and conditions, calculate the different metric values (such as information gain) of the different split options, and pick an option that provides the optimal value (for example, the highest information gain). When doing a prediction, the input data will traverse the tree based on the branching logic learned during the learning phase, and the terminal node (also known as the **leaf node**) will determine the final prediction. See the following figure (*Figure 3.2*) for the sample structure of a decision tree:

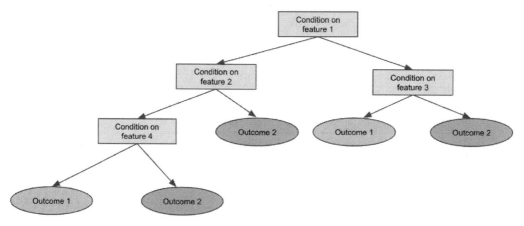

Figure 3.2 – Decision tree

The advantages that the decision tree has over linear regression and logistic regression are its ability to handle large datasets with complex non-linear relationships and co-linearity among the input features.

A decision tree works well with data without much preprocessing and can use categorical values and numerical values as it is. It can also handle missing features and large-scale differences among different features in the dataset. A decision tree is also easily explainable since it uses conditions to split the data to make decisions, and the decision path for an individual prediction can be easily visualized and analyzed. It is also a high-speed algorithm. On the negative side, a decision tree can be prone to outliers and overfitting. **Overfitting** is a model training problem where the model memorizes the training data and does not generalize well on unseen data, especially with large numbers of features and noise in the data.

Another key drawback for decision trees and tree-based algorithms in general is that they can't extrapolate outside of the inputs on which they were trained. For example, if you have a model predicting a housing price based on square footage and your training data contains ranges from 500 to 3,000 sq ft, a decision tree will not be able to extrapolate outside of the 3,000 sq ft, while a linear model would pick up the trend.

Random forest algorithm

A **random forest** algorithm is used extensively in real-world applications for e-commerce, healthcare, and finance for classification and regression tasks. Examples of these tasks include *insurance underwriting decisions*, *disease prediction*, *loan payment default prediction*, and *target marketing.*

As we have learned in the preceding decision tree section, a decision tree uses a single tree to make its decisions, and the root node of the tree (the first feature to split the tree) has the most influence on the final decision. The motivation behind the random forest algorithm is that multiple trees can make a better final decision. The way that a random forest works is to create multiple smaller **subtrees**, also called **weaker learner trees**, where each subtree uses a random subset of all the features to come to a decision, and the final decision is made by either majority voting (for classification) or averaging (for regression). This process of combining the decision from multiple models is also referred to as **ensemble learning**. Random forest algorithms also allow you to introduce different degrees of randomness, such as **bootstrap sampling** (using the same sample multiple times in a single tree) to make the model more generalized and less prone to overfitting. The following figure shows how the random forest algorithm processes input data instances using multiple subtrees and combines the outputs from the subtrees:

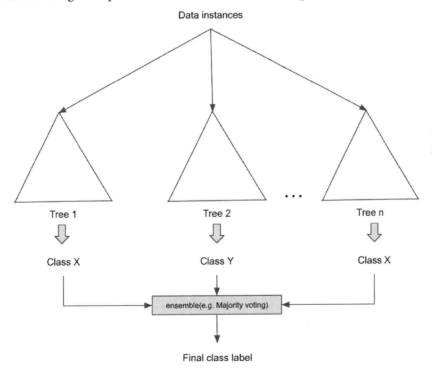

Figure 3.3 – Random forest

There are several advantages in using a random forest over a regular decision tree, such as parallelizable processing across multiple machines and the ability to handle outliers and imbalanced datasets. It is also able to handle a much higher dimension dataset because each tree uses a subset of the features. A random forest performs well with noisy datasets (datasets containing meaningless features or corrupted values). It is less prone to overfitting the data as a result of multiple trees making decisions independently. However, since it uses many trees to make a decision, the model interpretability does suffer a bit compared to a regular decision tree that can be easily visualized. It also takes more memory since it creates more trees.

Gradient boosting machine and XGBoost algorithms

Gradient boosting and **XGBoost** are also multi-tree-based ML algorithms. They have been widely used for many use cases such as *credit scoring, fraud detection*, and *insurance claim prediction*. While a random forest aggregates the result at the end by combining the results from weaker learner trees, gradient boosting aggregates the results from different trees sequentially.

A random forest builds on the idea of parallel independent weaker learners. The motivation for gradient boosting is based on the concept of a sequential weaker learner tree correcting the shortcoming (error) of the previous weaker tree. Gradient boosting has more hyperparameters to tune than a random forest and can achieve higher performance when it is tuned correctly. Gradient boosting also supports custom loss functions to give you the flexibility to model real-world applications. The following figure shows how the gradient boosting tree works:

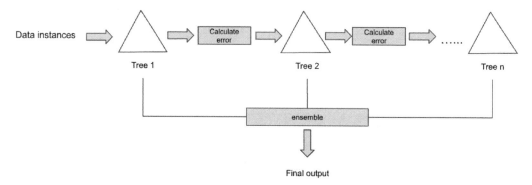

Figure 3.4 – Gradient boosting

Gradient boosting works well with imbalanced datasets, and it is good for use cases such as risk management and fraud detection where the dataset tends to be imbalanced. One major shortcoming of gradient boosting is that it does not parallelize as it creates trees sequentially. It is also prone to noise, such as outliers in the data, and can overfit easily as a result of this. Gradient boosting is less interpretable than a decision tree, but this can be easily overcome with tools such as variable importance (feature importance).

XGBoost is an implementation of gradient boosting. It has become very popular as a result of winning many **Kaggle** competitions. It uses the same underlying concept to build and tune the trees, but improves upon gradient boosting by providing support for training a single tree across multiple cores and multiple CPUs for faster training time, more powerful training regularization techniques to reduce the complexity of the model, and combat overfitting. XGBoost is also better at handling sparse datasets. In addition to XGBoost, there are other popular variations of gradient boosting trees, such as **LightGBM** and **CatBoost**.

K-nearest neighbor algorithm

K-nearest neighbor (**K-NN**) is a simple classification and regression algorithm. It is also a popular algorithm for implementing search systems and recommendation systems.

The fundamental assumption that K-NN works under is *similar things having close proximity*. The way to determine the proximity is to measure the distances between different data points. For classification tasks, K-NN first loads the data and their respective class labels. When we need to classify a new data point, we calculate its distances first, for example, the Euclidean distance to other loaded data points. We then retrieve the class labels for the top K (the K in K-NN) closest data points and use majority voting (the most frequent labels among the top K data points) to determine the class label for the new data point. The predicted scalar value will be the averaged values of the top K closest data points for regression tasks.

K-NN is simple to use and there is no need to train or tune the model with hyperparameters other than choosing the number of neighbors (K). The data points are simply loaded in the K-NN algorithm. Its results can be easily explainable, as each prediction can be explained by the properties of the nearest neighbors. In addition to classification and regression, it can also be used for search. However, the model grows in complexity as the number of data points increases, and it can become significantly slower with a large dataset for predictions. It also does not work well when the dataset dimension is high, and it is sensitive to noisy data and missing data. Outliers will need to be removed, and missing data will need to be imputed.

Multi-layer perceptron (MLP) network

As mentioned in the beginning, an **artificial neural network** (**ANN**) mimics how the human brain learns. The human brain has a huge number of neurons that are connected in a network to process information. Each neuron in a network processes inputs (electrical impulses) from another neuron, processes and transforms the inputs, and sends the output to neurons in the network. The following figure shows a picture of a human neuron:

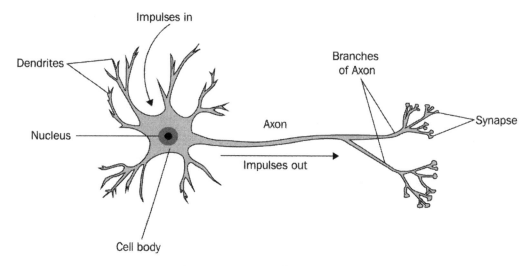

Figure 3.5 – Human brain neuron

An artificial neuron works similarly. The following figure shows an artificial neuron, which is mathematically a linear function plus an action function. An **activation function** transforms the output of the linear function, such as compressing the value between *0* and *1* (**sigmoid activation**), *-1* and *1* (**tanh activation**), or greater than 0 (**ReLU**). The idea for the activation function is to learn the non-linear relationship between input and output. You can also think of each neuron as a linear classifier, for example, logistic regression. The following figure shows the structure of an artificial neuron:

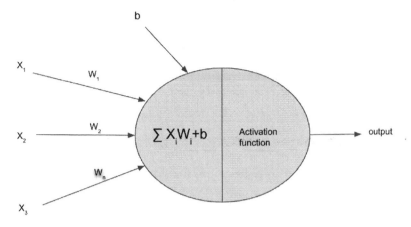

Figure 3.6 – Artificial neuron

When you stack a large number of neurons into different layers (*input layer*, *hidden layers*, and *output layer*) and connect all of the neurons together between two adjacent layers, we have an ANN called **multi-layer perceptron** (**MLP**). Here, the term *perceptron* means *artificial neuron*, and it was originally invented by Frank Rosenblatt in 1957. The idea behind MLP is that each hidden layer will learn some higher-level representation (features) of the previous layer, and those higher-level features capture the more important information in the previous layer. When the output from the final hidden layer is used for prediction, the network has extracted the most important information from the raw inputs for training a classifier or regressor. The following figure shows the architecture of an MLP network:

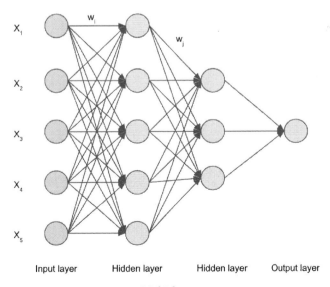

Figure 3.7 – Multi-layer perceptron

During model training, every neuron in every layer would have some influence on the final output, and their weights (W) are adjusted using a gradient descent to optimize the training objective. This process is called **backpropagation**, where the total error is propagated back into every neuron in every layer, and the weights for each neuron are adjusted for the portion of the total error associated with each neuron.

MLP is a general-purpose neural network that can be used for classification and regression. It can be used to solve similar problems as random forest and XGBoost. It is mainly used for tabular datasets, but can also work with other data formats, such as images and text. It can model complex nonlinear relationships in the dataset. It is also computationally efficient, as it is easily parallelizable. MLP normally requires more training data to train a performant model compared to traditional ML algorithms.

Algorithms for clustering

Clustering is a data mining technique to group items together based on item attributes. An example of clustering is to create different customer segments based on demographics data and historical transaction or behavior data. There are many different clustering algorithms. In this section, we will talk about the K-means clustering algorithm.

K-means algorithm

The **K-means** algorithm is used extensively in practical real-world applications, such as *customer segmentation analysis, documentation classification based on document attributes,* and *insurance fraud detection.*

K-means is one of the most popular clustering algorithms. It is used to find clusters of data points where similar data points belong to the same cluster. It is an unsupervised algorithm, as it does not require labels. The way it works is to start with random **centroids** (the center of clusters) for all K clusters and then find the best centroids by iterating the assignment of data points to the nearest centroid and moving the centroid to the mean. Some of the main benefits of using K-means are as follows:

- It guarantees convergence.
- It scales well with a large dataset.

However, to use K-means, you will need to manually choose the K (the number of clusters) – not always easy to do. Also, its performance is sensitive to the initial choices of random values, so you might not always find the optimal centroids. The centroids can also be easily dragged by outlier data points.

Algorithms for time series analysis

A **time series** is a list of sequential data points taken at different points in time. Examples of time series include daily stock prices over a period of time or weekly product sales for several months or years. Time series analysis has practical business values for many businesses, as it can help explain historical behaviors and forecast future business behaviors. Time series forecasting works under the principle that the future value of a variable has a dependency on the previous values at different times.

There are several key characteristics associated with time series data including *trend*, *seasonality*, and *stationarity*. Trend is the overall upward or downward direction of a time series over time. It helps understand the long-term movement of a time series. Seasonality helps capture patterns within an interval (usually within a year). It helps understand the seasonal time-dependent characteristics of a time series to help with forecasting. Stationarity indicates if the statistical properties (such as mean and variance) remain constant over time. It is important to understand if a time series is stationary or not, as forecasting on non-stationary time tends to be misleading. Many forecasting techniques work based on the assumption that the underlying time series data is stationary.

Now, let's take a look at some popular time series algorithms.

ARIMA algorithm

There are many practical real-world use cases for the **autoregressive integrated moving average** (**ARIMA**) algorithm, such as *budget forecasting*, *sales forecasting*, *patient visit forecasting*, and *customer support call volume forecasting*.

ARIMA has been around for decades, and it is an algorithm for time series forecasting (predicting the value of data in the future). The intuitions behind ARIMA are that the value of a variable in one period is related to its own values (versus the values of other variables in a linear regression model) in the previous periods (autoregressive), the deviation of the variable from the mean (moving average) is dependent on the previous deviations from the mean, and removing trend and seasonality with differencing `(the differences between raw data points from one period to another) to allow the time series to become stationary (statistical properties such as mean and variance are constant over time). The three components of ARIMA are expressed with the following formulas:

$$y_t = c + \emptyset_1 y_t - 1 + \emptyset_2 y_t - 2 + \cdots + \emptyset_p y_t - p + \varepsilon_t,$$

The **autoregressive** (**AR**) component is expressed as a regression of previous values $y_{t-1} \cdots y_{t-p}$ (also known as **lags**). The constant C represents a drift:

$$y_t = c + \varepsilon_t + \theta_1 \varepsilon_{t-1} + \theta_2 \varepsilon_{t-2} + \cdots + \theta_q \varepsilon_{t-q},$$

The **moving average (MA)** component is expressed as a weighted average of forecasting errors for the previous time periods, where it represents a constant:

$$y'_t = y_t - y_{t-1}$$

The **integrated component** (time series differencing) of a time series can be expressed as the difference between the values in one period from the previous period.

ARIMA is well suited to single time series (univariate) forecasting, as it does not require other variables to perform forecasting. It performs better than other simple forecasting techniques, such as simple moving average, exponential smoothing, or linear regression. It is also highly interpretable. However, ARIMA is mainly an backward-looking algorithm, so it does not forecast well for unexpected events. Also, ARIMA is a linear-based model, so it would not work well for time series data with complex non-linear relationships.

DeepAR algorithm

Deep learning-based forecasting algorithms address some of the shortcomings of traditional forecasting models (for example, ARIMA), such as complex non-linear relationships or the inability to take advantage of multivariate datasets. Deep learning-based models also make training a global model possible – meaning that you can train a single model that works with many similar target time series (for example, electricity consumption time series of all the customers) instead of creating one model per time series.

Deep Autoregressive (DeepAR) is an advanced neural network-based forecasting algorithm that can handle large datasets with multiple similar target time series. It supports related time series (for example, product prices or holiday schedules) to improve the accuracy of forecasting models.,This is especially useful for spiky events as a result of external variables.

DeepAR works by using a neural network called a **recurrent neural network (RNN)** to model the target time series, and combines that with other external supporting time series. At each time period, instead of taking the value of a single variable, the neural network input will take a single input vector that represents the values for variables (that is, values of data points for the multiple target time series and the values of data points for the multiple supporting time series), and jointly learn the patterns of the combined vectors over time (AR). This approach allows the network to learn the intrinsic non-linear relationship among all the different time series and extract common patterns exhibited by these time series. DeepAR trains a single global model that can work with multiple similar target time series for forecasting.

While DeepAR works well with complicated multivariate datasets, it requires very large amounts of data to be performant. Real-world practical use cases include large-scale retail forecasting for thousands or millions of items, with considerations for external events, such as marketing campaigns or holiday schedules.

Algorithms for recommendation

The **recommender** system is one of the most adopted ML technologies across industries such as retail, media and entertainment, finance, and healthcare.

The field of recommendation algorithms has evolved over the years. They work by predicting a user's preference toward an item mainly based on user or item attribute similarities or user-item interactions. Next, let's take a look at some common algorithms for the recommender system.

Collaborative filtering algorithm

Collaborative filtering is a common recommendation algorithm based on the concept that different people who share a common interest or taste on one set of items will likely share a common interest on other items. Essentially, it uses the collective experiences of different people to recommend items to users.

The following figure shows an item-user interaction matrix for movie ratings, and as you can see, it is a **sparse matrix**. This means that there are many empty entries in the matrix, which makes sense since no one would have watched every movie:

	Use 1 1	User 2	User 3 1	User 3	....	User n
Movie 1	5			4		
Movie 2	4		2			4
...						4
Movie n			3			

User-item interaction matrix

Figure 3.8 – User-item interaction matrix for collaborative filtering

Matrix factorization is one implementation of the collaborative filtering method. It is an embedding-based model where vector representations (embeddings) are learned for all the users (U) and items (V) in the user-item interaction matrix. The way to learn the embeddings is to ensure the product of the UV^T matrix would approximate the original matrix, so, to predict the value for a missing entry (the likely score a user would give to the unseen movie) in the original matrix, we just need to calculate the dot product between the user embedding and the item embedding.

Embedding is an important concept in ML, which I will cover more in the later section when we talk about algorithms for NLP. The main idea behind embedding is to create a mathematical representation for different entities in a way that the representations for similar entities are closer to each other in a multi-dimensional space represented by the embedding. You can think of embedding as a way to capture the latent semantics of the different objects.

Multi-arm bandit/contextual bandit algorithm

Collaborative filtering-based recommender systems require prior interaction data for identified users and items in order to work. When there are no prior interactions, or the user is anonymous, collaborative filtering will do poorly. This is also known as a **cold start problem**. A **multi-arm bandit** (**MAB**) based recommendation system is one approach to overcome the cold start problem. It works based on the concept of trial and error, and it is a form of reinforcement learning. It is analogous to a gambler who plays multiple slot machines at the same time evenly and tries to observe which machine provides a better overall return.

An MAB algorithm does not have any ready-to-use training data to train a model before it is deployed. It adopts a method called **online learning**, which means that it trains the model as the data is incrementally made available. At the beginning of an MAB learning, the MAB model would recommend all options (for example, products on e-commerce sites) with equal probabilities to users. As users start to interact (receiving rewards) with a subset of the items, the MAB model would start to offer items that it has received higher rewards for (for example, more interactions) more frequently. It continues to recommend new items at a smaller percentage to see if they would receive any interaction. This is also called the **explore** (offer new items) versus **exploit** (offer items with known good rewards) tradeoff.

Algorithms for computer vision problems

Computer vision is the ability for computers to understand visual representations (for example, images) to perform tasks such as identifying and classifying objects, detecting text, recognizing faces, and detecting activities. The computer vision tasks that we are solving today are mainly based on pattern recognition – meaning, we label images with object names and bounding boxes and train computer vision models to recognize the patterns from the images and make predictions on new images. Computer vision technology has many practical uses in the real world, such as *content management, security, augmented reality, self-driving cars, medical diagnosis, sports analytics*, and *quality inspection in manufacturing*. Next, we will deep dive into a couple of computer vision neural network architectures.

Convolution neural network

A convolution neural network (**CNN**) is a type of deep learning architecture that works well with image data. The way it learns is similar to how the animal visual cortex works. In the visual cortex context, a visual neuron responds to visual stimulation in a subregion of a visual field. The different subfields covered by different visual neurons partially overlap with each other to cover the entire visual field. In the context of a CNN, there are different filters that interact with the subregions in an image and respond to the information in a region.

A CNN is made of multiple repeating layers. Within each layer, there are different sublayers that are responsible for different functions.

The convolutional layer is responsible for extracting features from the input images. It uses a kind of filter called a **convolutional filter**, which is a matrix defined by height and width, to extract features. The convolutional layers convolve the image inputs (a multidimensional array) and send the output (extracted features) of a convolution layer to the next layer.

The pooling layer in a CNN reduces the dimensions of the extracted features from the convolutional layer by combining the multiple outputs into a single output. Two common pooling layers are **max pooling**, which takes the max value from the outputs, and **average pooling**, which averages the outputs into a single value.

After one or multiple convolutional layer/pooling layers, a fully connected layer is used to combine and flatten the outputs from the previous layer and feed them into an output layer for image classification. The following figure shows the architecture of a CNN:

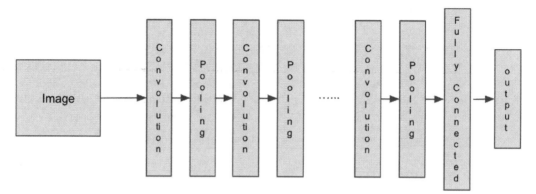

Figure 3.9 – CNN architecture

Training CNN-based models can be highly efficient, as it is highly parallelizable. While it is mainly used for computer vision tasks, we have also seen it applied to non-computer vision tasks, such as natural language processing.

ResNet

As computer vision tasks become increasingly complex, adding more layers helps make CNNs more powerful at image classification, as more layers progressively learn more complex features about the image. However, as more layers are added to a CNN architecture, the performance of the CNN degrades. This is also known as the **vanishing gradient problem**, which means signals from the original inputs (including important signals) are lost as they are processed by different layers of the CNN.

Residual network (**ResNet**) helps solve this problem by introducing a layer skipping technique. So, instead of processing signals layer by layer, ResNet provides another path for signals to skip layers. You can think of the skip layer connection as a highway that skips local exits. So, the signals from the earlier layers are carried over without getting lost. The following figure shows the architecture of ResNet:

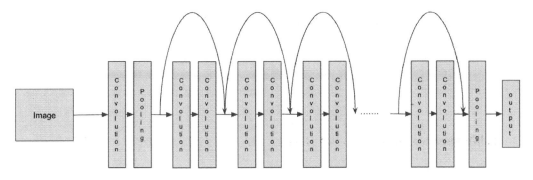

Figure 3.10 – ResNet architecture

ResNet can be used for different computer vision tasks such as *image classification, object detection* (detecting all objects in a picture), and producing models with much higher accuracy than a vanilla CNN network.

Algorithms for natural language processing problems

NLP is the study of the interaction between computer and human languages. Specifically, it is the processing and analysis of a large amount of natural language data. The goal is for computers to understand the meaning of human language and extract useful information for the human language data. NLP is a large data science domain. There are many NLP tasks, such as *document classification, topic modeling, speech to text, text to speech, entity extraction, language translation, reading comprehension, language generations,* and *questions and answering.*

ML algorithms cannot process raw text data directly. In order to train NLP models, the words in an input text need to be converted into numerical representations in the context of other words, sentences, or documents. Two popular methods for representing words and their relevance in a text are **bag-of-words (BOW)** and **term frequency–inverse document frequency (TF-IDF)**.

BOW is simply the count of a word appearing in a text (document). For example, if the input documents are I need to go to the bank to make a deposit and I am taking a walk along the river bank, and you count the number of appearances for each unique word in each input document, you will get *1* for the word *I*, and *3* for the word *to* in the first document, as an example. If we have a vocabulary for all the unique words in the two documents, the vector representation for the first document can be [1 1 3 1 1 1 1 1 0 0 0 0 0], where each position represents a unique word in the vocabulary (for example, the first position represents the word *I*, and the third position represents the word *to*). Now, this vector can be fed into an ML algorithm to train a model such as text classification. The main idea behind BOW is that a word that appears more frequently has stronger weights in a text.

TF-IDF has two components. The first component, *TF*, is the ratio of the number of times a vocabulary word appears in a document over the total number of words in the document. Using the preceding first document, the word *I* would have a TF value of *1/11* for the first sentence, and the word *walk* would have a TF value of *0/11*, since *walk* does not appear in the first sentence. While TF measures the importance of a word in the context of one text, the IDF component measures the importance of a word across all the documents. Mathematically, it is the log of the ratio of the number of documents over the number of documents where a word appears. The final value of TF-IDF for a word would be the *TF* term multiplied by the *IDF* term. In general, TF-IDF works better than BOW.

While techniques such as BOW and TF-IDF are good representations for NLP tasks, they don't capture any information on the semantic meaning of the word. They also result in very large and sparse input vectors. This is where the concept of **embedding** comes in.

Embedding is the technique of generating low-dimensional representations (mathematical vectors of real numbers) for words or sentences that captures the semantic meaning of the text. The intuition behind the technique of embedding is that those language entities with similar semantic meanings appear more frequently in similar contexts. The mathematical representations for semantically similar entities are closer to each other than entities with different semantic meanings in a multi-dimensional space. For example, if you have a number of words that represent sports such as *soccer*, *tennis*, and *bike*, their embeddings would be close to each other (measured by distance metrics such as cosine similarity between those embeddings) in the high-dimensional space represented by the embeddings. You can think of the embedding vector as representing the inherent meaning of the word, and each dimension in the vector represents a made-up attribute about the word. The following diagram is a visual depiction of what it means by being closer in the multidimensional space:

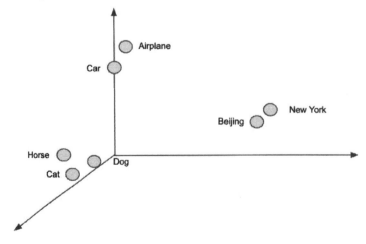

Figure 3.11 – Embedding representation

Most of the NLP tasks nowadays rely on embeddings as a prerequisite in order to achieve good results, as embedding provides more meaningful representations of the underlying text than other techniques (such as the count of words in a text). There are a number of ML algorithms for the different NLP tasks. Next, let's take a close look at some of the algorithms.

Word2Vec

Thomas Mikolov created **Word2Vec** in 2013. It supports two different techniques for learning embedding: **continuous bag-of-words** (**CBOW**) and **continuous-skip-gram**. CBOW tries to predict a word for a given window of surrounding words, and continuous-skip-gram tries to predict surrounding words for a given word. The training dataset for Word2Vec could be any running text available, such as **Wikipedia**. The process of generating a training dataset for CBOW is to run a sliding window across running text (for example, a window of five words) and choose one of the words as the target and the rest as inputs (the order of words is not considered). In the case of continuous-skip-gram, the target and inputs are reversed. With the training dataset, the problem can be turned into a multi-class classification problem, where the model will learn to predict the classes (for example, words in the vocabulary) for the target word and assign each predicted word with a probability distribution.

A simple one-hidden-layer MLP network can be used to train the Word2Vec embeddings. The inputs of the MLP network would be a matrix representing the surrounding words, and the outputs would be probability distributions for the target words. The weights learned for the hidden layer would be the actual embeddings for the word after it is fully trained and optimized.

As large-scale word embedding training can be expensive and time-consuming, Word2Vec embeddings are usually trained as a pre-training task so that they can be readily used for downstream tasks such as text classification or entity extraction. This approach of using embeddings as features for downstream tasks is called a **feature-based application**. There are pre-trained embeddings (for example, Tomas Mikolov' Word2Vec and Stanford's GloVe) in the public domain that can be used directly. The embeddings are a *1:1* mapping between each word and its vector representation.

Recurrent neural networks (RNN) and long short-term memory (LSTM)

As language comes in the form of word sequences, it needs to be modeled as such to capture the temporal relationship of the different words in a sequence. An RNN is a neural network that has been widely used for language-related ML tasks.

Unlike MLP or CNNs, where the input data is entered all at once and can be processed in parallel, an RNN takes and processes one data point input at a time (known as a **token**) in the sequence in a unit called the **cell**, and the output from the cell is used as an input for the next cell, in addition to the next data point in the input sequence. The number of cells in the sequence depends on the length of inputs (for example, the number of words), and each cell would perform the same function. This architecture allows inter-dependent semantic information (a word appears in a sentence depending on the previous words in the sentence to establish its semantic meaning) to be passed from one processing cell to another processing cell. The following figure shows what an RNN looks like:

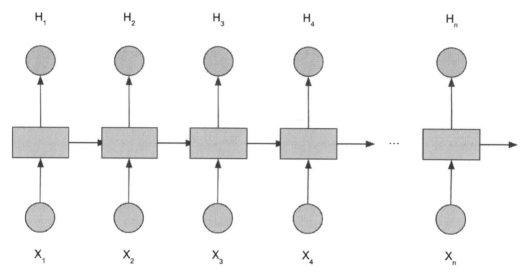

Figure 3.12 – An RNN

The ability to learn semantic relationships among character or word sequences makes RNN a popular algorithm for language modeling, where the goal is to generate the next language token (for example, character or word) given a preceding sequence of tokens.

An RNN also has the ability to summarize a sequence (for example, a sentence) and capture the inherent meaning of the sequence into a fixed-length vector representation. This makes an RNN a good fit for language tasks, such as language translation or summarization, where the goal is to take the semantic meaning of a sentence in one language and represent the same meaning in a different language or summarize longer sentences into more concise shorter sentences. This ability to summarize sentences into fixed-length vectors also makes an RNN useful for sentence classification.

When trained with a CNN together, an RNN can be used for image captioning tasks, where a CNN network summarizes images into fixed-length vectors, and the RNN uses the vectors to generate sentences that describe the images.

Since an RNN process inputs sequentially, it is hard to parallelize its computations, and training RNN-based models takes a long time compared to CNNs or MLP. Similar to the vanishing gradient problem associated with a large number of layers for a vanilla CNN, vanilla RNNs also suffer from the vanishing gradient problem when the sequence becomes long. RNN variations like **long short-term memory (LSTM)** allow additional hidden values to be passed from one cell to another and saved in the cells to capture important information in the early part of the long sequence.

For NLP tasks such as summarization and translation, to generate new sentences, the RNN (also known as the **decoder network**) needs to reference input tokens directly as additional inputs. Mechanisms such as the attention mechanism have been used to directly reference items in the input sequences from the generated outputs.

BERT

Word2Vec generates a single embedding representation for each word in the vocabulary, and the same embedding is used in different downstream tasks regardless of the context. As we know, a word could mean totally different things in different contexts (the word *bank* can mean a financial institution or the land along a body of water), and this requires word embeddings that consider context as part of the embedding generation process.

BERT, which stands for **Bidirectional Encoder Representations from Transformers**, is a language model that takes context into consideration by the following:

- Predicting randomly masked words in sentences (the context) and taking the order of words into consideration. This is also known as **language modeling**.

- Predicting the next sentence from a given sentence.

Released in 2018, this context-aware embedding approach provides better representation for words and can significantly improve language tasks such as *reading comprehension*, *sentiment analysis*, and *named entity resolution*. Additionally, BERT generates embeddings at subword levels (a segment between a word and a character, for example, the word *embeddings* is broken up into *em*, *bed*, *ding*, and *s*). This allows it to handle the **out-of-vocabulary (OOV)** issue, another limitation of Word2Vec, which only generates embeddings on known words and will treat OOV words simply as unknown.

To get word embeddings using BERT, instead of looking up *1:1* mapping as in the case of Word2Vec, you pass sentences to a trained BERT model and then extract the embeddings dynamically. In this case, the embeddings generated would be aligned with the context of the sentences. In addition to providing embeddings for words in the input sentences, BERT can also return the embeddings for the entire sentence. The following figure shows the building blocks of a BERT model for learning embeddings using input tokens. This is also known as **pre-training**:

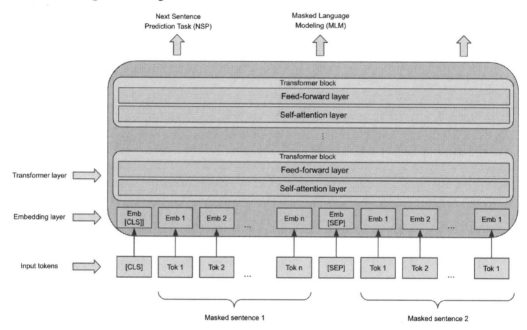

Figure 3.13 – BERT model pre-training

Architecturally, BERT mainly uses a building block called a **transformer**. A transformer has a stack of encoders and a stack of decoders inside it, and it transforms one sequence of inputs into another sequence. Each encoder has two components:

1. A self-attention layer mainly calculates the strength of the connection between one token (represented as a vector) and all other tokens in the input sentence, and this connection helps with the encoding of each token. One way to think about self-attention is which words in a sentence are more connected than other words in a sentence. For example, if the input sentence is *The dog crossed a busy street*, then we would say the words *dog* and *crossed* have stronger connections with the word *The* than the word *a* and *busy*, which would have strong connections with the word *street*. The output of the self-attention layer is a sequence of vectors; each vector represents the original input token as well as the importance it has with other words in the inputs.

2. A feed-forward network layer (single hidden layer MLP) extracts higher-level representation from the output of the self-attention layer.

Inside the decoder, there is also a self-attention layer and feed-forward layer, plus an extra encoder-decoder layer that helps the decoder to focus on the right places in the inputs.

In the case of BERT, only the encoder part of the transformer is used. BERT can be used for a number of NLP tasks, including *question answering*, *text classification*, *named entity extraction*, and *text summarization*. It achieved state-of-the-art performance in many of the tasks when it was released. BERT pre-training has also been adopted for different domains, such as scientific text and biomedical text, to understand domain-specific languages. The following figure shows how a pre-trained BERT model is used to train a model for a question-answering task using the fine-tuning technique:

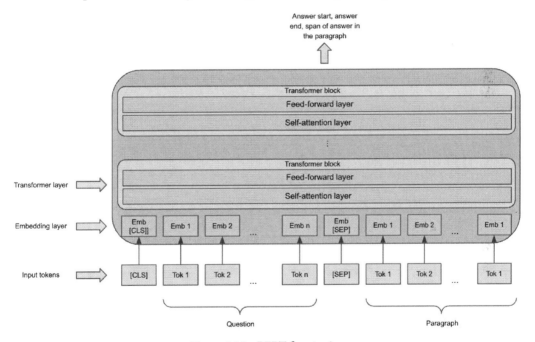

Figure 3.14 – BERT fine-tuning

While BERT's pre-trained embeddings can be extracted for downstream tasks such as text classification and question answering, a more straightforward way to use its pre-trained embeddings is through a technique called **fine-tuning**. With fine-tuning, an additional output layer is added to the BERT network to perform a specific task, such as question answering or entity extraction. During fine-tuning, the pre-trained model is loaded, and you plug in the task-specific input (for example, question/passage pairs in question answering) and output (start/end and span for the answers in the passage) to fine-tune a task-specific model. With fine-tuning, the pre-trained model weights are updated.

Generative pre-trained transformer

Unlike BERT, which requires fine-tuning using a large domain-specific dataset for the different downstream NLP tasks, the **Generative Pre-trained Transformer (GPT)**, developed by **OpenAI**, can learn how to perform a task with just seeing a few examples (or no example). This learning process is called **few-shot learning** or **zero-shot learning**. In a few-shot scenario, the GPT model is provided with a few examples, a task description, and a prompt, and the model will use these inputs and start to generate output tokens one by one. For example, when using **GPT**-3 for a translation task, an example of task definition would be *translate English to Chinese*. The training data would be a few examples of Chinese sentences translated from the English sentences. To use the trained model to translate a new English sentence, you provide the English sentence as a prompt, and the model will generate the translated text in Chinese. Note that, unlike the fine-tuning technique, few-shot or zero-shot learning does not update the model parameter weights.

GPT also uses Transformer as its main building block, and it is trained using next word prediction – meaning, given a sequence of input words, it predicts the word that should appear at the end of the sequence. Unlike BERT, which uses the Transformer encoder block, GPT uses the Transformer decoder block only. Similar to BERT, GPT also uses masked words to learn embeddings. However, it is different from BERT in that it does not randomly select masked words and predict the missing words. Instead, it does not allow the self-attention calculation to have access to words to the right of the target word to be calculated – this can be called masked self-attention.

The latest version of GPT is GPT-3, and it has shown very impressive results in a number of traditional NLP tasks, such as language modeling, language translation, and question answering, as well as many novel use cases, such as generating programming code or ML code, writing websites, and plot charts.

Latent Dirichlet Allocation algorithm

Topic modeling is the process of discovering common topics from a large number of documents and determining what top topics a document contains. A topic is usually presented by the associated top words. For example, a sport-related topic could have top words such as *sport*, *player*, *coach*, or *NHL*. Topic modeling is a very important natural language processing technique for document understanding, information retrieval, and document tagging and classification. A document can have one or more topics present in the content. The following figure shows the relationship between a document and various topics associated with the document:

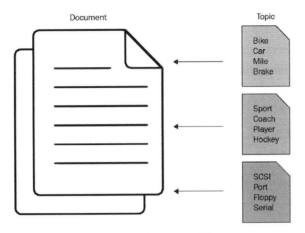

Figure 3.15 – Topic modeling

Latent Dirichlet Allocation (LDA) is one of the most popular ML algorithms for topic modeling. It works by calculating the probability of a word belonging to a topic and the probability of a topic belonging to a document. Let's explain how this works conceptually with an example. Say you have a large number of documents, and as you go through these documents, you want to identify words that frequently appear together in word clusters. Based on the count of word occurrences in a cluster, you can calculate the probabilities of different words belonging to a cluster (topic). The words with high probabilities would be considered top words that represent a topic. With a topic defined, you can then also calculate the probability of a topic belonging to a document. With LDA, you specify the number of topics to be discovered as input, and the output of LDA is a list of topics with top words weighed by their probability and a list of topics associated with each document.

LDA has many practical uses in the real world, such as *summarizing a large number of documents to a list of top topics* and *automatic document tagging and classification*. LDA is an unsupervised algorithm, and it discovers topics automatically. Its disadvantage is that it is hard to measure the overall quality of the model (that is, it is difficult to know if the topics generated are informative or not). You also need to tune the number of topics and interpret the result with a human-readable name for each topic produced by the model.

Generative model

A **generative model** is a type of ML model that can generate new data. For example, BERT and GPT are generative models, as they can generate new text. ML models like linear regression or MLP are called **discriminative models** in that they discriminate between different kinds of data instances, such as classifying something as one class or the other. Generative models model the joint probability, while a discriminative model models conditional probability.

Generative adversarial network

The **generative adversarial network (GAN)** is a generative model that tries to generate realistic data instances, such as images. It works by having a discriminative network (*Discriminator*) learning to tell if the instances generated by a *Generator* network are real or fake:

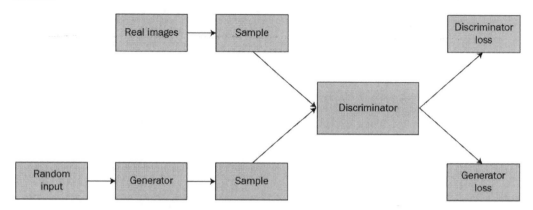

Figure 3.16 – Generative adversarial network

During training, the Discriminator network is provided with two data sources – one from a real source, used as positive examples, and one from the Generator source, the negative samples. The Discriminator will be trained to distinguish the real sample from the fake sample as a classifier, and it will optimize its loss to predict real/fake samples correctly from both sources. On the other hand, the Generator will be trained to produce fake data that the Discriminator cannot tell is fake or real, and it will be penalized when the Discriminator was able to tell its generated data is fake. Both networks learn using backpropagation. To generate data, the Generator is provided with random inputs. During training, the Generator and Discriminator are trained alternatively to allow both networks to train as a single connected network.

GAN has had a lot of success recently in generating realistic images that can fool humans. For example, it can be applied to many applications, such as translating sketches to realistic-looking images, converting text inputs and generating images corresponding to the text, and generating realistic human faces.

Now you have completed an overview of the different classic ML algorithms and deep learning networks. Next, let's practice with a hands-on exercise.

Hands-on exercise

In this hands-on exercise, we will build a **Jupyter Notebook** environment on your local machine and build and train an ML model in your local environment. The goal of the exercise is to get some familiarity with the installation process of setting up a local data science environment, and learn how to analyze the data, prepare the data, and train an ML model using one of the algorithms we covered in the preceding sections. First, let's take a look at the problem statement.

Problem statement

Before we start, let's first review the business problem that we need to solve. A retail bank is experiencing a high customer churn rate for its retail banking business. To proactively implement preventive measures to reduce potential churn, the bank needs to know who the potential churners are, so the bank can target those customers with incentives directly to prevent them from leaving. From a business operation perspective, it is much more expensive to acquire a new customer than offering incentives to keep an existing customer.

As an ML solutions architect, you have been tasked to run some quick experiments to validate the ML approach for this problem. There is no ML tooling available, so you have decided to set up a Jupyter environment on your local machine for this task.

Dataset description

You will use a dataset from the Kaggle site for bank customers' churn for modeling. You can access the dataset at `https://www.kaggle.com/mathchi/churn-for-bank-customers`. The dataset contains 14 columns for features such as credit score, gender, and balance, and a target variable column, `Exited`, to indicate if a customer churned or not. We will review those features in more detail in later sections.

Setting up a Jupyter Notebook environment

Now, let's set up a local data science environment for data analysis and experimentation. We will be using the popular Jupyter Notebook on your local computer. Setting up a Jupyter Notebook environment on a local machine consists of the following key components:

- **Python**: Python is a general-purpose programming language, and it is one of the most popular programming languages for data science work.

- **PIP**: PIP is a Python package installer used for installing different Python library packages, such as ML algorithms, data manipulation libraries, or visualization.

- **Jupyter Notebook**: Jupyter Notebook is a web application that can be used for authoring documents (called notebooks) that contain code, description, and/or visualizations. It is one of the most popular tools for data scientists to do experimentation and modeling.

Follow either the Mac or PC instructions given as follows, depending on your machine.

Installing Python 3 on macOS

Python 3 can be downloaded and installed directly from `https://www.python.org/downloads/`. An easier way is to install it using a package manager such as **Homebrew**. In the following section, we will use Homebrew to install `Python3`.

Installing Homebrew, Python3, and PIP3

Homebrew can be downloaded by following the instructions at `https://brew.sh/`. Installing Homebrew will also install Python 3. The specific steps are listed as follows:

1. Open up a terminal window on your Mac machine.

2. Inside the terminal window, type and run the following command to start installing Homebrew:

```
/bin/bash -c "$(curl -fsSL https://raw.githubusercontent.
com/Homebrew/install/HEAD/install.sh)"
```

3. Enter your Mac user password when prompted during the installation.

4. After the previous script completes, run the following command inside the **Terminal** window to get the latest versions of the packages:

```
brew update && brew upgrade python
```

5. Point to the Homebrew Python by typing and running the following command. It will make the current Terminal window use the Homebrew Python installation:

```
alias python=/usr/local/bin/python3
```

6. Verify the Python installation and version by running the following command inside the Terminal window:

```
python -version
```

At the time of writing this book, the latest Python version is 3.9.1.

7. To persist the setting of Homebrew Python for all Terminal windows, type and run the following command in the Terminal window depending on which shell you have on your Mac:

```
echo alias python=/usr/local/bin/python3 >> ~/.bashrc
```

Or, type and run the following command:

```
echo alias python=/usr/local/bin/python3 >> ~/.zshrc
```

Installing Jupyter Notebook on macOS

Now, we are ready to install the Jupyter Notebook on your machine:

1. Inside the Terminal window, run the following command:

```
brew install jupyter
```

2. Start the Jupyter Notebook by running the following command in your Terminal window:

```
jupyter notebook
```

Installing Python3 on a Windows machine

Download the Windows installer for Python 3.9.1 using the following URL:

https://www.python.org/ftp/python/3.9.1/python-3.9.1-amd64.exe

Run the installer and follow the instructions to complete the installation.

Installing PIP3

Follow the given steps to complete the installation:

1. Download https://bootstrap.pypa.io/get-pip.py and save it to a local folder on the PC.

2. Open a **Command Prompt** window and navigate to the folder where the file is saved.

3. Run the following command to install pip:

```
py get-pip.py
```

4. The preceding command will print out the directory where the `pip` utility is installed. Add the path of the `Pip` utility to the system path by running the following command:

```
set path= %path%;<path to the pip directory>
```

Installing Jupyter Notebook on Windows

With Python 3 and the pip utility installed, we can now install Jupyter Notebook by running the following command in the Command Prompt window:

```
pip install jupyter
```

Running the exercise

1. Now we have installed Python 3 and Jupyter Notebook, let's get started with the actual data science work. First, download the data files:

    (a) Let's create a folder called `MLSALab` on your local machine to store all the files. You can create the folder anywhere on your local machine as long as you can get to it. I have a Mac, so I created one directly inside the default user `Documents` folder.

    (b) Create another subfolder called `Lab1-bankchurn` under the `MLSALab` folder.

    (c) Visit the `https://www.kaggle.com/mathchi/churn-for-bank-customers` site and download the data file (an archive file) and save it in the `MSSALab/Lab1-bankchurn` folder. Create a Kaggle account if you do not already have one. Extract the archive file inside the folder, and you will see a file called `churn.csv`. You can now delete the archive file.

2. Launch Jupyter Notebook:

    (a) Inside the Terminal window (or the Command Prompt window for Windows systems), navigate to the `MLSALab` folder and run the following command to start the Jupyter Notebook server on your machine:

    ```
    jupyter notebook
    ```

    A browser window will open up and display the Jupyter Notebook environment (see the following screenshot). Detailed instructions on how Jupyter Notebook works is out of scope for this lab. If you are not familiar with how Jupyter Notebook works, you can easily find information on the internet:

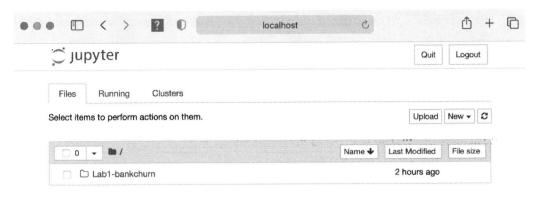

Figure 3.17 – Jupyter Notebook

(b) Click on the Lab1-bankchurn folder and you will see the churn.csv file.

3. Experimentation and model building: Now, let's create a new data science notebook inside the Jupyter Notebook environment. To do this, you click on the **New** dropdown and select **Python 3** (see following screenshot):

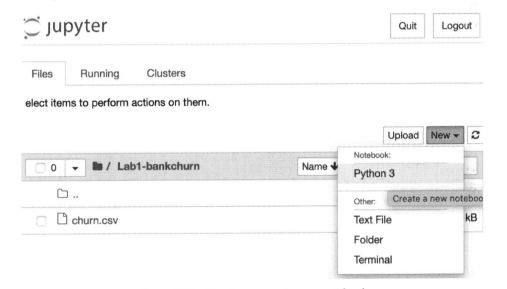

Figure 3.18 – Creating a new Jupyter notebook

4. You will see a screen similar to the following screenshot. This is an empty notebook that we will use to explore data and build models. The section next to **In [ ]:** is called a **cell**, and we will enter our code into the cell. To run the code in the cell, you click on the **Run** button on the toolbar. To add a new cell, you click on the + button on the toolbar:

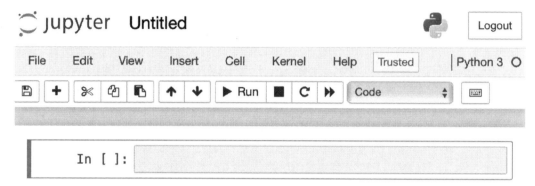

Figure 3.19 – Empty Jupyter notebook

5. First, let's configure the Jupyter environment to use the right Python library with the following code block by entering it in the first empty cell and running the cell by clicking on the **Run** button in the toolbar. Here, the `sys.executable` points to the `Python3` location we installed earlier, and the `sys.path` needs to include the additional path where the additional library package will be installed. Note, this code block is only needed for Mac. There is no need to run this code on a PC:

```
import sys
sys.executable = "/usr/local/bin/python3"
sys.path = sys.path + ['/usr/local/lib/python3.9/site-
packages']
```

6. Add a new cell by clicking on the + button in the toolbar, enter the following code block inside the first empty cell, and run the cell by clicking on the **Run** button in the toolbar. This code block downloads a number of Python packages for data manipulation (**pandas**), visualization (**matplotlib**), and model training and evaluation (**scikit-learn**). We will cover scikit-learn in greater detail in *Chapter 5, Open Source Machine Learning Libraries*. We will use these packages in the following sections:

```
! pip3 install pandas
! pip3 install matplotlib
! pip3 install scikit-learn
```

7.   Now, we can load and explore the data. Add the following code block in a new cell to load the Python library packages and load the data from the `churn.csv` file. You will see a table with 14 columns, where the `Exited` column is the target column:

```
import pandas as pd
churn_data = pd.read_csv("churn.csv")
churn_data.head()
```

8.   You can explore the dataset using a number of tools to understand information with the commands that follow, such as *dataset statistics*, the *pairwise correlation between different features*, and *data distributions*. The `describe()` function returns basic statistics about the data such as mean, standard deviation, min, and max, for each numerical column. The `hist()` function plots the histogram for the selected columns, and `corr()` calculates the correlation matrix between the different features in the data. Try them out one at a time in a new cell to understand the data:

```
# The following command calculates the various statistics
for the features.
churn_data.describe()
# The following command displays the histograms for the
different features.
# You can replace the column names to plot the histograms
for other features
churn_data.hist(['CreditScore', 'Age', 'Balance'])
# The following command calculate the correlations among
features
churn_data.corr()
```

9.   The dataset needs transformations in order to be used for model training. The following code block will convert the `Geography` and `Gender` values from categorical strings to ordinal numbers so they can be taken by the ML algorithm later. Please note that model accuracy is not the main purpose of this exercise, and we are performing ordinal transformation for demonstration purposes. Copy and run the following code block in a new cell:

```
from sklearn.preprocessing import OrdinalEncoder
encoder_1 = OrdinalEncoder()
encoder_2 = OrdinalEncoder()

churn_data['Geography_code'] = encoder_1.fit_
```

```
transform(churn_data[['Geography']])
  churn_data['Gender_code'] = encoder_2.fit_
transform(churn_data[['Gender']])
```

10. There are some columns not needed for model training. We can drop them using the following code block:

```
churn_data.drop(columns =
['Geography','Gender','RowNumber','Surname'],
inplace=True)
```

11. Now, the dataset has only the features we care about. Next, we need to split the data for training and validation. We also prepare each dataset by splitting the target variable, Exited, from the rest of the input features. Enter and run the following code block in a new cell:

```
# we import the train_test_split class for data split
from sklearn.model_selection import train_test_split

# Split the dataset into training (80%) and testing
(20%).
churn_train, churn_test = train_test_split(churn_data,
test_size=0.2)

# Split the features from the target variable "Exited" as
it is required for model training

# and validation later.
  churn_train_X = churn_train.loc[:, churn_train.columns
!= 'Exited']
  churn_train_y = churn_train['Exited']

churn_test_X = churn_test.loc[:, churn_test.columns !=
'Exited']
  churn_test_y = churn_test['Exited']
```

12. We are ready to train the model. Enter and run the following code block in a new cell. Here, we will use the random forest algorithm to train the model, and the fit() function kicks off the model training:

```
# We will use the Random Forest algorithm to train the
model
```

```
from sklearn.ensemble import RandomForestClassifier
bank_churn_clf = RandomForestClassifier(max_depth=2,
random_state=0)
 bank_churn_clf.fit(churn_train_X, churn_train_y)
```

13. Finally, we will test the accuracy of the model using the `test` dataset. Here, we get the predictions returned by the model using the `predict()` function, and then use the `accuracy_score()` function to calculate the model accuracy using the predicted values (`churn_prediction_y`) and the true values (`churn_test_y`) for the test dataset:

```
# We use the accuracy_score class of the sklearn library
to calculate the accuracy.
 from sklearn.metrics import accuracy_score


# We use the trained model to generate predictions using
the test dataset
churn_prediction_y = bank_churn_clf.predict(churn_test_X)


# We measure the accuracy using the accuracy_score class.
 accuracy_score(churn_test_y, churn_prediction_y)
```

Congratulations! You have successfully installed a Jupyter data science environment on your local machine and trained a model using the random forest algorithm. You have validated that an ML approach could potentially solve this business problem.

Summary

This chapter covered a number of ML algorithms for solving different types of ML tasks. You now should understand what algorithms can be used for the different kinds of ML problems. You have also created a simple data science environment on your local machine, used the scikit-learn ML libraries to explore and prepare data, and trained an ML model.

In the next chapter, we will discuss how data management intersects the ML life cycle and build a data management platform on AWS for the downstream ML tasks.

4
Data Management for Machine Learning

As a practitioner of **machine learning** (**ML**) solutions architecture, I often get asked to help provide architecture advice on data management platforms for ML workloads. While data management platform architecture is mainly considered a separate technical discipline, it is an integral part of ML workloads. To design a comprehensive ML platform, ML solutions architects need to be familiar with the key data architecture considerations for machine learning and know the technical design of a data management platform to meet the needs of data scientists and the automated ML pipelines. In this chapter, we will look at where data management intercepts with ML. We will talk about key considerations for designing a data management platform for ML. We will then deep dive into the core architecture components for a data management platform and the relevant **AWS** technologies and services for building a data management platform on AWS. Finally, you will get hands-on and create a **data lake** with support for **data catalog** management, **data discovery**, and **data processing** workflows on AWS.

Specifically, we will have the following main sections in the chapter:

- Data management considerations for ML

- Data management architecture for ML

- Hands-on exercise - data management for ML

Technical requirements

In this chapter, you will need access to an AWS account and AWS services such as **Amazon S3**, **Amazon Lake Formation**, **AWS Glue**, and **AWS Lambda**. If you do not have an AWS account, follow the official AWS website's instructions to create an account.

Data management considerations for ML

Data management is a broad and complex topic. Many organizations have dedicated data management teams and organizations to manage and govern the various aspects of a data platform. Traditionally, the main focus of data management has been meeting the needs of transactional systems or analytics systems. With the growing adoption of ML solutions, there are new business and technology considerations for data management platforms.

To understand where data management intersects with the ML workflow, let's bring back the ML life cycle, as shown in the following figure:

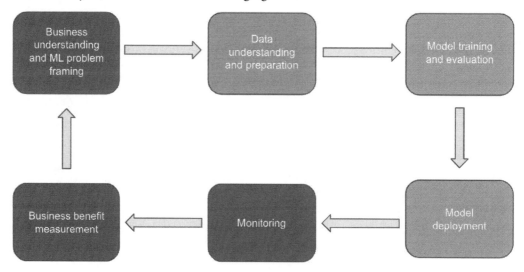

Figure 4.1 – Intersection of data management and the ML life cycle

At a high level, data management intersects with the ML life cycle in three stages: *data understanding and preparation*, *model training and evaluation*, and *model deployment*.

During the *data understanding and preparation* stage, data scientists will need to identify data sources that contain datasets for the modeling tasks and perform exploratory data analyses, such as data statistics, the correlation between the different features, and distribution of data samples, to understand the dataset. You also need to prepare the data for model training and validation, which would normally include the following:

- Data validation to detect errors and verify the data quality (for example, data range, data distribution, data types, or missing/null values)
- Data cleaning to fix the data errors
- Data enrichment to generate new signals through the joining of different datasets or data transformation

The data management capabilities required during this stage mainly include the following:

- The ability to search for curated data using various metadata such as dataset name, dataset description, field name, and data owner
- The ability to access both raw and processed datasets for exploratory data analysis.
- The ability to run queries against the selected dataset to get details, such as statistical details, data quality, and data samples
- The ability to retrieve data from the data management platform to a data science experimentation or model building environment for further processing and feature engineering
- The ability to run data processing against a large dataset

During the model training and validation stage, data scientists will need to create a training and validation dataset for formal model training. The data management capabilities required for this stage include the following:

- Data processing capabilities and an automated workflow to process raw/curated datasets into training/validation datasets of different formats for model training
- A data repository for storing and managing the training/validation datasets and their versioning
- The ability to serve the training/validation dataset to the model training infrastructure to train models

During the model deployment stage, the trained models will be used to serve predictions. The data management capabilities required for this stage include the following:

- Serving data needed for the feature processing as part of the input data when invoking the deployed models
- Serving pre-computed features as part of the inputs when invoking the deployed models

Unlike traditional data access patterns for building transactional or **business intelligence (BI)** solutions where developers can work with non-production data in lower environments for development purposes, data scientists need access to production data for model developments.

Now, we have discussed the considerations for ML data management. Next, let's deep dive into the data management architecture for ML.

Data management architecture for ML

Depending on the scope of your ML initiatives, you may want to consider different data management architecture patterns to support them.

For small-scale ML projects with limited data scope, team size, and cross-functional dependencies, consider purpose-built data pipelines that meet the project's specific needs. For example, suppose you only need to work with structured data from an existing data warehouse and a dataset from the public domain. In that case, you want to consider building a simple data pipeline that extracts the required data from the data warehouse and the public domain to a storage location owned by the project team on an as-needed schedule for further analysis and processing. The following figure shows a simple data management flow to support a small-scope ML project:

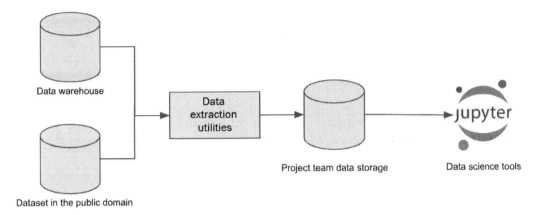

Figure 4.2 – Data architecture for an ML project with limited scope

For large, enterprise-wide ML initiatives, the data management architecture for ML is very similar to the enterprise architecture for analytics. Both need to support **data ingestion** from many different sources and centrally manage the data for various processing and access needs. Analytics data management mostly works with structured data, where an enterprise data warehouse is usually the core architecture backend. ML data management would need to work with structured, semi-structured, and unstructured data for different ML tasks, where a data lake architecture is usually adopted. ML data management is usually an integral part of the broader enterprise data management for both analytics and ML initiatives.

The following figure shows a logical enterprise data management architecture. It consists of several key components: data ingestion, data storage, data processing, data catalog, data security, and data access:

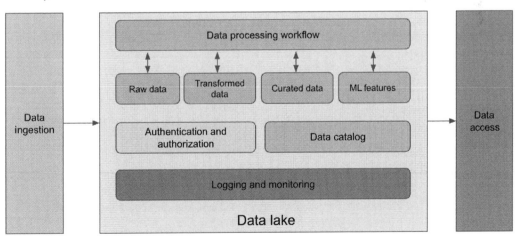

Figure 4.3 – Enterprise data management

Next, let's discuss each of the key components in detail and what a data management architecture looks like when built with AWS native services in the cloud.

Data storage and management

ML workloads require data of different formats from many sources, and the size of the dataset can be very large, especially when dealing with **unstructured data**. Cloud object data storage, such as Amazon S3 or **Hadoop Distributed File System (HDFS)** on a **Hadoop** cluster, is usually used as the storage medium for data. Functionally, you can think of cloud object storage as a file storage system where files of different formats can be stored. The files can also be organized using folder-like prefixes inside the object storage to help with the organization of objects. Also, note that prefixes are not physical folder structures. It is called **object storage** because each file is an independent *object*. Each object is bundled with metadata, and it is assigned with a unique identifier. Object storage is usually known for unlimited storage capacity, rich object analytics from the object metadata, API-based access, and low cost.

To effectively manage the large volumes of data in a cloud object storage medium, a data lake architecture backed up by cloud object storage is the recommended way to centralize data management and data access. Depending on the scope, the data lake can be scoped for the entire enterprise or individual line of business. A *data lake* is meant to store unlimited amounts of data and manage them in different life cycle stages, such as raw data, transformed data, curated data, and ML features. The main purpose of the data lake is to bring different data silos together into a single central repository for central data management and data access for both analytics needs and ML needs. A data lake can store different data formats, including structured data from databases, unstructured data such as documents, semi-structured data such as **JSON** and **XML**, and binary formats such as image, video, and audio. This capability is especially important for ML workloads since ML deals with data of different formats.

The data lake should be organized by different zones. For example, a *landing zone* should be established as the target for the initial data ingestion from different sources. After data pre-processing and data quality management processing, the data can be moved to the raw data zone. Data in the *raw data zone* can be further transformed and processed to meet different business and downstream consumption needs. To further ensure the reliability of the dataset for usage, the data can be curated and stored in the *curate data zone*. For ML tasks, ML features often need to be pre-computed and stored in an ML feature zone for reuse purposes.

AWS Lake Formation

AWS Lake Formation is an AWS data management service that simplifies the creation and management of a data lake on AWS. It provides four core functionalities:

- A data source crawler to infer the data structure from data files

- The creation and maintenance of a data catalog for the data in the data lake

- Data transformation processing

- Data security and access control

The following figure shows the core function of AWS Lake Formation:

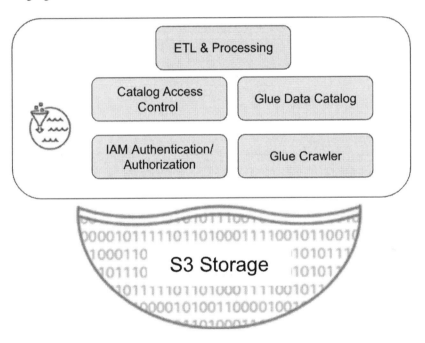

Figure 4.4 – AWS Lake Formation

Lake Formation integrates with AWS Glue, a serverless **Extract, Transform, Load (ETL)** and data catalog service, to provide data catalog management and data ETL processing functionality. We will cover ETL and data catalog components separately in later sections.

Lake Formation provides centralized data access management capability for managing data access permissions for the database, tables, or different registered S3 locations. For databases and tables, the permission can be granularly assigned to individual tables and columns and database functions, such as creating tables and inserting records.

Data ingestion

The data ingestion component is responsible for taking data of different formats (for example, structured, semi-structured, and unstructured) from different sources (for example, databases, social media, file storage, or IoT devices) and persisting data in storage, such as object data storage (for example, Amazon S3), data warehouses, or other data stores. The ingestion patterns should include both *real-time streaming* as well as *batch ingestion* to support different data sources.

There are different data ingestion technologies and tools for the different kinds of ingestion patterns. **Apache Kafka**, **Apache Spark Streaming**, and **Amazon Kinesis/ Kinesis Firehose** are some of the common tools for streaming data ingestion. Tools such as **Secure File Transfer Protocol** (**SFTP**) and AWS Glue can be used for batch-oriented data ingestion. AWS Glue supports different data sources and targets (for example, **Amazon RDS**, **MongoDB**, Kafka, **Amazon DocumentDB**, S3, and any databases that support JDBC connections).

When deciding on which tools to use for data ingestion, it is important to assess the tools and technologies based on practical needs. The following are some of the considerations when deciding on data ingestion tools:

- **Data format, size, and scalability**: Consider the needs for varying data formats, data size, and data velocity. ML projects could be using data from different sources and different formats (for example, tabular data such as **CSV** and **Parquet**, semi-structured data such as JSON/XML, and unstructured data such as documents or image/audio/video files). Do you need to scale the infrastructure up to handle large data ingestion volume when needed, and do you need to scale it down to reduce costs when the volume is low?

- **Ingestion patterns**: Consider the different data ingestion patterns you need to support. The tool or combination of several tools needs to support batch ingestion patterns (in other words, moving bulk data at different time intervals) and real-time streaming (moving data such as sensor data or website clickstreams in real time).

- **Data preprocessing capability**: The ingested data might need to be preprocessed before it lands in the target data store. So, consider tools with either built-in processing capability or those that integrate with external processing capability.

- **Security**: The tools need to provide security mechanisms for both authentication and authorization.

- **Reliability**: The tools need to provide failure recovery capability so critical data is not lost during the ingestion process. If there is no recovery capability, then make sure there is a capability for re-running ingestion jobs from the sources.

- **Support for different data sources and targets**: Ingestion tools need to support a wide range of data sources, such as databases, files, and streaming sources. The tool should also provide an API for data ingestion.

- **Manageability**: Manageability should be another consideration. Does the tool require self-management, or is it fully managed? Consider the trade-off before cost and operational complexity.

There are a number of AWS services for data ingestion into a data lake on AWS. You have Kinesis Data Streams, Kinesis Firehose, **AWS Managed Streaming for Kafka**, and AWS Glue streaming for streaming data requirements. For batch ingestion, you can have AWS Glue, SFTP, and AWS **Data Migration Service (DMS)**. In the following section, we will discuss how Kinesis Firehose and AWS Glue can be used for data ingestion management.

Kinesis Firehose

Kinesis Firehose is a fully managed service for loading streaming data into a data lake. By *fully managed*, we mean you don't manage the underlying infrastructure; instead, you interact with the service API for the ingestion, processing, and delivery of the data.

Kinesis Firehose supports the key requirements for scalable data ingestion:

- Support for different data sources such as websites, IoT devices, and video cameras using an ingestion agent or ingestion API.

- Support for different delivery targets, including Amazon S3, **Amazon Redshift** (an AWS data warehouse service), **Amazon ElasticSearch** (a managed search engine), and **Splunk** (a log aggregation and analysis product).

- Data processing capabilities through integration with AWS Lambda and **Kinesis Data Analytics**. AWS Lambda is a serverless compute service that runs custom functions written in **Python**, **Java**, **Node.js**, **Go**, **C#**, and **Ruby**. Check the official AWS documentation for more detail on how Lambda works. The following figure shows the data flow with Kinesis Firehose:

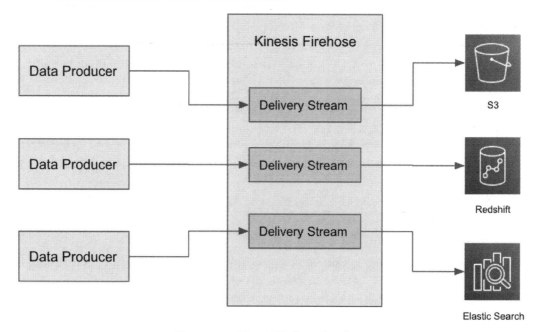

Figure 4.5 – Kinesis Firehose data flow

Kinesis works by creating *delivery streams* – that is, the underlying entity in the Firehose architecture that can accept streaming data from data producers. The delivery stream can have different delivery targets, such as S3 and Redshift. Depending on the data volume from the producers, you configure the throughput of the data stream by the number of shards (for example, each shard can ingest 1 MB/sec of data and can support 2 MB/sec for data read). Kinesis Firehose provides APIs for increasing and merging shards.

AWS Glue

AWS Glue is a fully managed serverless ETL service that can be used for ingesting data in batches. It connects to data sources such as transactional databases, data warehouses, and **NoSQL** databases, and performs data movement to different targets, such as Amazon S3, based on schedule or event triggers. If needed, it can also process and transform data before it delivers the data to the target. It supports a number of processing capabilities such as the **Python shell** (for running Python scripts) and **Apache Spark** (for Spark-based data processing).

AWS Lambda

AWS Lambda is the serverless compute platform on AWS. It works natively with many other AWS services, such as Amazon S3. A Lambda function can be triggered to execute by different events, such as the S3 `new file` event. Lambda functions can be developed to move data from different sources, such as a source S3 bucket to a target landing bucket in the data lake. AWS Lambda is not designed for large-scale data movement or processing; however, for simple data ingestion and processing jobs, it is a very effective tool.

Data cataloging

The data catalog is a critical component for data governance and for making the data in the central data storage discoverable by data analysts and data scientists. This is especially important for the data understanding and exploration phase of the ML life cycle when data scientists need to search and understand what data is available for their ML projects. Some of the key considerations for a data catalog technology include the following:

- **Metadata catalog**: Support for a central data catalog for the data lake metadata management. Examples of metadata are database names, table schemas, and table tags. A popular standard for metadata catalogs is the **Hive metastore catalog**.

- **Automated data cataloging**: The capability to automatically discover and catalog datasets and infer data schemas from different data sources, such as Amazon S3, relational databases, NoSQL databases, and logs. This is usually implemented as a crawler that crawls data sources and automatically identifies metadata, such as data column names and data types.

- **Tagging flexibility**: The ability to tag metadata entities (for example, databases, tables, fields) with custom attributes to support data search and discovery.

- **Integration with other tools**: The data catalog can be used by a wide range of data processing tools to access the underlying data, as well as native integration with data lake management platforms.

- **Search**: Search capability across a wide range of metadata in the catalog, such as database/table/field name, custom tags/description, and data type.

There are different technical options for building data catalogs. Here, we will discuss how AWS Glue can be used for data cataloging.

AWS Glue Catalog

In addition to the ETL functionality, AWS Glue also provides a built-in data catalog feature that integrates natively with AWS Lake Formation. The Glue catalog can be a drop-in replacement for the Hive metastore catalog, so any Hive metastore-compatible applications can work with the AWS Glue catalog.

The AWS Glue catalog structures its metadata hierarchy in the form of databases and tables. Databases are containers for tables that represent the data store. And just like regular databases, you can have multiple tables in a single database, and the tables can come from different data stores. However, each table can only belong to a single database. The databases and their tables can be queried using the SQL language using Hive metastore-compatible tools.

The AWS Glue catalog has a built-in crawler that can automatically crawl data sources, discover data schemas, and populate the central data catalog. The crawler supports the database and table creation for new data sources as well as incremental updates to the existing databases and tables. The crawler can run on-demand or be run by an event trigger, such as the completion of an AWS Glue ETL job.

When working together with AWS Lake Formation, the access permission to the databases and tables in the catalog can be managed through the Lake Formation entitlement layer.

Data processing

The data processing capability of a data lake provides the data processing frameworks and the underlying compute resources to process data for different purposes, such as data error correction, data transformation, data merging, data splitting, and ML feature engineering. Some of the common data processing frameworks include Python shell scripts and Apache Spark. The key requirements for data processing technology include the following:

- **Integration and interoperability with the underlying storage technology**: The capability to work with the underlying storage natively. This simplifies data access and movement from the storage to the processing layers.

- **Integration with the data catalog**: The capability to work with the data metastore catalog for querying the databases and tables in the data catalog.

- **Scalability**: The capability to scale up and scale down the compute resources based on the data volumes and processing velocity requirements.

- **Language and framework support**: Support for common data processing libraries and frameworks, such as Python and Spark.

Now, let's take a look at several available AWS services that can provide data processing capabilities in the data lake architecture.

AWS Glue ETL

In addition to supporting data movement and data catalogs, the ETL features of AWS Glue can be used for ETL and general-purpose data processing. AWS Glue ETL provides a number of built-in functions for data transformation, such as the drop of the NULL field and data filtering. It also provides general processing frameworks for Python and Spark to run Python scripts and Spark jobs. Glue ETL works natively with the Glue catalog for accessing the databases and tables in the catalog. Glue ETL can also access the Amazon S3 storage directly.

Amazon Elastic Map Reduce (EMR)

Amazon EMR is a fully managed big data processing platform on AWS. It is designed for large-scale data processing using the Spark framework and other Apache tools, such as **Apache Hive**, **Apache Hudi**, and **Presto**. It integrates with the Glue Data Catalog and Lake Formation natively for accessing databases and tables in Lake Formation.

AWS Lambda

AWS Lambda can also be used for data processing for small data volumes and files. Lambda can be triggered by real-time events, so it is a good option for lightweight, real-time data processing.

Data versioning

To establish the lineage for model training, we need to version-control the training/validation/testing dataset. **Data versioning** control is a hard problem as it requires both tools and people following best practices for it to work. During the model building process, it is very common for a data scientist to get a copy of a dataset, and perform their own cleansing and transformation to the data, then save the updated data back as a new version. This creates a huge challenge to data management in terms of duplication and linking the data to the different upstream and downstream tasks.

Data versioning for the entire data lake is out of scope for this book. Instead, we will discuss a couple of architecture options for the versioning control of training datasets.

S3 partitions

For each newly created or updated dataset, save it in a new S3 partition with a prefix (for example, the unique S3 folder name) for each dataset. While this approach potentially creates data duplication, it is a clean and simple way to separate different datasets for model training. The datasets should be generated by a controlled processing pipeline to enforce the naming standards and should be made readonly for the downstream applications to ensure immutability. The following sample shows an S3 partition structure with multiple versions of a training dataset:

```
s3://project1/<date>/<unique version id 1>/train_1.txt
s3://project1/<date>/<unique version id 1>/train_2.txt
s3://project1/<date>/<unique version id 2>/train_1.txt
s3://project1/<date>/<unique version id 2>/train_2.txt
```

In this example, the two versions of the dataset are separated by two different S3 prefixes.

Purpose-built data version tools

There are a number of open source tools, such as **DVC**, for data versioning control. For example, DVC works with any Git-compliant code repo and can use S3 as the storage backend for the training dataset. Each dataset version is associated with a unique commit ID that can uniquely identify a version of data.

ML feature store

For large enterprises, common reusable ML features such as curated customer profile data and standardized product sales data should be centrally managed to reduce the ML project life cycle, especially during the data understanding and data preparation stages. Depending on the scope, you can build custom feature stores that meet the basic requirements, such as insertion and lookup of organized features for ML model training. Or, you can implement commercial-grade feature store products, such as **Amazon SageMaker Feature Store** (an AWS ML service that we will cover in later chapters). SageMaker Feature Store has online and offline capability for training and inference, metadata tagging, feature versioning, and advanced search.

Data serving for client consumption

The central data management platform needs to provide different methods, such as APIs or Hive metastore-based methods, for online access of the data. Also, consider data transfer tools to support data movement from the central data management platform to other data-consuming environments for different data consumption patterns. Consider tools that have built-in data serving capabilities or that can be easily integrated with external data serving tools.

There are several data serving patterns for supplying data to data science environments. Let's discuss the following two data access patterns.

Consumption via API

With this pattern, the consumption environments/applications can pull data directly from the data lake using Hive metastore-compliant tools or through direct access to S3. Amazon services such as **Amazon Athena** (a big data query tool), Amazon EMR (a big data processing tool), and **Amazon Redshift Spectrum** (a feature of Amazon Redshift are used for querying data lake data indexed in Glue catalogs). This pattern is good when you don't need to make a copy of the data and only need to select a subset of the data as part of the downstream data processing tasks.

Consumption via data copy

With this pattern, a subset of the data in the data lake is copied to the storage of the consumption environment for different processing and consumption needs. For example, the more recent data can be loaded into Amazon Redshift in an analytics environment or delivered to S3 buckets owned by a data science environment.

Data pipeline

Data pipelines automate the process of data movement and transformation. For example, you might need to build a data pipeline that ingests data from the source, performs data validation and cleansing, enriches the dataset with new data and transformation, and then performs feature engineering and creates the training/validation/testing dataset for the ML model training and validation tasks. There are various workflow tools for building data pipelines, and many data management tools come with built-in data pipeline features.

AWS Glue workflows

AWS Glue workflows are a built-in workflow management feature of AWS Glue that can be used to orchestrate different Glue jobs, such as data ingestion, data processing, and feature engineering. A Glue workflow is made of two types of components: a *trigger* component and a *node* component. A trigger component can be a schedule trigger, an event trigger, or an on-demand trigger. A node can be either a crawler job or an ETL job. A schedule trigger or an on-demand trigger are used to kick off a workflow run, and an event trigger is a success/failure event emitted after the crawler job or ETL job. A workflow is a series of triggers and ETL or crawler jobs.

AWS Step Functions

AWS Step Functions is a workflow orchestration tool. It integrates with other AWS data processing services, such as AWS Glue and Amazon EMR. It can be used to build a workflow to run the different steps in a workflow, for example, data ingestion, data processing, or feature engineering.

Authentication and authorization

Data lake access for administration and data consumption needs to be authenticated and authorized. Federated authentication, or AWS **Identity and Access Management (IAM)**, authenticates users to verify user identities. For access to data catalog resources and the underlying data storage, AWS Lake Formation uses both the built-in Lake Formation access control and AWS IAM. The built-in Lake Formation permission model uses the database `grant/revoke` commands to control permission to different resources (for example, database and tables) and database actions (for example, `create table`). When a requestor makes a request to access a resource, both IAM policy and Lake Formation permissions are enforced and verified before access is granted.

There are several personas involved in the administration of the data lake and consumption of the data lake resources:

- **Lake Formation administrator**: A Lake Formation administrator has the permission to manage all aspects of a Lake Formation data lake in an AWS account. Examples include granting/revoking permissions to access data lake resources by other users, register data stores in S3, and creating/deleting databases. When you create Lake Formation, you will need to register an administrator. An administrator can be an AWS IAM user or IAM role. You can add more than one administrator to a Lake Formation data lake.

- **Lake Formation database creator**: A Lake Formation database creator has been granted permission to create databases in Lake Formation. A database creator can be an IAM user or IAM role.

- **Lake Formation database user**: A Lake Formation database user can be granted permission to perform different actions against a database. Example permissions include create table, drop table, describe table, and alter table. A database user can be an IAM user or IAM role.

- **Lake Formation data user**: A Lake Formation data user can be granted permission to perform different actions against database tables and columns. Example permissions include insert, select, describe, delete, alter, and drop. A data user can be an IAM user or an IAM role.

Running queries against the Lake Formation database and table is done through supported AWS services such as Amazon Athena and Amazon EMR. When accessing Lake Formation to run the query through these services, the principals (IAM user, group, and role) associated with these services are verified for appropriate access permission to the database, tables, and S3 location of the data by Lake Formation. If access is allowed, then Lake Formation provides a temporary credential to the service to run the query.

Data governance

Data governance ensures the data assets are trusted, secured, cataloged, and their access is monitored and audited. Data can be trusted when data flows are identified and documented and data qualities are measured and reported. To ensure data is protected and secured, data needs to be classified, and the appropriate access permissions should be applied. To have visibility into who has done what with which data, you should implement monitoring and audits.

When data is ingested and then further processed from the landing zone to other zones, **data lineage** should be established and documented. For example, when running a data pipeline with data ingestion and processing tools, such as AWS Glue, AWS EMR, or AWS Lambda, the following data points can be captured to establish data lineage:

- Data source name, location, and ownership details

- Data processing job history and details (such as job name, ID, associated processing script, and owner of the job)

- Artifacts generated by the data processing jobs (for example, S3 `uri` for the target data)

- Data metrics at different stages (for example, number of records, size, schema, and feature statistics) as a result of the data processing

A central data operational data store should be created for storing all the data lineage and processing metrics. AWS DynamoDB, a fully managed NoSQL database, is a good technology option for storing this type of data, as it is designed for low latency and high transaction access:

- **Data quality**: Automated data quality checks should be implemented at different stages, and quality metrics should be reported. For example, after the source data is ingested into the landing zone, an AWS Glue quality check job can run to check the data quality using tools such as the open source **Deequ** library. Data quality metrics (such as counts, schema validation, missing data, wrong data type, or statistical deviations from the baseline) and reports can be generated for reviews. Optionally, manual or automated operational data cleansing processes should be established to correct data quality issues.

- **Data cataloging**: Create a central data catalog and run Glue crawlers on datasets in the data lake to automatically create an inventory of data and populate the central data catalog. Enrich the catalogs with additional metadata to track other information to support discovery and data audits, such as the business owner, data classification, and data refresh date. For ML workloads, data science teams also generate new datasets (for example, new ML features) from the existing datasets in the data lake for model training purposes. These datasets should also be registered and tracked in a data catalog, and different versions of the data should be retained and archived for audit purposes.

- **Data access provisioning**: A formal process should be established for requesting and granting access to datasets and Lake Formation databases and tables. An external ticketing system can be used to manage the workflow for requesting access and granting access.

- **Monitoring and auditing**: Data access should be monitored, and access history should be maintained. Amazon S3 server access logging can be enabled to track access to all S3 objects directly. AWS Lake Formation also records all accesses to Lake Formation datasets in **AWS CloudTrail** (AWS CloudTrail provides event history in an AWS account to enable governance, compliance, and operational auditing). With Lake Formation auditing, you can get details such as event source, event name, SQL queries, and data output location.

Now, we have covered the core concepts and architecture patterns for building a data management platform for ML. Next, let's get hands-on with the architecture and technologies we have covered and build a simple data lake and data processing pipeline.

Hands-on exercise – data management for ML

In this hands-on exercise, you will build a data management platform for a fictitious retail bank to support an ML workflow. We will build the data management platform on AWS using various AWS technologies. If you don't have an AWS account, you can create one by following the instructions at `https://aws.amazon.com/console/`.

The data management platform we create will have the following key components:

- A data lake environment for data management
- A data ingestion component for ingesting files to the data lake
- A data discovery and query component
- A data processing component

The following diagram shows the data management architecture we will build in this exercise:

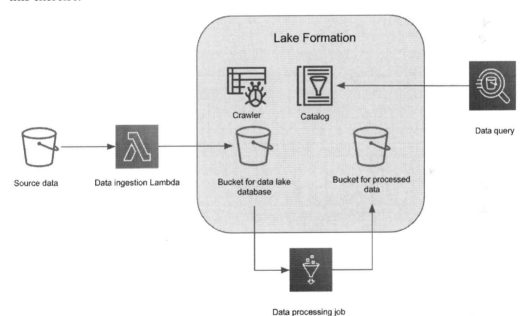

Figure 4.6 – Data management architecture for the hands-on exercise

Let's get started with building out this architecture on AWS.

Creating a data lake using Lake Formation

We will build the data lake architecture using AWS Lake Formation. After you log on to the **AWS Management Console**, create an S3 bucket called `MLSA-DataLake-<your initials>`. We will use this bucket as the storage for the data lake. If you get a message that the bucket name is already in use, try adding some random characters to the name to make it unique. If you are not familiar with how to create S3 buckets, follow the instructions at the following link:

`https://docs.aws.amazon.com/AmazonS3/latest/user-guide/create-bucket.html`

After the bucket is created, follow these steps to get started with creating a data lake:

1. **Register Lake Formation administrators**: We need to add Lake Formation administrators to the data lake. The administrators will have full permission to manage all aspects of the data lake. To do this, navigate to the Lake Formation management console, click on the **Admin and database creators** link, and then click on the **Grant** button for the **Data Lake administrator** section and add your own IAM user ID to the list (the user ID you currently use to log in to the AWS Management Console). You can find your own user ID in the top-right portion of the AWS Management Console banner. Note that you will need to log in to the AWS Management Console using a user ID with administrator rights to register new Lake Formation administrators.

2. **Register S3 storage**: Next, we need to register the S3 bucket (`MLSA-DataLake-<your initials>`) you created earlier in Lake Formation so it will be managed and accessible through Lake Formation. To do this, you click on the **Dashboard** link and then click on **Register Location**. Browse and select the bucket you created and click on **Register Location**. This S3 bucket will be used by Lake Formation to store data for the databases and manage its access permission.

3. **Create database**: Now, we are ready to set up a database called `bank_customer_db` for managing retail customers. Before we register the database, let's first create a folder called the `bank_customer_db` folder under the `MLSA-DataLake-<your initials>` bucket. This folder will be used to store data files associated with the database. To do this, you click on the **Create database** button on the Lake Formation dashboard and follow the instructions on the screen to create the database.

You have successfully created a data lake powered by Lake Formation and created a database for data management. Next, let's create a data ingestion pipeline to move files into the data lake.

Creating a data ingestion pipeline

With the database ready, we can now ingest data to the new database. As discussed in the previous section, there could be many different data sources as other S3 buckets, such as databases (for example, Amazon RDS), streaming (for example, social media feeds), and logs (CloudTrail). There are also many different services for building a data ingestion pipeline, such as AWS Glue, Amazon Kinesis, and AWS Lambda. In this part of the exercise, we will build an Amazon Lambda function job that will ingest data from other S3 buckets to this new database:

1. **Create a source S3 bucket and download data files**:

   Let's create another S3 bucket, called `customer-data-source`, to represent the data source where we will ingest the data from. Now, download the sample data files from the following link:

   `https://github.com/PacktPublishing/The-Machine-Learning-Solutions-Architect-Handbook/tree/main/Chapter04/Archive.zip`

   Then, save it to your local machine. Extract the archived files and upload them to the `customer-data-source` bucket. There should be two files (`customer_data.csv` and `churn_list.csv`).

2. **Create Lambda function**:

   Now, we will create the Lambda function that will ingest data from the `customer-data-source` bucket to the `MLSA-DataLake-<your initials>` bucke:

   I. To get started, navigate to the AWS Lambda management console, click on the **Functions** link in the left pane, and click on the **Create Function** button in the right pane. Choose **Author from scratch**, then enter `datalake-s3-ingest` for the function name, and select `Python 3.8` as the runtime.

   II. On the next screen, click on **Add trigger**, select S3 as the trigger, and select the `customer-data-source` bucket as the source. For **Event Type**, choose the `Put` event and click on the **Add** button to complete the step. This trigger will allow the Lambda function to be invoked when there is an S3 bucket event, such as saving a file into the bucket.

III. Next, let's create the function by replacing the default function template with the following code block. Replace the `desBucket` variable with the name of the actual bucket:

```
import json
import boto3
def lambda_handler(event, context):
    s3 = boto3.resource('s3')
    for record in event['Records']:
        srcBucket = record['s3']['bucket']['name']
        srckey = record['s3']['object']['key']
        desBucket = "MLSA-DataLake-<your initials>"
        desFolder = srckey[0:srckey.find('.')]
        desKey = "bank_customer_db/" + desFolder +
"/" + srckey
        source= { 'Bucket' : srcBucket,'Key':srckey}
        dest ={ 'Bucket' : desBucket,'Key':desKey}
        s3.meta.client.copy(source, desBucket,
desKey)
    return {
        'statusCode': 200,
        'body': json.dumps('files ingested')
    }
```

IV. The new function will also need S3 permission to copy files (*objects*) from one bucket to another. For simplicity, just add the `AmazonS3FullAccess` policy to the **execution IAM role** associated with the function. You can find the IAM role by clicking on the **Permission** tab for the Lambda function.

3. **Trigger data ingestion**:

You can now trigger the data ingestion process by uploading the `customer_detail.csv` and `churn_list.csv` files to the `customer-data-source` bucket and verify the process completion by checking the `MLSA-DataLake-<your initials>/bank_customer_db` folder for the two files.

You have now successfully created an AWS Lambda-based data ingestion pipeline to automatically move data from a source S3 bucket to a target S3 bucket. Next, let's create an AWS Glue catalog using the Glue crawler.

Creating a Glue catalog

To allow discovery and querying of the data in the `bank_customer_db` database, we need to create a data catalog. Here, we will use an AWS Glue crawler to crawl the files in the `bank_customer_db` S3 folder and generate the catalog:

1. **Grant permission for Glue:**

    I. First, let's grant permission for AWS Glue to access the `bank_customer_db` database. We will create a new IAM role for the Glue service to assume on your behalf. To do this, create a new IAM service role called `AWSGlueServiceRole_data_lake`, and attach the `AWSGlueServiceRole` and `AmazonS3FullAccess` IAM managed policies to it. Make sure you select `Glue` as the service when you create the role. If you are not familiar with how to create a role and attach a policy, follow the instructions at the following link: `https://docs.aws.amazon.com/IAM/latest/UserGuide`.

    II. After the role is created, click on **Data permission** in the left pane of the Lake Formation management console and then click the **Grant** button in the right pane.

    III. On the new pop-up screen, select `AWSGlueServiceRole_data_lake` and `bank_customer_db` and click on **Grant**. `AWSGlueServiceRole_data_lake` will be used later for configuring the Glue crawler job.

2. **Configure Glue crawler job:**

    Launch the Glue crawler by clicking on the **Crawler** link in the Lake Formation management console. A new browser tab for Glue will open up. Click on the **Add Crawler** button to get started. Enter `bank_customer_db_crawler` as the name of the crawler and click on **Next**. On the next screen, keep **Data store** and **Crawl all folders** checked. On the **Add a data store** screen, select **S3** and enter `s3://MLSA-DataLake-<your initials>/bank_customer_db/churn_list/` for the **include path** field.

    On the next **Add another data store** screen, choose **Yes**, select **S3**, and then enter `s3://MLSA-DataLake-<your initials>/bank_customer_db/customer_data/`.

    On the next **Choose an IAM role** screen, select **Choose existing IAM role**, and select `AWSGlueServiceRole_data_lake`, which you used earlier.

    Select **Run on demand** as the frequency on the **Create a scheduler for this crawler** screen.

Choose `bank_customer_db` on the **Configure the crawler's output** screen and select **Finish** on the final screen to complete the setup.

On the **Crawler** screen, select the `bank_customer_db_crawler` job you just created, click on **Run crawler**, and wait for the status to say `Ready`.

Navigate back to the Lake Formation management console and click on the **Tables** link. You will now see two new tables created (`churn_list` and `customer_data`).

You have now successfully configured an AWS Glue crawler that automatically discovers table schemas from data files and creates data catalogs for the new data.

You now have created the Glue Data Catalog for the newly ingested data. You are now ready to discover and query the data in the data lake.

Discovering and querying data in the data lake

To support the data discovery and data understanding phase of the ML workflow, we will need to provide data discovery and data query capabilities in the data lake.

By default, Lake Formation already provides a list of tags, such as data type classification (for example, CSV), for tables in the database to search. Let's add a few more tags for each table to make it more discoverable:

1. Select the `customer_data` table, click on the **Action** dropdown, and select **Edit**. On the edit screen, add the following tags and hit **Save**:

   - `department: customer`
   - `contact: joe`

2. Select the `churn_list` table, and add the following tags:

   - `department: operations`
   - `contact: jenny`

3. Let's also add some metadata to the table fields as well. Select the `customer_data` table, click on **Edit Schema**, select the `creditscore` field, click on **Add** to add a column property, and enter the following:

   - `description: credit score is the FICO score for each customer`

4. Follow the same previous steps and add the following column property for the
    `exited` field in the `churn_list` table:

    - `description: churn flag`

5. We are now ready to do some searches using metadata inside the Lake Formation
    management console. Try typing the following words separately in the text box for
    Find table by properties to search for tables and see what's returned:

    - `FICO`

    - `csv`

    - `churn flag`

    - `operations`

    - `customer`

    - `jenny`

    - `creditscore`

    - `customerid`

    Now you have found the table you are looking for, let's query the table and see that
    actual data.

6. Select the table you want to query and click on the **View data** button in the **Actions**
    drop-down menu. This should bring you to the **Amazon Athena** screen. You should
    see a query tab already created, and the query is already executed. The results are
    displayed at the bottom of the screen. You can run any other SQL query to explore
    the data further, such as joining the `customer_data` and `churn_list` tables by
    the `customerid` field:

```
SELECT * FROM "customer_db"."customer_data", "customer_
db"."churn_list" where "customer_db"."customer_
data"."customerid" = "customer_db"."churn_
list"."customerid" ;
```

You have now learned how to discover the data in Lake Formation and run queries against
the data in a Lake Formation database and tables. Next, let's run a data processing job
using the Amazon Glue ETL service to make the data ready for ML tasks.

Creating an Amazon Glue ETL job to process data for ML

The customer_data and churn_list tables contain features that are useful for ML. However, they need to be joined and processed so they can be used for training ML models. One option is for the data scientists to download these datasets and process them in a **Jupyter notebook** for model training. Another option is to process the data using a separate processing engine so that the data scientists can work with the processed data directly. Here, we will set up an AWS Glue job to process the data in the customer_data and churn_list tables and transform them into new ML features that are ready for model training directl:

1. First, create a new S3 bucket called MLSA-DataLake-Serving-<your initials>. We will use this bucket to store the output training datasets from the Glue job.

2. To start creating the Glue job, click on the **Jobs** link on the Lake Formation console. Then, click on the **Add Job** button, and enter customer_churn_process as the job name.

3. Select AWSGlueService_Role as the IAM role, and under the **This job runs** section, select the **A new script to be authored by you** option.

4. Click **Next** to proceed to the next screen, and then click on the **Save job and edit script** button.

5. On the **Script edit** screen, copy the following code blocks to the code section, and then click on **Save** and then the **Run job** button. Make sure to replace default_bucket with your own bucket in the code. The following code block first joins the churn_list and customer_data tables using the customerid column as the key, then transforms the gender and geo columns with an index, creates a new DataFrame with only the relevant columns, and finally saves the output file to an S3 location using the date and generated version ID as partitions. The code uses default values for the target bucket, prefix variables, and generates a date partition and version partition for the S3 location. The job can also accept input arguments for these parameters.

   The following code block sets up default configurations, such as SparkContext and a default bucket:

   ```
   import sys
   from awsglue.utils import getResolvedOptions
   from awsglue.transforms import Join
   from pyspark.context import SparkContext
   ```

```
from awsglue.context import GlueContext
from awsglue.job import Job
import pandas as pd
from datetime import datetime
import uuid
from pyspark.ml.feature import StringIndexer
glueContext = GlueContext(SparkContext.getOrCreate())
logger = glueContext.get_logger()
current_date = datetime.now()
default_date_partition = f"{current_date.year}-{current_
date.month}-{current_date.day}"
default_version_id = str(uuid.uuid4())
default_bucket = "<your default bucket name>"
default_prefix = "ml-customer-churn"
target_bucket = ""
prefix = ""
day_partition =""
version_id = ""
try:
      args = getResolvedOptions(sys.argv,['JOB_
NAME','target_bucket','prefix','day_partition','version_
id'])
      target_bucket = args['target_bucket']
      prefix = args['prefix']
      day_partition = args['day_partition']
      version_id = args['version_id']
except:
      logger.error("error occured with getting
arguments")
if target_bucket == "":
      target_bucket = default_bucket
if prefix == "":
      prefix = default_prefix
if day_partition == "":
      day_partition = default_date_partition
if version_id == "":
      version_id = default_version_id
```

The following code joins the `customer_data` and `churn_list` tables into a single table using the `customerid` column as the key:

```
# catalog: database and table names
db_name = "customer_db"
tbl_customer = "customer_data"
tbl_churn_list = "churn_list"
# Create dynamic frames from the source tables
customer = glueContext.create_dynamic_frame.from_
catalog(database=db_name, table_name=tbl_customer)
churn = glueContext.create_dynamic_frame.from_
catalog(database=db_name, table_name=tbl_churn_list)
# Join the frames to create customer churn dataframe
customer_churn = Join.apply(customer, churn,
'customerid', 'customerid')
customer_churn.printSchema()
```

The following code block transforms several data columns from string labels to label indices and writes the final file to an output location in S3:

```
# ---- Write out the combined file ----
current_date = datetime.now()
str_current_date = f"{current_date.year}-{current_date.
month}-{current_date.day}"
random_version_id = str(uuid.uuid4())
output_dir = f"s3://{target_bucket}/{prefix}/{day_
partition}/{version_id}"
s_customer_churn = customer_churn.toDF()
gender_indexer = StringIndexer(inputCol="gender",
outputCol="genderindex")
s_customer_churn = gender_indexer.fit(s_customer_churn).
transform(s_customer_churn)
geo_indexer = StringIndexer(inputCol="geography",
outputCol="geographyindex")
s_customer_churn = geo_indexer.fit(s_customer_churn).
transform(s_customer_churn)
s_customer_churn = s_customer_
churn.select('geographyindex',
'estimatedsalary','hascrcard','numofproducts', 'balance',
'age', 'genderindex', 'isactivemember', 'creditscore',
'tenure', 'exited')
```

```
s_customer_churn = s_customer_churn.coalesce(1)
s_customer_churn.write.option("header","true").
format("csv").mode('Overwrite').save(output_dir)
logger.info("output_dir:" + output_dir)
```

6. After the job completes, check the `s3://MLSA-DataLake-Serving-<your initials>/ml-customer-churn/<date>/<guid>/` location in S3 and see whether a new CSV file was generated. Open the file and see whether you see the new processed dataset in the file.

You have now successfully built an AWS Glue job for data processing and feature engineering for ML. Try creating a crawler to crawl the newly processed data in the `MLSA-DataLake-Serving-<your initials>` bucket to make it available in the Glue catalog and run some queries against it. You should see a new table created with multiple partitions (for example, `ml-customer-churn`, `date`, and `GUID`) for the different training datasets. You can query the data by using the `GUID` partition as a query condition.

Building a data pipeline using Glue workflows

Now, let's create a pipeline that will first run a data ingestion job, then create a database catalog for the data and run a data processing job to generate the training dataset:

1. To start, click on the **Workflows** link in the left pane of the Glue management console.

2. Click on **Add Workflow** and enter a name for your workflow on the next screen. Then, click on the **Add Workflow** button.

3. Select the workflow you just created and click on **Add Trigger**. Select the **Add New** tab, and then enter a name for the trigger and select the `on-demand` trigger type.

4. On the workflow UI designer, you will see a new **Add Node** icon show up. Click on the **Add Node** icon, select the **Crawler** tab, and select `bank_customer_db_crawler`, then, click on **Add**.

5. On the workflow UI designer, click on the **Crawler** icon, and you will see a new **Add Trigger** icon show up. Click on the **Add Trigger** icon, select the **Add new** tab, and select **After ANY event** as the trigger logic, and then click on **Add**.

6. On the workflow UI designer, click on the **Add Node** icon, select the **jobs** tab, and select the `customer_churn_process` job.

7. On the workflow UI designer, the final workflow should look like the following diagram:

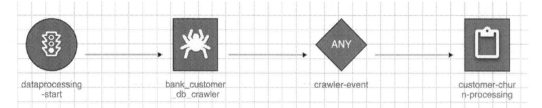

Figure 4.7 – Glue data flow design

8. Now, you are ready to run the workflow. Select the workflow and select **Run** from the **Actions** dropdown. You can monitor the running status by selecting the **Run ID** and clicking on **View run details**. You should see something similar to the following screenshot:

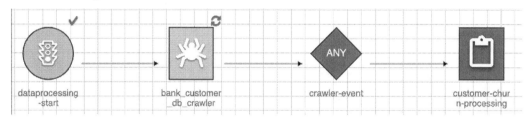

Figure 4.8 – Glue workflow execution

9. Try deleting the `customer_data` and `churn_list` tables and re-run the workflow. See whether the new tables are created again. Check the `s3://MLSA-DataLake-Serving-<your initials>/ml-customer-churn/<date>/` S3 location to verify a new folder is created with a new dataset.

Congratulations! You have completed the hands-on lab and learned how to build a simple data lake and its supporting components to allow data cataloging, data querying, and data processing.

Summary

In this chapter, we covered data management considerations for ML and what an enterprise data management platform could look like for ML. Now, you should know where data management intersects with the ML life cycle and how to design a data lake architecture on AWS. To put the learning into practice, you also built a data lake using Lake Formation. You practiced data ingestion, processing, and data cataloging for data discovery, querying, and downstream ML tasks. You have also developed hands-on skills with AWS data management tools, including AWS Lake Formation, AWS Glue, AWS Lambda, and Amazon Athena.

In the next chapter, we will start covering architecture and technologies for building data science environments using open source technologies.

5
Open Source Machine Learning Libraries

There are multiple technologies available for building **machine learning** (**ML**) and data science solutions, in both open source and commercial product spaces. To maintain greater flexibility and customization of their machine learning platforms, some organizations have chosen to invest in in-house data science and engineering teams to build data science platforms using open source technology stacks. Some organizations, however, have adopted commercial products to focus their effort on solving business and data challenges. Some organizations have chosen hybrid architecture to leverage both open source and commercial products for their machine learning platform. As an machine learning solution architecture practitioner, I often need to explain to others what open source machine learning technologies are available and how they can be used for building machine learning solutions.

In the next several chapters, we will focus on various open source technologies for experimentation, modeling building, and building machine learning platforms. In this chapter, you will learn about machine learning libraries such as **scikit-learn**, **Spark**, **TensorFlow**, and **PyTorch**. We will discuss these machine learning libraries' core functionalities and how we can apply them to various steps in a machine learning life cycle, such as data processing, model building, and model evaluation. You will also get hands-on with a couple of machine learning libraries and learn to use them for model training.

Specifically, we will be covering the following main topics:

- Core features of open source machine learning libraries
- Understanding the scikit-learn machine learning library
- Understanding the Apache Spark ML machine learning library
- Understanding the TensorFlow machine learning library and hands-on lab
- Understanding the PyTorch machine learning and hands-on lab

Technical requirements

In this chapter, you will need access to your local machine where you installed the **Jupyter** environment from *Chapter 3*, *Machine Learning Algorithms*.

You can find the code samples used in this chapter at `https://github.com/PacktPublishing/The-Machine-Learning-Solutions-Architect-Handbook/tree/main/Chapter05`.

Core features of open source machine learning libraries

At their core, machine learning libraries are just software libraries written in different programming languages. What makes them different from other software libraries are the functions they support. In general, most ML libraries have support for the following key features via different library sub-packages:

- **Data manipulation and processing**: This includes support for different data tasks such as loading data of different formats, data manipulation, data analysis, data visualization, and data transformation.

- **Model building and training**: This covers support for built-in machine learning algorithms as well as capabilities for building custom algorithms. Most ML libraries also have built-in support for the commonly used loss functions (such as mean squared error or cross-entropy) and a list of optimizers (such as gradient descent or adam) to choose from. Some libraries also provide advanced support for distributed model training across multiple CPU/GPU devices or compute nodes.

- **Model evaluation**: This includes packages for evaluating the performance of trained models, such as model accuracy or error rates.

- **Model saving and loading**: This includes support for saving the models to various formats for persistence, and support for loading saved models into memory for predictions.

- **Model serving**: This includes model serving features to expose trained machine learning models behind an API, usually a RESTful API web service.

A machine learning library usually supports one or more programming languages such as **Python**, **Java**, or **Scala** to meet different needs. Python is one of the most popular languages for machine learning, and most of the machine learning libraries provide support for the Python interface. The backend and underlying algorithms for these libraries are, however, mainly written in compiled languages, such as **C++** and **Cython**, to optimize performance. Next, we will take a closer look at some of the most common machine learning libraries.

Understanding the scikit-learn machine learning library

scikit-learn (`https://scikit-learn.org/`) is an open source machine learning library for Python. Initially released in 2007, it is one of the most popular machine learning libraries for solving many machine learning tasks, such as classification, regression, clustering, and dimensionality reduction.

scikit-learn is widely used by companies in different industries and academics for solving real-world business cases such as churn prediction, customer segmentation, recommendations, and fraud detection.

scikit-learn is built mainly on top of three foundational libraries: **NumPy**, **SciPy**, and **matplotlib**. NumPy is a Python-based library for managing large, multidimensional arrays and matrices, with additional mathematical functions to operate on the arrays and matrices. SciPy provides scientific computing functionality, such as optimization, linear algebra, and Fourier Transform. Matplotlib is used for plotting data for data visualization. scikit-learn is a sufficient and effective tool for a range of common data processing and model-building tasks.

Installing scikit-learn

You can easily install the scikit-learn package on different operating systems such as Mac, Windows, and Linux. The `scikit-learn` library package is hosted on the **Python Package Index** site (`https://pypi.org/`) and the **Anaconda** package repository (`https://anaconda.org/anaconda/repo`). To install it in your environment, you can use either the **PIP** package manager or the **Conda** package manager. A package manager allows you to install and manage the installation of library packages in your operating system.

To install the `scikit-learn` library using the PIP or Conda package manager, you can simply run `pip install -U scikit-learn` to install it from the PyPI index or run `conda install scikit-learn` if you want to use a Conda environment. You can learn more about PIP at `https://pip.pypa.io/` and Conda at `http://docs.conda.io`.

Core components of scikit-learn

`scikit-learn` provides a full range of Python classes for machine learning, from data processing to building repeatable pipelines. The following diagram shows the main components in the scikit-learning library package:

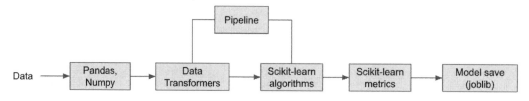

Figure 5.1 – scikit-learn components

Now, let's take a closer look at how these components support the various phases of the machine learning life cycle:

- **Preparing data**: For data manipulation and processing, the pandas library is commonly used. It provides core data loading and saving functions, as well as utilities for data manipulations such as data selection, data arrangement, and data statistical summaries. pandas is built on top of NumPy. The pandas library also comes with some visualization features such as pie charts, scatter plots, and boxplots.

  scikit-learn provides a list of transformers for data processing and transformation, such as imputing missing values, encoding categorical values, normalization, and feature extraction for text and images. You can find the full list of transformers at https://scikit-learn.org/stable/data_transforms.html. You also have the flexibility to create custom transformers.

- **Model training**: scikit-learn provides a long list of machine learning algorithms (also known as estimators) for classification and regression (for example, logistic regression, K nearest neighbors, and random forest), as well as clustering (for example, k-means). You can find the full list of algorithms at https://scikit-learn.org/stable/index.html. The following sample code shows the syntax for using the RandomForestClassifier algorithm to train a model using a labeled training dataset:

```
from sklearn.ensemble import RandomForestClassifier
model = RandomForestClassifier (max_depth, max_features,
n_estimators
model.fit(train_X, train_y)
```

- **Model evaluation**: scikit-learn has utilities for hyperparameter tuning and cross-validation, as well as metrics classes for model evaluations. You can find the full list of model selection and evaluation utilities at https://scikit-learn.org/stable/model_selection.html. The following sample code shows the accuracy_score class for evaluating the accuracy of classification models:

```
from sklearn.metrics import accuracy_score
acc = accuracy_score (true_label, predicted_label)
```

- **Model saving**: `scikit-learn` can save model artifacts using Python object serialization (`pickle` or `joblib`). The serialized `pickle` file can be loaded into memory for predictions. The following sample code shows the syntax for saving a model using the `joblib` class:

```
import joblib
joblib.dump(model, "saved_model_name.joblib")
```

- **Pipeline**: `scikit-learn` also provides a pipeline utility for stringing together different transformers and estimators as a single processing pipeline, and it can be reused as a single unit. This is especially useful when you need to preprocess data for modeling training and model prediction, as both require the data to be processed in the same way:

```
from sklearn.pipeline import Pipeline
from sklearn.preprocessing import StandardScaler
from sklearn.ensemble import RandomForestClassifier


pipe = Pipeline([('scaler', StandardScaler()), (RF,
RandomForestClassifier()])
pipe.fit(X_train, y_train)
```

As you can see, it is quite easy to get started with the `scikit-learn` machine learning package to experiment with and build machine learning models. `scikit-learn` is well suited for common regression, classification, and clustering machine learning tasks running on a single machine. However, if you need to train machine learning on large datasets or multiple machines, then `scikit-learn` normally would not be the right option, unless the algorithm (for example, `SGDRegressor`) supports incremental training. Next, we will look at some machine learning libraries that can handle machine learning model training at a large scale.

Understanding the Apache Spark ML machine learning library

Apache Spark is a distributed data processing framework for large-scale data processing. It allows Spark-based applications to load and process data across a cluster of distributed machines in memory to speed up the processing time.

A Spark cluster consists of a master node and worker nodes for running different Spark applications. Each application that runs in a Spark cluster has a driver program and its own set of processes, which are coordinated by the **SparkSession** object in the driver program. The `SparkSession` object in the driver program connects to a cluster manager (for example, Mesos, YARN, Kubernetes, or Spark's standalone cluster manager), which is responsible for allocating resources in the cluster for the Spark application. Specifically, the cluster manager acquires resources on worker nodes called **executors** to run computations and store data for the Spark application. Executors are configured with resources such as the number of CPU cores and memory to meet task processing needs. Once the executors have been allocated, the cluster manager sends the application code (Java JAR or Python files) to the executors. Finally, `SparkContext` sends the tasks to the executors to run. The following diagram shows how a driver program interacts with a cluster manager and executor to run a task:

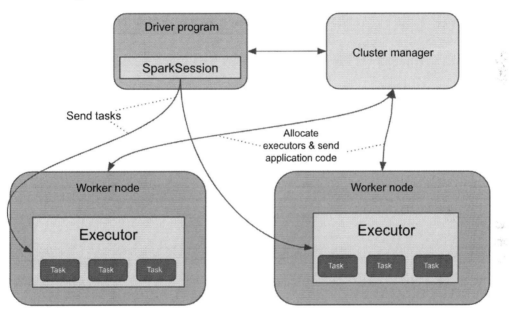

Figure 5.2 – Running a Spark application on a Spark cluster

Each Spark application gets its own set of executors, which stay up for the duration of the application. The executors for different applications are isolated from each other, and they can only share data through external data storage.

The machine learning package for Spark is called `MLlib`, which runs on top of the distributed Spark architecture. It is capable of processing and training models with a large dataset that does not fit into the memory of a single machine. It provides APIs in different programming languages, including Python, Java, Scala, and R. From a structure perspective, it is very similar to that of the `scikit-learn` library.

Spark is highly popular and adopted by companies of all sizes across different industries. Large companies such as **Netflix**, **Uber**, and **Pinterest** use Spark for large-scale data processing and transformation, as well as running machine learning models.

Installing Spark ML

Spark ML libraries are included as part of the Spark installation. PySpark is the Python API for Spark, and it can be installed like a regular Python package using PIP (`pip install pyspark`). Note that `PySpark` requires Java and Python to be installed on the machine before it can be installed. You can find Spark's installation instructions at `https://spark.apache.org/docs/latest/`.

Core components of the Spark ML library

Similar to the `scikit-learn` library, Spark and Spark ML provide a full range of functionality for building machine learning models, from data preparation to model evaluation and model persistence. The following diagram shows the core components that are available in Spark for building machine learning models:

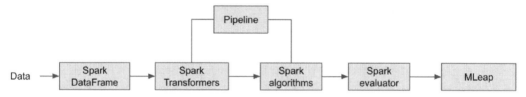

Figure 5.3 – Core components of Spark ML

Now, let's take a closer look at the core functions supported by the Spark and Spark ML library packages:

- **Preparing data**: Spark supports Spark DataFrame, a distributed collection of data that can be used for data join, aggregation, filtering, and other data manipulation needs. Conceptually, a Spark DataFrame is equivalent to a table in a relational database. A Spark DataFrame can be distributed (that is, partitioned) across many machines, which allows fast data processing in parallel. Spark DataFrame also operates on a model called the lazy execution model. **Lazy execution** defines a set of transformations (for example, adding a column or filtering column) and the transformations are only executed when an action (such as calculating the min/max of a column) is needed. This allows an execution plan for the different transformations and actions to be generated to optimize the execution's performance.

To start using the Spark functionality, you need to create a Spark session. A Spark session creates a `SparkContext` object, which is the entry point to the Spark functionality. The following sample code shows how to create a Spark session:

```
from pyspark.sql import SparkSession
spark = SparkSession.builder.appName('appname').
getOrCreate()
```

A Spark DataFrame can be constructed from many different sources, such as structured data files (for example, CSV or JSON) and external databases. The following code sample reads a CSV file into a Spark DataFrame:

```
dataFrame = spark.read.format('csv').load(file_path)
```

There are many transformers for data processing and transformation in Spark, such as `Tokenizer` (breaks text down into individual words) and `StandardScalar` (normalizes a feature into unit deviation and/or zero mean). You can find a list of supported transformers at `https://spark.apache.org/docs/2.1.0/ml-features.html`.

To use a transformer, first, you must initiate it with parameters, then call the `fit()` function on the DataFrame that contains the data, and finally call the `transform()` function to transfer the features in the DataFrame:

```
from pyspark.ml.feature import StandardScaler


scaler = StandardScaler(inputCol="features",  outputCol=
"scaledFeatures", withStd=True, withMean=False)
scalerModel = scaler.fit(dataFrame)
scaledData = scalerModel.transform(dataFrame)
```

- **Model training**: Spark ML supports a large number of machine learning algorithms for classification, regression, clustering, recommendation, and topic modeling. You can find a list of Spark ML algorithms at `https://spark.apache.org/docs/1.4.1/mllib-guide.html`. The following code sample shows how to train a logistic regression model:

```
from pyspark.ml.classification import LogisticRegression
lr_algo = LogisticRegression(maxIter regParam,
elasticNetParam)
lr_model = lr_algo.fit(dataFrame)
```

- **Model evaluation**: For model selection and evaluation, Spark ML provides utilities for cross-validation, hyperparameter tuning, and model evaluation metrics. You can find the list of evaluators at `https://spark.apache.org/docs/latest/api/python/reference/api/pyspark.ml.evaluation.MulticlassClassificationEvaluator.html?highlight=model%20evaluation`:

```
from pyspark.ml.evaluation import
BinaryClassificationEvaluator

dataset = spark.createDataFrame(scoreAndLabels, ["raw",
"label"])
evaluator = BinaryClassificationEvaluator()
evaluator.setRawPredictionCol("raw")

evaluator.evaluate(dataset)
evaluator.evaluate(dataset, {evaluator.metricName:
"areaUnderPR"})
```

- **Pipeline**: Spark ML also supports the pipeline concept, similar to that of `scikit-learn`. With the pipeline concept, you can sequence a series of transformation and model training steps as a unified repeatable step:

```
from pyspark.ml import Pipeline
from pyspark.ml.classification import LogisticRegression
from pyspark.ml.feature import HashingTF, Tokenizer

lr_tokenizer = Tokenizer(inputCol, outputCol)
lr_hashingTF = HashingTF(inputCol=tokenizer.
getOutputCol(), outputCol)
lr_algo = LogisticRegression(maxIter, regParam)

lr_pipeline = Pipeline(stages=[lr_tokenizer, lr_
hashingTF, lr_algo])
lr_model = lr_pipeline.fit(training)
```

- **Model saving**: The Spark ML pipeline can be serialized into a serialization format called an `MLeap` bundle, which is an external library from Spark. A serialized `MLeap` bundle can be deserialized back into Spark for batch scoring or a `Mleap` runtime to run real-time APIs. You can find more details about `MLeap` at `https://combust.github.io/mleap-docs/`. The following code shows the syntax for serializing a Spark model into `MLeap` format:

```
import mleap.pyspark
from pyspark.ml import Pipeline, PipelineModel

lr_model.serializeToBundle("saved_file_path", lr_model.
transform(dataframe))
```

Spark provides a unified framework for large-scale data processing and machine learning model training. It is well-suited for classic machine learning tasks. It also has some basic support for neural network training, such as the multilayer perceptron.

Next, we will take a look at a couple of machine learning libraries that focus on providing support for deep learning.

Understanding the TensorFlow deep learning library

Initially released in 2015, TensorFlow is a popular open source machine learning library, primarily backed up by Google, that is mainly designed for deep learning. TensorFlow has been used by companies of all sizes for training and building state-of-the-art deep learning models for a range of use cases, including computer vision, speech recognition, question-answering, text summarization, forecasting, and robotics.

TensorFlow is based on the concept of a computational graph (that is, a dataflow graph), in which the data flow and operations that are performed on the data are constructed as a graph. TensorFlow takes input data in the form of an n-dimensional array/matrix, which is known as a tensor, and performs mathematical operations on this tensor, such as add or matrix multiplication. An example of a tensor could be a scalar value (for example, 1.0), a one-dimensional vector (for example, [1.0, 2.0, 3.0]), a two-dimensional matrix (for example, [[1.0, 2.0, 3.0], [4.0, 5.0, 6.0]]), or even higher dimensional matrices. The following diagram shows a sample computational graph for performing a sequence of mathematical operations on tensors:

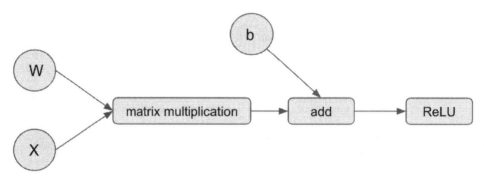

Figure 5.4 – Data flow diagram

In the preceding computational diagram, the rectangular nodes are mathematical operations, while the circles represent tensors. This particular diagram shows a computational graph for performing an artificial neuron tensor operation, which is to perform a matrix multiplication of W and X, followed by the addition of b, and, lastly, apply a *ReLU* action function. The equivalent mathematical formula is as follows:

$$f(x) \ = \ ReLU(Wx + b)$$

In the earlier versions (such as version 1.0) of TensorFlow, all computational graphs are static, meaning the graph needs to be constructed in advance, and it cannot be modified when it is being executed. During the construction step of the computational graph, the mathematical operations defined in the graph are not executed. A separate execution step is required to perform the operations and get the result. Static graphs are more performant as they need to be compiled for optimal execution before the actual execution. The following code constructs a simple graph that adds two constant numbers together. `print(tf.__version__)` displays the version of TensorFlow that's been installed:

```
import tensorflow as tf
print(tf.__version__)


A = tf.constant (1)
```

```
B = tf.constant (2)
C = tf.add (A, B)
print (C)
```

If you run the preceding code, you might expect to get an output of 3; however, you will get a 0 instead because the graph has not been executed. Each statement here only helps construct the graph. To run the graph, you need to execute the graph using a TensorFlow session object. If you run the following code, you will see the correct output:

```
sess = tf.Session()
sess.run(C)
```

In TensorFlow 2.x, the computational graph can be both static and dynamic. A dynamic graph is executed when each statement is executed. If you run the same code using TensorFlow 2.x, you will get an output of 3 on the print (C) statement:

```
import tensorflow as tf
print(tf.__version__)


A = tf.constant (1)
B = tf.constant (2)
C = tf.add (A, B)
print (C)
```

A dynamic graph is not as performant as a static graph, but it is much easier for development and debugging. And in most cases, the performance difference is small.

Installing Tensorflow

TensorFlow can be installed using the pip install --upgrade tensorflow command in a Python-based environment. After installation, TensorFlow can be used just like any other Python library package.

Core components of TensorFlow

The TensorFlow library provides a rich set of features for different machine learning steps, from data preparation to model serving. The following diagram shows the core building blocks of the TensorFlow library:

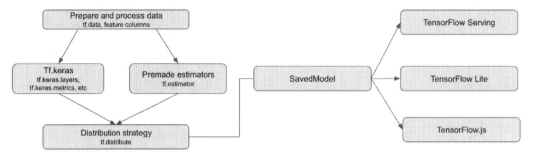

Figure 5.5 – TensorFlow components

Training a machine learning model using TensorFlow 2.x involves the following main steps:

- **Preparing the dataset**: TensorFlow 2.x provides a `tf.data` library for efficiently loading data from sources (such as files), transforming data (such as changing the values of the dataset), and setting up the dataset for training (such as configuring batch size or data prefetching). These data classes provide efficient ways to pass data to the training algorithms for optimized model training. The TensorFlow **Keras** API also provides a list of built-in classes (MNIST, CIFAR, IMDB, MNIST Fashion, and Reuters News wires) for building simple deep learning models. You can also feed a NumPy array or Python generator (a function that behaves like an iterator) to a model in TensorFlow for model training, but `tf.data` is the recommended approach.

- **Defining the neural network**: TensorFlow 2.x provides multiple ways to use or build a neural network for model training. You can use the premade estimators (the `tf.estimator` class) such as `DNNRegressor` and `DNNClassifier` to train models. Or, you can create custom neural networks using the `tf.keras` class, which provides a list of primitives such as `tf.keras.layers` for constructing neural network layers and `tf.keras.activation` such as ReLU, **Sigmoid**, and **Softmax** for building neural networks. Softmax is usually used as the last output of a neural network for a multiclass problem. It takes a vector of real numbers (positive and negative) as input and normalizes the vector as a probability distribution to represent the probabilities of different class labels, such as the different types of hand-written digits. For binary classification problems, Sigmoid is normally used and it returns a value between 0 and 1.

- **Defining the loss function**: TensorFlow 2.x provides a list of built-in loss functions such as **mean squared error (MSE)** and **mean absolute error (MAE)** for regression tasks and cross-entropy loss for classification tasks. You can find more details about MSE and MAE at `https://en.wikipedia.org/wiki/Mean_squared_error` and `https://en.wikipedia.org/wiki/Mean_absolute_erro`. You can find a list of supported loss functions in the `tf.keras.losses` class. You can find more details about the different losses at `https://keras.io/api/losses/`. If the built-in loss functions do not meet your needs, you can also define custom loss functions.

- **Selecting the optimizer**: TensorFlow 2.x provides a list of built-in optimizers for model training, such as the **Adam** optimizer and the **Stochastic Gradient Descent (SGD)** optimizer for parameters optimization, with its `tf.keras.optimizers` class. You can find more details about the different supported optimizers at `https://keras.io/api/optimizers/`. Adam and SGD are two of the most commonly used optimizers.

- **Selecting the evaluation metrics**: TensorFlow 2.x has a list of built-in model evaluation metrics (for example, accuracy and cross-entropy) for model training evaluations with its `tf.keras.metrics` class. You can also define custom metrics for model evaluation during training.

- **Compiling the network into a model**: This step compiles the defined network, along with the defined loss function, optimizer, and evaluation metrics, into a computational graph that's ready for model training.

- **Fitting the model**: This step kicks off the model training process by feeding the data to the computational graph through batches and multiple epochs to optimize the model parameters.

- **Evaluating the trained model**: Once the model has been trained, you can evaluate the model using the `evaluate()` function against the test data.

- **Saving the model**: The model can be saved in TensorFlow **SavedModel** serialization format or **Hierarchical Data Format (HDF5)** format.

- **Model serving**: TensorFlow comes with a model serving framework called TensorFlow Serving, which we will cover in greater detail in *Chapter 7, Open Source Machine Learning Platform*.

The TensorFlow library is designed for large-scale production-grade data processing and model training. As such, it provides capabilities for large-scale distributed data processing and model training on a cluster of servers against a large dataset. We will cover large-scale distributed data processing and model training in a *Chapter 10, Advanced ML Engineering*.

Hands-on exercise – training a TensorFlow model

In this exercise, you will learn how to install the TensorFlow library in your local Jupyter environment and build and train a simple neural network model. Launch a Jupyter notebook that you have previously installed on your machine. If you don't remember how to do this, visit the *Hands-on lab* section of *Chapter 3, Machine Learning Algorithms*.

Once the Jupyter notebook is running, create a new folder by selecting the **New** dropdown and then **Folder**. Rename the folder `TensorFlowLab`. Open the `TensorFlowLab` folder, create a new notebook inside this folder, and rename the notebook `Tensorflow-lab1.ipynb`. Now, let's get started:

1. Inside the first cell, run the following code to install TensorFlow:

   ```
   ! pip3 install --upgrade tensorflow
   ```

2. Now, we must import the library and load the sample training data. We will use the built-in `fashion_mnist` dataset that comes with the `keras` library to do so. Next, we must load the data into a `tf.data.Dataset` class and then call its `batch()` function to set up a batch size. Run the following code block in a new cell to load the data and configure the dataset:

   ```
   import numpy as np
   import tensorflow as tf
   tf.enable_eager_execution()


   train, test = tf.keras.datasets.fashion_mnist.load_data()
   images, labels = train
   labels = labels.astype(np.int32)
   images = images/256
   train_ds = tf.data.Dataset.from_tensor_slices((images,
   labels))
   train_ds = train_ds.batch(32)
   ```

3. Let's see what the data looks like. Run the following code block in a new cell to view the sample data:

   ```
   from matplotlib import pyplot as plt

   print ("label:" + str(labels[0]))
   ```

```
pixels = images[0]
plt.imshow(pixels, cmap='gray')
plt.show()
```

4. Next, we must build a simple MLP network with two hidden layers (one with `100` nodes and one with `50` nodes) and an output layer with `10` nodes (each node represents a class label). Then, we must compile the network using the **Adam** optimizer, use the cross-entropy loss as the optimization objective, and use the accuracy as the measuring metric. The Adam optimizer is a variation of **gradient descent (GD)**, and it improves upon GD mainly in the area of the adaptive learning rate for updating the parameters to improve model convergence, whereas GD uses a constant learning rate for parameter updating. Cross-entropy measures the performance of a classification model, where the output is the probability distribution for the different classes adding up to 1. The cross-entropy error increases when the predicted distribution diverges from the actual class label. To kick off the training process, we must call the `fit()` function. We will run the training for `10` epochs. One epoch is one pass of the entire training dataset:

```
model = tf.keras.Sequential([
    tf.keras.layers.Flatten(),
    tf.keras.layers.Dense(100, activation="relu"),
    tf.keras.layers.Dense(50, activation="relu"),
    tf.keras.layers.Dense(10)
    tf.keras.layers.Softmax()
])
model.compile(optimizer='adam',
              loss=tf.keras.losses.
SparseCategoricalCrossentropy(),
              metrics=[tf.keras.metrics.
SparseCategoricalAccuracy()])

model.fit(train_ds, epochs=10)
```

When the model is training, you should see a loss metric and accuracy metrics are being reported for each epoch.

5. Now that the model has been trained, we need to validate its performance using the test dataset. In the following code, we are creating a `test_ds` for the test data:

```
images_test, labels_test = test
labels_test = labels_test.astype(np.int32)
```

```
images_test = images_test/256

test_ds = tf.data.Dataset.from_tensor_slices((images_
test, labels_test))
test_ds = train_ds.batch(32)
test_ds = train_ds.shuffle(30)

results = model.evaluate(test_ds)
print("test loss, test acc:", results)
```

6. You can also use the standalone keras.metrics to evaluate the model. Here, we are getting the prediction results and using tf.keras.metrics.Accuracy to calculate the accuracy of predictions against the true values in test[1]:

```
predictions = model.predict(test[0])
predicted_labels = np.argmax(predictions, axis=1)
m = tf.keras.metrics.Accuracy()
m.update_state(predicted_labels, test[1])
m.result().numpy()
```

7. To save the model, run the following code in a new cell. It will save the model in SavedModel serialization format:

```
model.save(filepath='model', save_format='tf')
```

8. Open the model directory. You should see that several files have been generated, such as saved_model.pb, and several files under the variables subdirectory.

Congratulations! You have successfully installed the TensorFlow package in your local Jupyter environment and trained a deep learning model.

With that, you have learned about TensorFlow and how to use it to train deep learning models. Next, let's take a look at PyTorch, another highly popular deep learning library for experimentation and production-grade ML model training.

Understanding the PyTorch deep learning library

PyTorch is an open source machine learning library that was designed for deep learning using GPUs and CPUs. It was released in 2016, and it is a highly popular machine learning framework with a large following and many adoptions. Many technology companies, including tech giants such as **Facebook**, **Microsoft**, and **Airbnb**, all use PyTorch heavily for a wide range of deep learning use cases, such as computer vision and natural language processing.

PyTorch strikes a good balance of performance (using a C++ backend) with ease of use with default support for dynamic computational graphs and interoperability with the rest of the Python ecosystem. For example, with PyTorch, you can easily convert between NumPy arrays and PyTorch tensors. To allow for easy backward propagation, PyTorch has built-in support for automatically computing gradients, a vital requirement for gradient-based model optimization.

The PyTorch library consists of several key modules, including tensors, **Autograd**, **Optimizer**, and **Neural Network**. Tensors are used to store and operate multidimensional arrays of numbers. You can perform various operations on tensors such as matrix multiplication, transpose, return max number, and dimensionality manipulation. PyTorch supports automatic gradient calculation with its Autograd module. When performing a forward pass, the Autograd module simultaneously builds up a function that computes the gradient. The Optimizer module provides various algorithms such as SGD and Adam for updating model parameters. The Neural Network module provides modules that represent different layers of a neural network such as the linear layer, embedding layer, and dropout layer. It also provides a list of loss functions that are commonly used for training deep learning models.

Installing PyTorch

PyTorch can run on different operating systems, including Linux, macOS, and Windows. You can follow the instructions at `https://pytorch.org/` to install it in your environment. For example, you can use the `pip install torch` command to install it in a Python-based environment.

Core components of PyTorch

Similar to TensorFlow, PyTorch also supports the end-to-end machine learning workflow, from data preparation to model serving. The following diagram shows what different PyTorch modules are used to train and serve a PyTorch model:

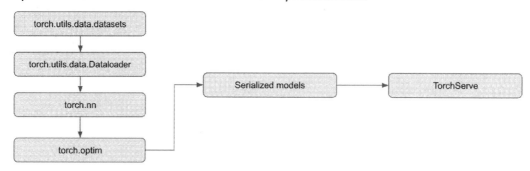

Figure 5.6 – PyTorch modules for model training and serving

The steps involved in training a deep learning model are very similar to that of TensorFlow model training. We'll look at the PyTorch-specific details in the following steps:

1. **Preparing the dataset**: PyTorch provides two primitives for dataset and data loading management: `torch.utils.data.Dataset` and `torch.utils.data.Dataloader`. `Dataset` stores data samples and their corresponding labels, while `Dataloader` wraps around the dataset and provides easy and efficient access to the data for model training. `Dataloader` provides functions such as `shuffle`, `batch_size`, and `prefetch_factor` to control how the data is loaded and fed to the training algorithm.

    As the data in the dataset might need to be transformed before training is performed, `Dataset` allows you to use a user-defined function to transform the data.

2. **Defining the neural network**: PyTorch provides a high-level abstraction for building neural networks with its `torch.nn` class. `torch.nn` provides built-in support for different neural network layers such as linear layers and convolutional layers, as well as activation layers such as Sigmoid and ReLU. It also has container classes such as `nn.Sequential` for packaging different layers into a complete network. Existing neural networks can also be loaded into PyTorch for training.

3. **Defining the loss function**: PyTorch provides several built-in loss functions in its `torch.nn` class, such as `nn.MSELoss` and `nn.CrossEntropyLoss`.

4. **Selecting the optimizer**: PyTorch provides several optimizers with its `nn.optim` classes. Examples of optimizers include `optim.SGD`, `optim.Adam`, and `optim.RMSProp`. All the optimizers have a `step()` function that updates model parameters with each forward pass. There's also a backward pass that calculates the gradients.

5. **Selecting the evaluation metrics**: The PyTorch `ignite.metrics` class provides several evaluation metrics such as Precision, Recall, and `RootMeanSquaredError` for evaluating model performances. You can learn more about precision and recall at `https://en.wikipedia.org/wiki/Precision_and_recall`. You can also use the `scikit-learn` metrics libraries to help evaluate models.

6. **Training the model**: Training a model in PyTorch involves three main steps in each training loop: forward pass the training data, backward pass the training data to calculate the gradient, and performing the optimizer step to update the gradient.

7. **Saving/loading the model**: The `torch.save()` function saves a model in a serialized pickle format. The `torch.load()` function loads a serialized model into memory for inference. A common convention is to save the files with the `.pth` or `.pt` extension. You can also save multiple models into a single file.

8. **Model serving**: PyTorch comes with a model serving library called `TorchServe`, which we will cover in more detail *Chapter 7, Open Source Machine Learning Platforms*.

The PyTorch library supports large-scale distributed data processing and model training, which we will cover in more detail in *Chapter 10, Advanced ML Engineering*.

Now that you have learned about the fundamentals of PyTorch, let's get hands-on through a simple exercise.

Hands-on exercise – building and training a PyTorch model

In this hands-on exercise, you will learn how to install the PyTorch library in your local machine and train a simple deep learning model using PyTorch. Launch a Jupyter notebook that you have previously installed on your machine. If you don't remember how to do this, visit the *Hands-on lab* section of *Chapter 3, Machine Learning Algorithms*. Now, let's get started:

1. Create a new folder called `pytorch-lab` in your Jupyter notebook environment and create a new notebook file called `pytorch-lab1.ipynb`. Run the following command in a cell to install PyTorch and the `torchvision` package. `torchvision` contains a set of computer vision models and datasets. We will use the pre-built MNIST dataset in the `torchvision` package for this exercise:

```
!pip3 install torch
!pip3 install torchvision
```

2. The following sample code shows the previously mentioned main components. Be sure to run each code block in a separate Jupyter notebook cell for easy readability.

   First, we must import the necessary library packages and load the MNIST dataset from the `torchvision` dataset class:

```
import numpy as np
import matplotlib.pyplot as plt
import torch
from torchvision import datasets, transforms
from torch import nn, optim

transform = transforms.Compose([transforms.ToTensor(),
transforms.Normalize((0.5,), (0.5,),)])
trainset = datasets.MNIST('pytorch_data/train/',
download=True, train=True, transform=transform)
valset = datasets.MNIST('pytorch_data/test/',
download=True, train=False, transform=transform)
trainloader = torch.utils.data.DataLoader(trainset,
batch_size=64, shuffle=True)
```

3. Next, we must construct an MLP neural network for classification. This MLP network has two hidden layers with ReLU activation for the first and second layers. The MLP model takes an input size of 784, which is the flattened dimension of a 28x28 image. The first hidden layer has 128 nodes (neurons), while the second layer has 64 nodes (neurons). The final layer has 10 nodes because we have 10 class labels:

```python
model = nn.Sequential(nn.Linear(784, 128),
                      nn.ReLU(),
                      nn.Linear(128, 64),
                      nn.ReLU(),
                      nn.Linear(64, 10))
```

4. Let's show a sample of the image data:

```python
images, labels = next(iter(trainloader))
pixels = images[0][0]
plt.imshow(pixels, cmap='gray')
plt.show()
```

5. Now, we must define a **cross-entropy loss function** for the training process since we want to measure the error in the probability distribution for all the labels. Internally, PyTorch's CrossEntropyLoss automatically applies a softmax to the network output to calculate the probability distributions for the different classes. For the optimizer, we have chosen the Adam optimizer with a learning rate of 0.003. The view() function flattens the two-dimensional input array (28x28) into a one-dimensional vector since our neural network takes one-dimensional vector input:

```python
criterion = nn.CrossEntropyLoss()
images = images.view(images.shape[0], -1)
output = model(images)
loss = criterion(output, labels)
optimizer = optim.Adam(model.parameters(), lr=0.003)
```

6. Now, let's start the training process. We are going to run 15 epochs. Unlike the TensorFlow Keras API, where you just call a `fit()` function to start the training, PyTorch requires you to build a training loop and specifically run the forward pass (`model(images)`), run the backward pass to learn (`loss.backward()`), update the model weights (`optimizer.step()`), and then calculate the total loss and the average loss. For each training step, `trainloader` returns one batch (a batch size of 64) of training data samples. Each training sample is flattened into a 784-long vector. The optimizer is reset with zeros for each training step:

```python
epochs = 15
for e in range(epochs):
    running_loss = 0
    for images, labels in trainloader:
        images = images.view(images.shape[0], -1)
        optimizer.zero_grad()
        output = model(images)
        loss = criterion(output, labels)
        loss.backward()
        optimizer.step()
        running_loss += loss.item()
    else:
        print("Epoch {} - Training loss: {}".format(e,
running_loss/len(trainloader)))
```

When the training code runs, it should print out the average loss for each epoch.

7. To test the accuracy using the validation data, we must run the validation dataset through the trained model and use `scikit-learn.metrics.accuracy_score()` to calculate the model's accuracy:

```
valloader = torch.utils.data.DataLoader(valset, batch_
size=valset.data.shape[0], shuffle=True)

val_images, val_labels = next(iter(valloader))

val_images = val_images.view(val_images.shape[0], -1)

predictions = model (val_images)

predicted_labels = np.argmax(predictions.detach().
numpy(), axis=1)


from sklearn.metrics import accuracy_score

accuracy_score(val_labels.detach().numpy(), predicted_
labels)
```

8. Finally, we must save the model to a file:

```
torch.save(model, './model/my_mnist_model.pt')
```

Congratulations! You have successfully installed PyTorch in your local Jupyter environment and trained a deep learning PyTorch model.

Summary

In this chapter, we covered several popular open source machine learning library packages, including `scikit-learn`, Spark ML, TensorFlow, and PyTorch. You should now be familiar with the core building blocks for each of these libraries and how they can be used to train a machine learning model. You have also learned to use the TensorFlow and PyTorch frameworks to build simple artificial neural networks, train deep learning models, and persist these trained models to files. These model files can be loaded into model serving environments to generate predictions.

In the next chapter, we will cover **Kubernetes** and how it can be used as a foundational infrastructure for building open source machine learning solutions.

6
Kubernetes Container Orchestration Infrastructure Management

While it is fairly straightforward to build a local data science environment with open source technologies for individual uses in simple **machine learning** (**ML**) tasks, it is quite challenging to configure and maintain a data science environment for many users for different ML tasks and track ML experiments. Building an end-to-end ML platform is a complex process, and there are many different architecture patterns and open source technologies available to help. In this chapter, we will cover **Kubernetes**, an open source container orchestration platform that can serve as the foundational infrastructure for building open source ML platforms. We will discuss the core concept of Kubernetes, its networking architecture and components, and its security and access control. You will also get hands-on with Kubernetes to build a Kubernetes cluster and use it to deploy containerized applications.

Specifically, we will cover the following topics:

- Introduction to containers
- Kubernetes overview and core concepts
- Kubernetes networking
- Kubernetes security and access control
- Hands-on lab – building a Kubernetes infrastructure on **AWS**

Technical requirements

In this chapter, you will continue to use services in your AWS account for the hands-on portion of the chapter. We will be using several AWS services, including the AWS **Elastic Kubernetes Service** (**EKS**), AWS **CloudShell**, and AWS **EC2**. All code files used in this chapter are located on GitHub:

```
https://github.com/PacktPublishing/The-Machine-Learning-
Solutions-Architect-Handbook/tree/main/Chapter06.
```

Let's begin the chapter with a quick introduction to containers.

Introduction to containers

A **container** is a form of operating system virtualization, and it has been a very popular computing platform for software deployment and running modern software based on micro-services architecture. A container allows you to package and run computer software with isolated dependencies. Compared to server virtualization, such as Amazon EC2 or **VMware** virtual machines, containers are more lightweight and portable, as they share the same operating system and do not contain operating system images in each container. Each container has its own filesystem, shares of computing resources, and process space for the custom applications running inside it.

While containers may seem like a relatively new transformative technology, the concept of containerization technology was actually born in the 1970s with the **chroot system** and **Unix Version 7**. However, container technology did not gain much attraction in the software development community for the next two decades and remained dormant. While it picked up some steam and made remarkable advances from 2000 to 2011, it was the introduction of **Docker** in 2013 that started a renaissance of container technology.

You can run all kinds of applications inside containers, such as simple programs like data processing scripts or complex systems like databases. The following diagram shows how container deployment is different from other types of deployment. Note that a container runtime can also run in the guest operating system of a virtualized environment to host containerized applications:

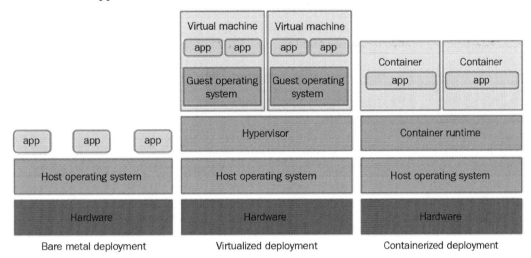

Figure 6.1 – The differences between bare metal, virtualized, and container deployment

Containers are packaged as Docker images, which are made of all the files (such as installation, application code, and dependencies) that are essential to run the containers and the applications in them. One way to build a Docker image is the use of a **Dockerfile** – that is, a plain-text file that provides specifications on how to build a Docker image. Once a Docker image is created, it can be executed in a container runtime environment. The following is an example `Dockerfile` for building a Docker image to create a runtime environment based on the **Ubuntu** operating system (the FROM instruction) and install various **Python** packages, such as `python3`, `numpy`, `scikit-learn` and `pandas` (the RUN instructions):

```
FROM ubuntu:18.04

RUN apt-get -y update && apt-get install -y --no-install-
recommends \
        wget \
        python3-pip \
        nginx \
        ca-certificates \
    && rm -rf /var/lib/apt/lists/*
```

```
RUN ln -s /usr/bin/python3 /usr/bin/python
RUN ln -s /usr/bin/pip3 /usr/bin/pip
RUN pip --no-cache-dir install numpy==1.16.2 scipy==1.2.1
scikit-learn==0.20.2 pandas flask gunicorn
```

To build a Docker image from this `Dockerfile`, you can use the Docker `build` command, which is a utility that comes as part of the Docker installation.

Now we have an understanding of containers, next, let's dive into Kubernetes.

Kubernetes overview and core concepts

While it is feasible to deploy and manage the life cycle of a small number of containers and containerized applications directly in a compute environment, it can get very challenging when you have a large number of containers to manage and orchestrate across a large number of servers. This is where Kubernetes comes in. Initially released in 2014, **Kubernetes (K8s)** is an open source system for managing containers at scale on clusters of servers (the abbreviation K8s is derived by replacing *ubernete* with the digit 8).

Architecturally, Kubernetes operates a master node and one or more worker nodes in a cluster of servers. The master node, also known as the **control plane**, is responsible for the overall management of the cluster, and it has four key components:

- API server
- Scheduler
- Controller
- etcd

The master node exposes an **API server** layer that allows programmatic control of the cluster. An example of an API call could be the deployment of a web application on the cluster. The control plane also tracks and manages all configuration data in a key-value store called **etcd** that is responsible for storing all the cluster data, such as the desired number of container images to run, compute resource specification, and size of storage volume for a web application running on the cluster. Kubernetes uses an object type called **controller** to monitor the current states of Kubernetes resources and take the necessary actions (for example, request the change via the API server) to move the current states to the desired states if there are differences (such as the difference in the number of the running containers) between the two states. The controller manager in the master node is responsible for managing all the Kubernetes controllers. Kubernetes comes with a set of built-in controllers such as **scheduler**, which is responsible for scheduling **Pods** (units of deployment that we will discuss in more detail later) to run on worker nodes when there is a change request. Other examples include **Job controller**, which is responsible for running and stopping one or more Pods for a task, and **Deployment controller**, which is responsible for deploying Pods based on a deployment manifest, such as a deployment manifest for a web application. The following figure (*Figure 6.2*) shows the core architecture components of a Kubernetes cluster:

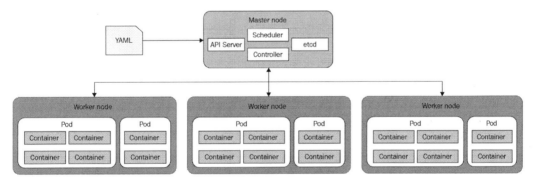

Figure 6.2 – Kubernetes architecture

To interact with a Kubernetes cluster control plane, you can use the `kubectl` command-line utility, the Kubernetes Python client (`https://github.com/kubernetes-client/python`), or access directly using the RESTful API. You can get a list of supported `kubectl` commands at `https://kubernetes.io/docs/reference/kubectl/cheatsheet/`.

There are a number of unique technical concepts that are core to the Kubernetes architecture. The following are some of the main concepts that Kubernetes operates around:

- **Namespaces**: Namespaces organize clusters of worker machines into virtual sub-clusters. They are used to provide logical separation of resources owned by different teams and projects while still allowing ways for different namespaces to communicate. A namespace can span multiple worker nodes, and it can be used to group a list of permissions under a single name to allow authorized users to access resources in a namespace. Resource usage controls can be enforced to namespaces such as quotas for CPU and memory resources. Namespaces also make it possible to name resources with identical names if the resources reside in the different namespaces to avoid naming conflicts. By default, there is a `default` namespace in Kubernetes. You can create additional namespaces as needed. The default namespace is used if a namespace is not specified.

- **Pods**: Kubernetes deploys computing in a logical unit called a Pod. All Pods must belong to a Kubernetes namespace (either the default namespace or a specified namespace). One or more containers can be grouped into a Pod, and all containers in the Pod are deployed and scaled together as a single unit and share the same context, such as Linux namespaces and filesystems. Each Pod has a unique IP address that's shared by all the containers in a Pod. A Pod is normally created as a workload resource, such as a Kubernetes Deployment or Kubernetes Job.

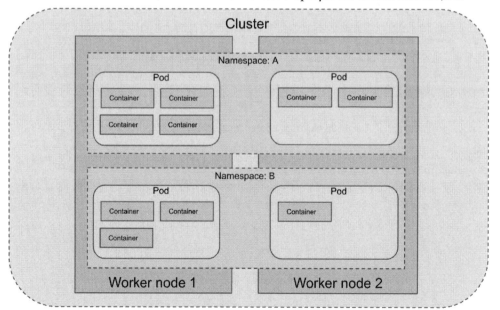

Figure 6.3 – Namespaces, Pods, and containers

The preceding figure (*Figure 6.3*) shows the relationship between namespaces, Pods, and containers in a Kubernetes cluster. In this figure, each namespace contains its own set of Pods and each Pod can contain one or more containers running in it.

- **Deployment**: A deployment is used by Kubernetes to create or modify Pods that run containerized applications. For example, to deploy a containerized application, you create a configuration manifest file (usually in a YAML file format) that specifies details, such as the container deployment name, namespaces, container image URI, number of Pod replicas, and the communication port for the application. After the deployment is applied using a Kubernetes client utility (kubectl), the corresponding Pods running the specified container images will be created on the worker nodes. The following example creates a deployment of Pods for an Nginx server with the desired specification:

```
apiVersion: apps/v1  # k8s API version used for creating
this deployment
kind: Deployment  # the type of object. In this case, it
is deployment
metadata:
  name: nginx-deployment  # name of the deployment
spec:
  selector:
    matchLabels:
      app: nginx  # an app label for the deployment.
This can be used to look up/select Pods
  replicas: 2  # tells deployment to run 2 Pods matching
the template
  template:
    metadata:
      labels:
        app: nginx
    spec:
      containers:
      - name: nginx
        image: nginx:1.14.2  # Docker container image
used for the deployment
        ports:
        - containerPort: 80  # the networking port to
communicate with the containers
```

The following figure shows the flow of applying the preceding deployment manifest file to a Kubernetes cluster and creates two Pods to host two copies of the Nginx container:

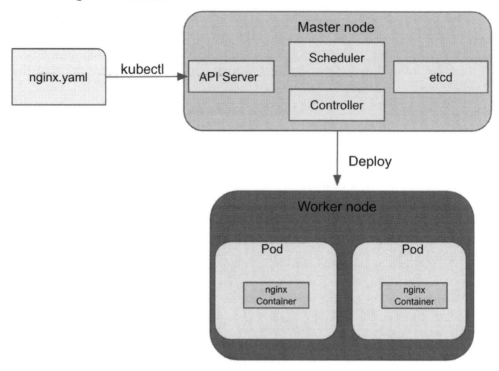

Figure 6.4 – Creating an Nginx deployment

After the deployment, a Deployment controller monitors the deployed container instances. If an instance goes down, the controller will replace it with another instance on the worker node.

- **Kubernetes Job**: A Kubernetes Job is a controller that creates one or more Pods to run some tasks, and ensures the job is successfully completed. If a number of Pods fail due to node failure or other system issues, a Kubernetes Job will recreate the Pods to complete the task. A Kubernetes Job can be used to run batch-oriented tasks, such as running batch data processing scripts, ML model training scripts, or ML batch inference scripts on a large number of inference requests. After a job is completed, the Pods are not terminated, so you can access the job logs and inspect the detailed status of the job. The following is an example template for running a training job:

```
apiVersion: batch/v1
kind: Job # indicate that his is the Kubernetes Job
```

```
resource
metadata:
  name: train-job
spec:
  template:
    spec:
      containers:
      - name: train-container
        imagePullPolicy: Always # tell the job to always
pulls a new container image when it is started
        image: <uri to Docker image containing training
script>
        command: ["python3", "train.py"] # tell the
container to run this command after it is started
      restartPolicy: Never
  backoffLimit: 0
```

- **Kubernetes custom resources (CRs) and operators**: Kubernetes provides a list of built-in resources, such as Pods or deployment for different needs. It also allows you to create CRs and manage them just like the built-in resources, and you can use the same tools (such as kubectl) to manage them. When you create the **custom resource** (**CR**) in Kubernetes, Kubernetes creates a new API (for example, <custom resource name>/<version>) for each version of the resource. This is also known as *extending* the Kubernetes APIs. To create a CR, you create a **custom resource definition** (**CRD**) YAML file. To register the CRD in Kubernetes, you simply run kubectl apply -f <name of the CRD yaml file> to apply the file. And after that, you can use it just like any other Kubernetes resource. For example, to manage a custom model training job on Kubernetes, you can define a CRD with specifications such as algorithm name, data encryption setting, training image, input data sources, number of job failure retries, number of replicas, and job liveness probe frequency.

A Kubernetes operator is a controller that operates on a custom resource. The operator watches the CR types and takes specific actions to make the current state match the desired state, just like what a built-in controller does. For example, if you want to create a training job for the training job CRD mentioned previously, you create an operator that monitors training job requests and performs application-specific actions to start up the Pods and run the training job throughout the life cycle. The following figure (*Figure 6.5*) shows the components involved with an operator deployment:

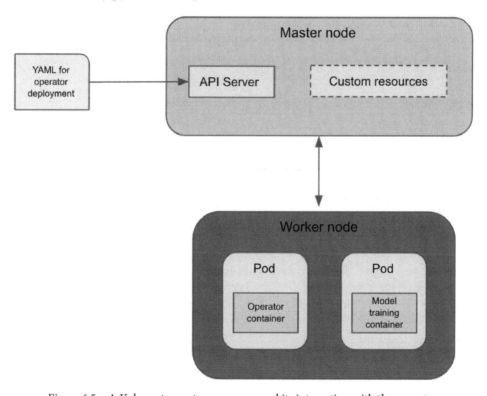

Figure 6.5 – A Kubernetes custom resource and its interaction with the operator

The most common way to deploy an operator is to deploy a CR definition and the associated controller. The controller runs outside of the Kubernetes control plane, similar to running a containerized application in a Pod.

Networking on Kubernetes

Kubernetes operates a flat private network among all the resources in a Kubernetes cluster. Within a cluster, all Pods can communicate with each other cluster-wide without an **network address translation (NAT)**. Kubernetes gives each Pod its own cluster private IP address, and the IP is the same IP seen by the Pod itself and what others see it as. All containers inside a single Pod can reach each container's port on the localhost. All nodes in a cluster have their individually assigned IPs as well and can communicate with all Pods without an NAT. The following figure (*Figure 6.6*) shows the different IP assignments for Pods and nodes, and communication flows from different resources:

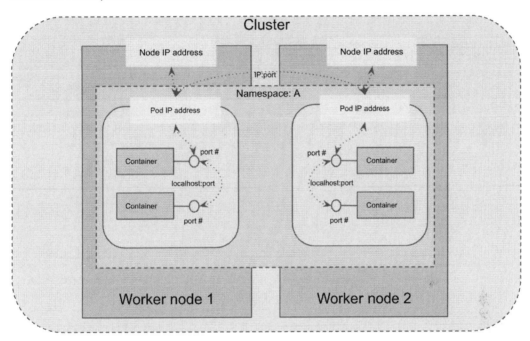

Figure 6.6 – IP assignments and communication flow

Sometimes you might need a set of Pods running the same application container (the container for an **Nginx** application) for high availability and load balancing, for example. Instead of calling each Pod by its private IP separately to access the application running in a Pod, you want to call an abstraction layer for this set of Pods, and this abstraction layer can dynamically send traffic to each Pod behind it. In this case, you can create a Kubernetes Service as an abstraction layer for a logical set of Pods. A Kubernetes Service can dynamically select the Pod behind it by matching an `app` label for the Pod using a Kubernetes feature called `selector`. The following example shows the specification that would create a service called `nginx-service` that sends traffic to Pods with the app `nginx` label on port `9376`. A service is also assigned with its own cluster private IP address, so it is reachable by other resources inside a cluster:

```
apiVersion: v1
kind: Service
metadata:
  name: nginx-service
spec:
  selector:
    app: nginx
  ports:
    - protocol: TCP
      port: 80
      targetPort: 9376
```

In addition to using `selector` to automatically detect Pods behind the service, you can also manually create an `Endpoint` and map a fixed IP and port to a service, as shown in the following example:

```
apiVersion: v1
kind: Endpoints
metadata:
  name: nginx-service
subsets:
  - addresses:
      - ip: 192.0.2.42
    ports:
      - port: 9376
```

While nodes, Pods, and services are all assigned with cluster private IPs, these IPs are not routable from outside of a cluster. To access Pods or services from outside of a cluster, you have the following options:

- **Access from a node or Pod**: You can connect to the shell of a running Pod using the kubectl exe command, and access other Pods, nodes, and services from the shell.

- **Kubernetes Proxy**: You can start the Kubernetes Proxy to access services by running the kubectl proxy --port=<port number> command on your local machine. Once the proxy is running, you can access nodes, Pods, or services. For example, you can access a service using the following scheme:

```
http://localhost:<port number>/api/v1/proxy/
namespaces/<NAMESPACE>/services/<SERVICE NAME>:<PORT
NAME>
```

- **NodePort**: NodePort opens a specific port on all the worker nodes, and any traffic sent to this port on the IP address of any of the nodes is forwarded to the service behind the port. The nodes' IPs need to be routable from external sources. The following figure (*Figure 6.7*) shows the communication flow using NodePort:

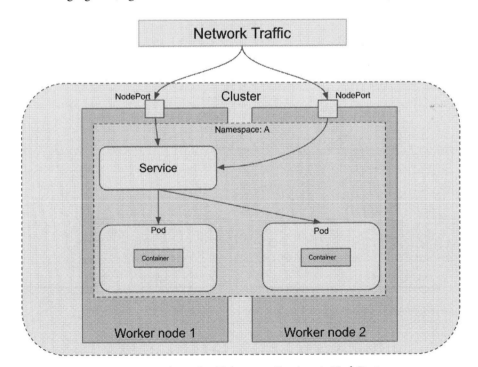

Figure 6.7 – Accessing Kubernetes Service via NodePort

`NodePort` is simple to use, but it has some limitations, such as one service per `NodePort`, a fixed port range to use (`3000` to `32767`), and you need to know the IPs of individual worker nodes.

- **Load balancer**: A load balancer is a standard way to expose services to the internet. With a load balancer, you get a public IP address that's accessible to the internet, and all traffic sent to the IP address will be forwarded to the service behind the load balancer. A load balancer is not part of Kubernetes and it is provided by whatever cloud infrastructure a Kubernetes cluster resides on (for example, AWS). The following figure (*Figure 6.8*) shows the communication flow from a load balancer to services and Pods:

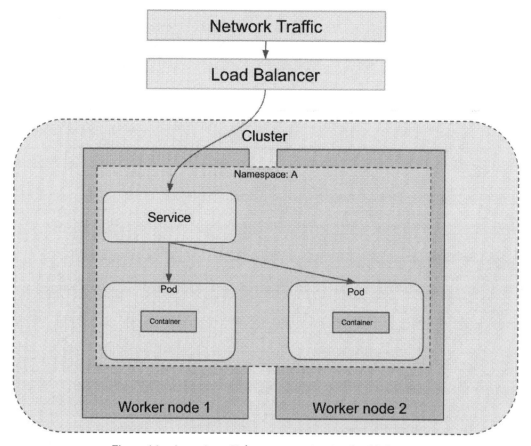

Figure 6.8 – Accessing a Kubernetes service via a load balancer

A load balancer allows you to choose the exact port to use and can support multiple ports per service. However, it does require a separate load balancer per service.

- **Ingress**: An Ingress gateway is the entry point to a cluster. It acts as a load balancer and routes incoming traffic to the different services based on routing rules.

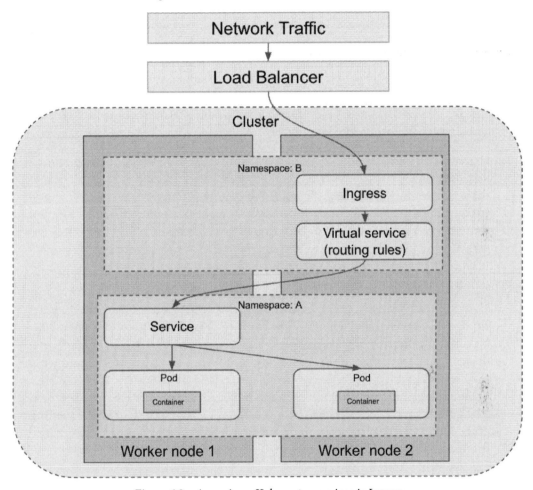

Figure 6.9 – Accessing a Kubernetes service via Ingress

An Ingress is different from a load balancer and `NodePort` in that it acts as a proxy to manage traffic to clusters. It works with the `NodePort` and load balancer and routes the traffic to the different services. The Ingress way is becoming more commonly used, especially in combination with a load balancer.

Service mesh

In addition to network traffic management from outside of the cluster, another important aspect of Kubernetes network management is to control the traffic flow between different Pods and services within a cluster. For example, you might want to allow certain traffic to access a Pod or service while denying traffic from other sources. This is especially important for applications built on microservices architecture, as there could be many services or Pods that need to work together. Such a network of microservices is also called a **service mesh**. As the number of services grows large, it becomes challenging to understand and manage the networking requirements, such as *service discovery*, *network routing*, *network metrics*, and *failure recovery*. **Istio** is an open source service mesh management software that makes it easy to manage a large service mesh on Kubernetes, and it provides the following core functions:

- **Ingress**: Istio provides an Ingress gateway that can be used to expose Pods and services inside a service mesh to the internet. It acts as a load balancer that manages the inbound and outbound traffic for the service mesh. A gateway only allows traffic to come in/out of a mesh – it does not do routing of the traffic. To route traffic from the gateway to service inside the service mesh, you create an object called `Virtual Service` to provide routing rules to route incoming traffic to different destinations inside a cluster, and you create a binding between virtual services and the gateway object to connect the two together.

- **Network traffic management**: Istio provides easy rule-based network routing to control the flow of traffic and API calls between different services. When Istio is installed, it automatically detects services and endpoints in a cluster. Istio uses an object called `Virtual Service` to provide routing rules to route incoming traffic to different destinations inside a cluster. Istio uses a load balancer called `gateway` to manage the inbound and outbound traffic for the network mesh. The `gateway` load balancer only allows traffic to come in/out of a mesh – it does not do routing of the traffic. To route traffic from the gateway, you create a binding between virtual services and the `gateway` object.

In order to manage the traffic in and out of a Pod, an Envoy proxy component (aka `sidecar`) is injected into a Pod, and it intercepts and decides how to route all traffic. The Istio component that manages the traffic configurations of the sidecars and service discovery is called the `Pilot`. The `Citadel` component manages authentication for service to service and end user. The `Gallery` component is responsible for insulating other Istio components from the underlying Kubernetes infrastructure. The following figure shows the architecture of Istio on Kubernetes:

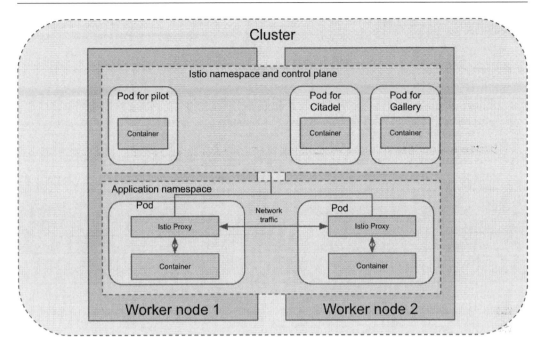

Figure 6.10 – Istio architecture

- **Security**: Istio provides authentication and authorization for inter-service communications.

- **Observability**: Istio captures metrics, logs, and traces of all service communications within a cluster. Examples of metrics include network latency, errors, and saturation. Examples of traces include call flows and service dependencies within a mesh.

Istio can handle a wide range of deployment needs, such as load balancing and service-to-service authentication. It can even extend to other clusters.

Security and access management

Kubernetes has many built-in security features. These security features allow you to implement fine-grained network traffic control and access control to different Kubernetes APIs and services. In this section, we will discuss network security, authentication, and authorization.

Network security

By default, Kubernetes allows all Pods in a cluster to communicate with each other. To prevent unintended network traffic among different Pods, **network policies** can be established to specify how Pods can communicate with each other. You can think of a network policy as a network firewall that contains a list of allowed connections. Each network policy has a `podSelector` field, which selects a group of Pods enforced by the network policy and the allowed traffic direction (ingress or egress). The following sample policy denies all ingress traffic to all Pods, as there are no specific ingress policies defined:

```
apiVersion: networking.k8s.io/v1
kind: NetworkPolicy
metadata:
  name: default-deny-ingress
spec:
  podSelector: {}
  policyTypes:
  - Ingress
```

Network traffic is allowed if there is at least one policy that allows it.

Authentication and authorization to APIs

Access to Kubernetes APIs can be authenticated and authorized for both users and Kubernetes **service accounts** (a service account provides an identity for processes running in a Pod).

Users are handled outside of Kubernetes, and there are a number of user authentication strategies for Kubernetes:

- **X.509 client certificate**: A signed certificate is sent to the API server for authentication. The API server verifies this with the certificate authority to validate the user.

- **Single sign-on with OpenID Connect (OIDC)**: The user authenticates with the OIDC provider and receives a bearer token (**JSON Web Token (JWT)**) that contains information about the user. The user passes the bearer token to the API server, which verifies the validity of the token by checking the certificate in the token.

- **HTTP basic authentication**: HTTP basic authentication requires a user ID and password to be sent as part of the API request, and it validates the user ID and password against a password file associated with the API server.

- **Authentication proxy**: The API server extracts the user identity in the HTTP header and verifies the user with the certificate authority.

- **Authentication webhook**: An external service is used for handling the authentication for the API server.

Service accounts are used to provide identity for processes running in a Pod. They are created and managed in Kubernetes. Service accounts need to reside within a namespace, by default. There is also a *default* service account in each namespace. If a Pod is not assigned a service account, the default service account will be assigned to the Pod. A service account has an associated authentication token, saved as a Kubernetes Secret, and used for API authentication. A Kubernetes Secret is used for storing sensitive information such as passwords, authentication tokens, and SSH keys. We will cover secrets in more detail later in this chapter.

After a user or service account is authenticated, the request needs to be authorized to perform allowed operations. Kubernetes authorizes authenticated requests using the API server in the control plane, and it has several modes for authorization:

- **Attribute-based access control** (**ABAC**): Access rights are granted to users through policies. Note that every service account has a corresponding username. The following sample policy allows the `joe` user access to all APIs in all namespaces.

```
{
    "apiVersion": "abac.authorization.kubernetes.io/
v1beta1",
    "kind": "Policy",
    "spec": {
        "user": "joe",
        "namespace": "*",
        "resource": "*",
        "apiGroup": "*"
    }
}
```

The following policy allows the `system:serviceaccount:kube-system:default` service account access to all APIs in all namespaces:

```
{
    "apiVersion": "abac.authorization.kubernetes.io/
v1beta1",
    "kind": "Policy",
```

```
  "spec": {
    "user": "system:serviceaccount:kube-system:default",
    "namespace": "*",
    "resource": "*",
    "apiGroup": "*"
  }
}
```

- **Role-based access control (RBAC):** Access rights are granted based on the role of a user. RBAC authorizes using the `rbac.authorization.k8s.io` API group. The RBAC API works with four Kubernetes objects: `Role`, `ClusterRole`, `RoleBinding`, and `ClusterRoleBinding`.

`Role` and `ClusterRole` contain a set of permissions. The permissions are *additive*, meaning there are no deny permissions, and you need to explicitly add permission to resources. The `Role` object is namespaced and is used to specify permissions within a namespace. The `ClusterRole` object is non-namespaced, but can be used for granting permission for a given namespace or cluster-scoped permissions. The following `yaml` file provides get, watch, and list access to all Pods resources in the default namespace for the core API group:

```
apiVersion: rbac.authorization.k8s.io/v1
kind: Role
metadata:
  namespace: default
  name: pod-reader
rules:
- apiGroups: [""]
  resources: ["pods"]
  verbs: ["get", "watch", "list"]
```

The following policy allows get, watch, and list access for all Kubernetes nodes across the cluster:

```
apiVersion: rbac.authorization.k8s.io/v1
kind: ClusterRole
metadata:
  name: nodes-reader
rules:
```

```
- apiGroups: [""]
  resources: ["nodes"]
  verbs: ["get", "watch", "list"]
```

RoleBinding and ClusterRoleBinding grant permissions defined in a
Role or ClusterRole object to a user or set of users with reference to a Role or
ClusterRole object. The following policy binds the joe user to the pod-reader role:

```
apiVersion: rbac.authorization.k8s.io/v1
kind: RoleBinding
metadata:
  name: read-pods
  namespace: default
subjects:
- kind: User
  name: joe
  apiGroup: rbac.authorization.k8s.io
roleRef:
  kind: Role
  name: pod-reader
  apiGroup: rbac.authorization.k8s.io
```

The following RoleBinding object binds a service account, SA-name, to the
ClusterRole nodes-reader:

```
apiVersion: rbac.authorization.k8s.io/v1
kind: ClusterRoleBinding
metadata:
  name: read-secrets-global
subjects:
- kind: ServiceAccount
  name: SA-name
  namespace: default
roleRef:
  kind: ClusterRole
  name: secret-reader
  apiGroup: rbac.authorization.k8s.io
```

Kubernetes has a built-in feature for storing and managing sensitive information such as passwords. Instead of storing this sensitive information directly in plain text in a Pod, you can store this information as Kubernetes Secrets, and provide specific access to them using Kubernetes RBAC to create and/or read these secrets. By default, secrets are stored as unencrypted plain-text Base64-encoded strings, and data encryption at rest can be enabled for the secrets. The following policy shows how to create a secret for storing AWS access credentials:

```
apiVersion: v1
kind: Secret
metadata:
  name: aws-secret
type: Opaque
data:
  AWS_ACCESS_KEY_ID: XXXX
  AWS_SECRET_ACCESS_KEY: XXXX
```

There are several ways to use a secret in a Pod:

- As environment variables in the Pod specification template:

```
apiVersion: v1
kind: Pod
metadata:
  name: secret-env-pod
spec:
  containers:
  - name: mycontainer
    image: redis
    env:
      - name: SECRET_AWS_ACCESS_KEY
        valueFrom:
          secretKeyRef:
            name: aws-secret
            key: AWS_ACCESS_KEY_ID
      - name: SECRET_AWS_SECRET_ACCESS_KEY
```

```
            valueFrom:
              secretKeyRef:
                name: aws-secret
                key: AWS_SECRET_ACCESS_KEY
      restartPolicy: Never
```

The application code inside the container can access the secrets just like other environment variables.

- As a file in a volume mounted on a Pod:

```
apiVersion: v1
kind: Pod
metadata:
  name: pod-ml
spec:
  containers:
  - name: pod-ml
    image: <Docker image uri>
    volumeMounts:
    - name: vol-ml
      mountPath: "/etc/aws"
      readOnly: true
  volumes:
  - name: vol-ml
    Secret:
      secretName: aws-secret
```

In the previous examples, you will see files in the /etc/aws folder for each corresponding secret name (such as SECRET_AWS_ACCESS_KEY) that contains the values for the secrets.

Running ML workloads on Kubernetes

We now know what containers are and how they can be deployed on a Kubernetes cluster. We also know how to configure networking on Kubernetes to allow Pods to communicate with each other and how to expose a Kubernetes container for external access outside of the cluster using different networking options.

Kubernetes can function as the foundational infrastructure for running ML workloads. For example, you can run a **Jupyter Notebook** as a containerized application on Kubernetes as your data science environment for experimentation and model building. You can also run a model training job as a Kubernetes Job if you need additional resources, and then serve the model as a containerized web service application or run batch inferences on trained models as a Kubernetes Job. In the following hands-on exercise, you will learn how to use Kubernetes as the foundational infrastructure for running ML workloads.

Hands-on – creating a Kubernetes infrastructure on AWS

In this section, you will create a Kubernetes environment using the Amazon EKS. Let's first look at the problem statement in the following section.

Problem statement

As a ML solutions architect, you have been tasked to evaluate Kubernetes as a potential infrastructure platform for building an ML platform for one business unit in your bank. You need to build a sandbox environment on AWS and demonstrate that you can deploy a Jupyter Notebook as a containerized application for your data scientists to use.

Lab instruction

In this hands-on exercise, you are going to create a Kubernetes environment using the Amazon EKS. The EKS is a managed service for Kubernetes on AWS that creates and configures a Kubernetes cluster with both master and worker nodes automatically. The EKS provisions and scales the control plane, including the API server and backend persistent layer. The EKS runs the open source Kubernetes and is compatible with all Kubernetes-based applications.

After the EKS cluster is created, you will explore the EKS environment to inspect some of its core components, and then you will learn to deploy a containerized Jupyter Notebook application and make it accessible from the internet.

Let's complete the following steps to get started:

1. Launch the AWS CloudShell service.

    Log on to your AWS account, select the **Oregon** region, and launch the AWS CloudShell. CloudShell is an AWS service that provides a browser-based **Linux** terminal environment to interact with AWS resources. With CloudShell, you authenticate using your AWS console credential and can easily run **AWS CLI**, **AWS SDK**, and other tools.

2. Install the `eksctl` utility.

    Run the following commands one by one in the CloudShell terminal. The `eksctl` utility is a command-line utility for managing the EKS cluster. We will use the `eksctl` utility to create a Kubernetes cluster on Amazon EKS in *Step 4*:

    ```
    curl --silent --location "https://github.com/weaveworks/
    eksctl/releases/latest/download/eksctl_$(uname -s)_amd64.
    tar.gz" | tar xz -C /tmp
    ```

    ```
    chmod +x /tmp/eksctl
    ```

    ```
    sudo mv /tmp/eksctl ./bin/eksctl
    ```

    ```
    export PATH=$PATH:/home/cloudshell-user/bin
    ```

3. Install the AWS IAM Authenticator.

    Inside the CloudShell service, run the following commands one by one to download the **AWS IAM Authenticator** software. The AWS IAM Authenticator software authenticates to the Kubernetes cluster running on Amazon EKS with an AWS credential:

    ```
    curl -o aws-iam-authenticator https://amazon-eks.s3.us-
    west-2.amazonaws.com/1.19.6/2021-01-05/bin/linux/amd64/
    aws-iam-authenticator
    ```

    ```
    chmod +x ./aws-iam-authenticator
    ```

    ```
    sudo mv aws-iam-authenticator ./bin/aws-iam-authenticator
    ```

4. Build a new EKS cluster.

    Run the following command to create a cluster configuration file:

    ```
    cat << EOF > cluster.yaml
    ---
    apiVersion: eksctl.io/v1alpha5
    kind: ClusterConfig

    metadata:
      name: eksml-cluster
      version: "1.18"
      region: us-west-2

    managedNodeGroups:
    - name: kubeflow-mng
      desiredCapacity: 3
      instanceType: m5.large
    EOF
    ```

    Run the following command to start creating an EKS cluster in the **Oregon** region inside your AWS account. It will take about 15 minutes to complete running the setup:

    ```
    eksctl create cluster -f cluster.yaml
    ```

    The command will launch a `cloudformation` template and this will create the following resources:

    A. An Amazon EKS cluster with two worker nodes inside a new Amazon **virtual private cloud** (**VPC**). Amazon EKS provides fully managed Kubernetes master nodes, so you won't see the master nodes inside your private VPC.

    B. An EKS cluster configuration file saved in the `/home/cloudshell-user/.kube/config` directory on CloudShell. The `config` file contains details such as the API server `url` address, the name of the admin user for managing the cluster, and the client certificate for authenticating to the Kubernetes cluster. The `kubectl` utility uses information in the `config` file to connect and authenticate to the Kubernetes API server.

C. EKS organizes worker nodes into logical groups called `nodegroup`. Run the following command to look up the `nodegroup` name. You can look up the name of the cluster in the EKS management console. The name of the node group should look something like *ng-xxxxxxxx*.

```
eksctl get nodegroup --cluster=<cluster name>
```

5. Install the `kubectl` utility.

   Run the following commands to download the `kubectl` utility:

```
curl -LO "https://storage.googleapis.com/kubernetes-
release/release/$(curl -s https://storage.googleapis.com/
kubernetes-release/release/stable.txt)/bin/linux/amd64/
kubectl"
```

```
chmod +x ./kubectl
```

```
sudo mv ./kubectl ./bin/kubectl
```

6. Explore the cluster.

   Now the cluster is up, let's explore it a bit. Try running the following commands in the CloudShell terminal and see what is returned:

Items to explore	kubectl command syntax
Get cluster info.	`kubectl cluster-info`
List all API resources.	`kubectl api-resources`
List available namespaces.	`kubectl get namespaces`
List worker nodes.	`kubectl get nodes`
List Pods in all namespaces.	`kubectl get pods -A`
List services in all namespaces.	`kubectl get services -A`
List all clusterroles.	`kubectl get clusterroles`
List all roles in all namespaces.	`kubectl get roles -A`
List all service accounts in all namespaces.	`kubectl get sa -A`
Describe admin clusterrole.	`kubectl describe clusterrole admin`
List all secrets.	`kubectl get secret -A`
List all deployments.	`kubectl get deployments -A`
List networkpolicies.	`kubectl get networkpolicies -A`

Table 6.1 – kubectl commands

7. Deploy a Jupyter Notebook.

Let's deploy a Jupyter Notebook server as a containerized application. Copy and run the following code block. It should create a file called `deploy_Jupyter_notebook.yaml`. We will use a container image from the Docker Hub image repository:

```
cat << EOF > deploy_Jupyter_notebook.yaml
apiVersion: apps/v1
kind: Deployment
metadata:
  name: jupyter-notebook
  labels:
    app: jupyter-notebook
spec:
  replicas: 1
  selector:
    matchLabels:
      app: jupyter-notebook
  template:
    metadata:
      labels:
        app: jupyter-notebook
    spec:
      containers:
      - name: minimal-notebook
        image: jupyter/minimal-notebook:latest
        ports:
        - containerPort: 8888
EOF
```

Now, let's create a deployment by running the following:

```
kubectl apply -f deploy_Jupyter_notebook.yaml.
```

Check to make sure the Pod is running by running `kubectl get pods`.

Check the logs of the Jupyter server Pod by running `kubectl logs <name of notebook pod>`. Find the section in the logs that contains `http://jupyter-notebook-598f56bf4b-spqn4:8888/?token=XXXXXXX...`, and copy the token (XXXXXX...) portion. We will use the token for *Step 8*.

You can also access the pod using an interactive shell by running `kubectl exec --stdin --tty <name of notebook pod> -- /bin/sh`. Run `ps aux` to see a list of running processes. You will see a process related to the Jupyter Notebook.

8. Expose the Jupyter Notebook to the internet.

At this point we have a Jupyter server running in a Docker container in a Kubernetes Pod on top of two EC2 instances in an AWS VPC but we can't get to it because the Kubernetes cluster doesn't expose a route to the container. We will create a Kubernetes service to expose the Jupyter Notebook server to the internet so it can be accessed from a browser.

Run the following code block to create a specification file for a new Service. It should create a file called `jupyter_svc.yaml`:

```
cat << EOF > jupyter_svc.yaml
apiVersion: v1
kind: Service
metadata:
  name: jupyter-service
  annotations:
    service.beta.kubernetes.io/aws-load-balancer-type:
alb
spec:
  selector:
    app: jupyter-notebook
  ports:
    - protocol: TCP
      port: 80
      targetPort: 8888
  type: LoadBalancer
EOF
```

After the file is created, run `kubectl apply -f jupyter_svc.yaml` to create the service. A new Kubernetes Service called `jupyter-service`, as well as a new `LoadBalancer` object should be created. You can verify the service by running `kubectl get service`. Note and copy the `EXTERNAL-IP` address associated with the `jupyter-service` service.

Paste the EXTERNAL-IP address to a new browser window, and enter the token you copied earlier into the **Password or token** field (*Figure 6.11*) to log in. You should see a Jupyter Notebook window showing up:

Figure 6.11 – Jupyter login screen

The following diagram shows the environment that you have created after working through the hands-on exercise.

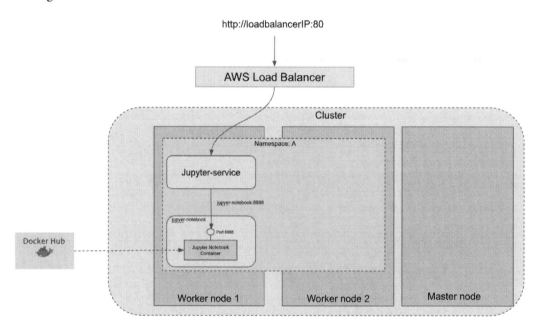

Figure 6.12 – Jupyter notebook deployment on the EKS cluster

Congratulations, you have successfully created a new Amazon EKS cluster on AWS and deployed a Jupyter Server instance as a container on the cluster. We will re-use this EKS cluster for the next chapter. However, if you don't plan to use this EKS for a period of time, it is recommended to shut down the cluster to avoid unnecessary costs.

Summary

In this chapter, we covered Kubernetes, a container management platform that can serve as the infrastructure foundation for building open source ML platforms. Now, you should be familiar with what containers are and how Kubernetes works. You have also learned how to set up a Kubernetes cluster on AWS using the AWS EKS service and use the cluster to deploy a containerized Jupyter Notebook application to set up a basic data science environment. In the next chapter, we will cover a number of open source ML platforms that work on top of the Kubernetes infrastructure for building ML platforms.

Section 3: Technical Architecture Design and Regulatory Considerations for Enterprise ML Platforms

In *Section 3*, we will discuss architecture and business requirements beyond just data scientists, looking at enterprise ML platforms, security, and governance. We will cover advanced science and engineering topics for machine learning.

This section comprises the following chapters:

- *Chapter 7, Open Source Machine Learning Platforms*
- *Chapter 8, Building a Data Science Environment Using AWS ML Services*
- *Chapter 9, Building an Enterprise ML Architecture with AWS ML Services*
- *Chapter 10, Advanced ML Engineering*
- *Chapter 11, ML Governance, Bias, Explainability, and Privacy*
- *Chapter 12, Building ML Solutions Using AI Services and ML Platforms*

7

Open Source Machine Learning Platforms

In the previous chapter, we covered how **Kubernetes** can be used as the foundational infrastructure for running **machine learning** (**ML**) tasks, such as running model training jobs or building data science environments such as **Jupyter notebook** servers. However, to perform these tasks at scale and more efficiently for large organizations, you will need to build ML platforms with the capabilities to support the full data science life cycle. These capabilities include scalable data science environments, model training services, model registries, and model deployment capabilities.

In this chapter, we will discuss the core components of an ML platform and additional open source technologies that can be used for building ML platforms. We will start with technologies for building a data science environment that can support a large number of users for experiments, and then discuss other technologies for model training, model registries, model deployment, and ML pipeline automation.

Specifically, we will cover the following topics:

- The core components of an ML platform
- Open source technologies for building ML platforms
- Hands-on exercise – building an ML platform with an open source ML framework

Let's get started by taking a quick look at the technical requirements for this chapter and reviewing the core components of an ML platform.

Technical requirements

For the hands-on exercise in this chapter, we will continue to use the **AWS** Kubernetes environment you created in *Chapter 6, Kubernetes Container Orchestration Infrastructure Management*.

The sample source code used in this chapter can be found at `https://github. com/PacktPublishing/The-Machine-Learning-Solutions-Architect- Handbook/tree/main/Chapter07`.

Core components of an ML platform

An ML platform is a complex system as it consists of multiple environments for running different tasks and has complex workflow processes to orchestrate. In addition, an ML platform needs to support many roles, such as data scientists, ML engineers, infrastructure engineers, and operation team members. The following are the core components of an ML platform:

- **Data science environment**: The data science environment provides data analysis tools, such as Jupyter notebooks, code repositories, and ML frameworks. Data scientists and ML engineers mainly use the data science environment to perform data analysis and data science experiments, and also to build and tune models.

- **Model training environment**: The model training environment provides a separate infrastructure for different model training requirements. While data scientists and ML engineers can run small-scale model training directly inside their local Jupyter environment, they need a separate dedicated infrastructure for large-scale model training. Running model training in a separate infrastructure also allows for better control of the environments for more consistent model training process management and model lineage management. The model training environment is normally managed by infrastructure engineers and operations teams.

- **Model registry**: After models are trained, they need to be tracked and managed in a model registry for model inventory and lineage management, model versioning control, model discovery, and model life cycle management (such as in the staging environment or in the production environment). The model registry is especially important when you have a large number of models to manage. Data scientists can register models directly in the registry as they perform experiments in their data science environment. Models can also be registered as part of automated ML model pipeline executions.

- **Model serving environment**: To generate predictions using trained ML models for client applications, you will need to host the models in a model serving infrastructure behind an API endpoint in real time. This infrastructure should also support *batch transform* capabilities. There are different types of model serving frameworks available.

- **Continuous integration (CI)/continuous deployment (CD)** and **workflow automation**: Lastly, you need to establish CI/CD and workflow automation capabilities to streamline the data processing, model training, and model deployment processes, which in turn will increase the ML deployment velocity, consistency, reproducibility, and observability.

In addition to these core components, there are other platform architecture factors to consider, such as security and authentication, logging and monitoring, and governance and control. In the following sections, we will discuss some open sources technologies that can be used to build an end-to-end ML platform.

Open source technologies for building ML platforms

While it is possible to run different ML tasks by creating and deploying different standalone ML containers in a Kubernetes cluster, this can become quite complex to manage when you have to do this at scale for a large number of users and ML workloads. This is where open source technologies such as **Kubeflow**, **MLflow**, **Seldon Core**, **GitHub**, and **Airflow** come in. Next, let's take a closer look at how these open source technologies can be used for building data science environments, model training services, model inference services, and ML workflow automation.

Using Kubeflow for data science environments

Kubeflow is a Kubernetes-based, open source ML platform that provides a number of ML-specific components. Kubeflow runs on top of Kubernetes and provides the following capabilities:

- A central UI dashboard
- A Jupyter notebook server for code authoring and model building
- A Kubeflow pipeline for ML pipeline orchestration
- **KFServing** for model serving
- Training operators for model training support

The following figure (*Figure 7.1*) shows how Kubeflow can provide the various components needed for a data science environment. Here, we will focus on its support for Jupyter notebook servers.

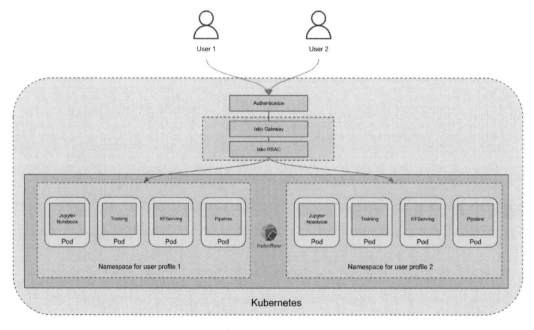

Figure 7.1 – A Kubeflow-based data science environment

Kubeflow provides a multi-tenant Jupyter notebook server environment with built-in authentication and authorization support. Let's discuss each of these core components in detail:

- **Jupyter notebook**: As a data scientist, you can use the Kubeflow Jupyter notebook server to author and run your **Python** code to explore data and build models inside the Jupyter notebook. Kubeflow can spawn multiple notebook servers, with each server belonging to a single Kubernetes namespace that corresponds to a team, project, or user. Each notebook server runs a container inside a **Kubernetes Pod**. By default, a Kubeflow notebook server provides a list of notebook container images hosted in public container image repositories to choose from. You can also create custom notebook container images to run custom notebook servers. To enforce standards and consistency, Kubeflow administrators can provide a list of standard images for users to use. When creating a notebook server, you select the namespace to run the notebook server in, specify the **Universal Resource Identifier** (**URI**) of the container image for the notebook server, and specify the resource requirements, such as the number of CPUs/GPUs and memory size.

- **Authentication and authorization**: You access the notebook server through the Kubeflow UI dashboard, which provides an authentication service through the **Dex Open ID Connection** (**OIDC**) provider. Dex is an identity service that uses OIDC to provide authentication for other applications. Dex can federate with other authentication services such as the **Active Directory** service. Each notebook is associated with a default Kubernetes service account (`default-editor`) that can be used for entitlement purposes (such as granting the notebook permission to access various resources in the Kubernetes cluster). Kubeflow uses **Istio role-based access control** (**RBAC**) to control in-cluster traffic. The following **YAML** file grants the `default-editor` service account (which is associated with the Kubeflow notebook) access to the Kubeflow pipeline service by attaching the `ml-pipeline-services` service role to it:

```yaml
apiVersion: rbac.istio.io/v1alpha1
kind: ServiceRoleBinding
metadata:
  name: bind-ml-pipeline-nb-admin
  namespace: kubeflow
spec:
  roleRef:
    kind: ServiceRole
    name: ml-pipeline-services
  subjects:
```

```
  - properties:
      source.principal: cluster.local/ns/admin/sa/
default-editor
```

- **Multi-tenancy**: Kubeflow allows multiple users to access the same Kubeflow environment with support for resource isolation by users (for example, resources such as notebook servers). It does this by creating a separate namespace for each user, and it uses Kubernetes RBAC and Istio RBAC to control access to the different namespaces and their resources. For team-based collaboration, the owner of a namespace can grant other users access to the namespace directly by using the **Manage Contributor** function inside the Kubeflow dashboard UI.

To add a new Kubeflow user, you create a new user profile, which in turn creates a new namespace for the profile. The following YAML file, once applied using kubectl, creates a new user profile called test-user with an email of test-user@kubeflow.org, and it also creates a new namespace called test-user:

```
apiVersion: kubeflow.org/v1beta1
kind: Profile
metadata:
  name: test-user
spec:
  owner:
    kind: User
    name: test-user@kubeflow.org
```

You can run the kubectl get profiles and kubectl get namespaces commands to verify that the profile and namespaces have been created.

After a user is created and added to the Kubeflow Dex authentication service, the new user can log in to the Kubeflow dashboard and access the Kubeflow resources (such as a Jupyter notebook server) under the newly created namespace.

Now we reviewed how Kubeflow can be used to provide a multi-user Jupyter notebook environment for experimentation and model building. Next, let's see how to build a model training environment.

Building a model training environment

As discussed earlier, an ML platform usually provides a separate model training service and infrastructure to support large-scale and automated model training in an ML pipeline. This dedicated training service should be accessible from an experimentation environment (such as a Jupyter notebook) so that data scientists can launch model training jobs as part of their experiments, and it should also be accessible from an ML automation pipeline.

In a Kubernetes-based environment, there are two main approaches for model training:

- Model training using **Kubernetes Jobs**
- Model training using **Kubeflow training operators**

You can choose which approach to use depending on your training needs. Now, let's take a closer look at each one of them in detail:

- **Model training using Kubernetes Jobs**: As we discussed in *Chapter 6, Kubernetes Container Orchestration Infrastructure Management*, a Kubernetes Job creates one or more containers and runs them through to completion. This pattern is well suited for running certain types of ML model training jobs, as an ML job runs a training loop to completion and does not run forever. For example, you can package a container with a Python training script and all the dependencies that train a model and use the Kubernetes Job to load the container and kick off the training script. When the script completes and exits, the Kubernetes job also ends. The following sample YAML file kicks off a model training job if submitted with the `kubectl apply` command:

```
apiVersion: batch/v1
kind: Job
metadata:
  name: train-churn-job
spec:
  template:
    spec:
      containers:
        - name: train-container
          imagePullPolicy: Always
          image: <model training uri>
```

```
          command: ["python", "train.py"]
        restartPolicy: Never
    backoffLimit: 4
```

You can query the status of the job using the `kubectl get jobs` command and see the detailed training logs using the `kubectl logs <pod name>` command.

- **Model training using Kubeflow training operators**: A Kubernetes Job can launch a model training container and run a training script inside the container to completion. Since the controller for a Kubernetes Job does not have application-specific knowledge about the training job, it can only handle generic Pod deployment and management for the running jobs, such as running the container in a Pod, monitoring the Pod, and handling generic Pod failure. However, some model training jobs, such as distributed training job in a cluster, require the special deployment, monitoring, and maintenance of stateful communications among various Pods. This is where the Kubernetes training operator pattern can be applied.

Kubeflow comes with a list of pre-built training operators (such as the **TensorFlow**, **Pytorch**, and **XGBoost** operators) for complex model training jobs. Each Kubeflow training operator has a **custom resource (CR)** (for example, `TFJob` CR for TensorFlow jobs) that defines the training job's specific configurations, such as the type of Pod in the training job (for example, `master`, `worker`, or `parameter server`), or runs policies on how to clean up resources and how long a job should run. The controller for the CR is responsible for configuring the training environment, monitoring the training job's specific status, and maintaining the desired training job's specific state. For example, the controller can set environment variables to make the training cluster specifications (for example, types of Pods and indices) available to the training code running inside the containers. The controller can also inspect the exit code of a training process and fail the training job if the exit code indicates a permanent failure. The following YAML file sample template represents a specification for running training jobs using the TensorFlow operator (`tf-operator`):

```
apiVersion: "kubeflow.org/v1"
kind: "TFJob"
metadata:
  name: "distributed-tensorflow-job"
spec:
  tfReplicaSpecs:
    PS:
      replicas: 1
```

```
        restartPolicy: Never
      template:
        spec:
          containers:
            - name: tensorflow
              image: <model training image uri>
              command:
  Worker:
    replicas: 2
    restartPolicy: Never
    template:
      spec:
        containers:
          - name: tensorflow
            image: <model training image uri>
            command:
```

In this example template, the specification will create one copy of the parameter servers (which aggregate model parameters across different containers) and two copies of the workers (which run model training loops and communicate with the parameter servers). The operator will process the TFJob object according to the specification, keep the TFJob object stored in the system with the actual running services and Pods, and replace the actual state with the desired state. You can submit the training job using kubectl apply -f <TFJob specs template> and can get the status of the TFJob with the kubectl get tfjob command.

As a data scientist, you can submit Kubernetes training jobs or Kubeflow training jobs using the kubectl utility, or from your Jupyter notebook environment using the **Python** (**SDK**). For example, TFJob object has a Python SDK called kubeflow.tfjob, and Kubernetes has a client SDK called kubernetes.client for interacting with the Kubernetes and Kubeflow environments from your Python code. You can also invoke training jobs using the Kubeflow Pipeline component, which we will cover later in the *Kubeflow pipeline* section.

Registering models with a model registry

A **model registry** is an important component in model management and governance, and it is a key link between the model training stage and the model deployment stage. There are several open source options for implementing a model registry in an ML platform, and in this section, we will take a look at the MLflow model registry for model management.

The MLflow model registry

MLflow is an open source ML platform, and it is designed for managing the stages of the ML life cycle, including experiment management, model management, reproducibility, and model deployment. It has the following four main components:

- Experiment tracking
- ML project packaging
- Model packaging
- Model registry

The model registry component of MLflow provides a central model repository for saved models. It captures model details such as model lineage, model version, annotation, and description, and also captures model stage transitions from staging to production (so the status of the model state is clearly described).

To use the MLflow model registry in a team environment, you need to set up an MLflow tracking server with a database as a backend and storage for the model artifacts. MLflow provides a UI and an API to interact with its core functionality, including its model registry. Once the model is registered in the model registry, you can add, modify, update, transition, or delete the model through the UI or the API. The following figure shows an architecture setup for an MLflow tracking server and its associated model registry:

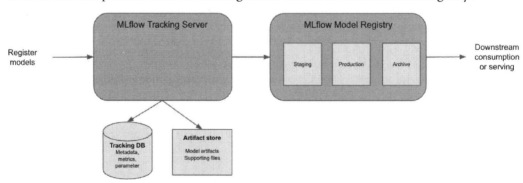

Figure 7.2 – The MLflow tracking server and model registry

One of the main drawbacks of the MLflow model registry is that it does not support user permission management, so any user with access to the tracking server will be able to access and manage all the models in the registry. An external custom entitlement layer will be implemented to manage user-based access to different resources in the model registry. The MLflow tracking server does not provide built-in authentication support either, so an external authentication server, such as **Nginx**, is needed to provide authentication support.

Serving models using model serving services

After a model is trained and saved, you can use it for generating predictions by simply loading the saved model into an ML package and calling the model prediction function supported by the package. However, for large-scale and complex model serving requirements, you will need to consider implementing a dedicated model serving infrastructure to meet those needs. Now, let's take a look at several open source model serving frameworks.

The Gunicorn and Flask inference engine

Gunicorn and **Flask** are often used for building custom model-serving web frameworks. The following figure (*Figure 7.3*) shows a typical architecture that uses Flask, Gunicorn, and Nginx as the building blocks for a model serving service.

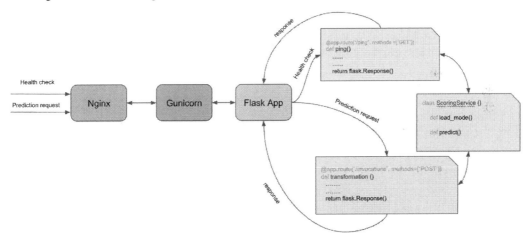

Figure 7.3 – A model serving architecture using Flask and Gunicorn

Flask is a Python-based micro web framework for building web apps quickly. It is lightweight and has almost no dependencies on external libraries. With Flask, you can define different invocation routes and associate handler functions to handle different web calls (such as health check calls and model invocation calls). To handle model prediction requests, the Flask app would load the model into memory and call the predict function on the model to generate the prediction. Flask comes with a built-in web server, but it does not scale well as it can only support one request at a time.

This is where Gunicorn comes in. Gunicorn is a web server for hosting web apps (such as the Flask apps), and it can handle multiple requests in parallel and distribute the traffic to the hosted web apps efficiently. When it receives a web request, it will invoke the hosted Flask app to handle the request (such as invoking the function to generate model prediction).

In addition to serving prediction requests as web requests, an enterprise inference engine also needs to handle secure web traffic (such as SSL/TLS traffic), as well as load balancing when there are multiple web servers. This is where Nginx comes in. Nginx can serve as a load balancer for multiple web servers and can handle termination for SSL/TLS traffic more efficiently, so web servers do not have to handle it.

A Flask/Gunicorn-based model serving architecture can be a good option for hosting simple model serving patterns. But for more complicated patterns, such as serving different versions of models, A/B testing, or large model serving, this architecture will have limitations. The Flask/Gunicorn architecture pattern also requires custom code (such as the Flask app) to work, as it does not provide built-in support for the different ML models.

Next, let's review some purpose-built model serving frameworks and see how they are different from the custom Flask-based inference engine.

The TensorFlow Serving framework

TensorFlow Serving is a production-grade, open source model serving framework, and provides out-of-the-box support for serving TensorFlow models behind a RESTFul endpoint. It manages the model life cycle for model serving and provides access to versioned and multiple models behind a single endpoint. There is also built-in support for canary deployments. A **canary deployment** allows you to deploy a model to support a subset of traffic. In addition to the real-time inference support, there is also a batch scheduler feature that can batch multiple prediction requests and perform a single joint execution. With TensorFlow Serving, there is no need to write custom code to serve the model. The following figure (*Figure 7.4*) shows the architecture of TensorFlow Serving:

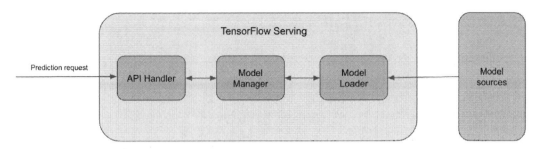

Figure 7.4 – TensorFlow Serving architecture

The *API handler* provides APIs for TensorFlow Serving. It comes with a built-in, lightweight HTTP server to serve RESTful-based API requests. It also supports **gRPC** (a **remote procedure call** protocol) traffic. gRPC is a more efficient and fast networking protocol, but it is more complicated to use than the REST protocol. TensorFlow Serving has a concept called a *servable*, which refers to the actual objects that handle a task, such as model inferences or lookup tables. For example, a trained model is represented as a *servable*, and it can contain one or more algorithms and lookup tables or embeddings tables. The API handler uses the servable to fulfill client requests.

The *model manager* manages the life cycle of servables, including loading the servables, serving the servables, and unloading the servables. When a servable is needed to perform a task, the model manager provides the client with a handler to access the servable instances. The model manager can manage multiple versions of a servable. This allows gradual rollout of different versions of a model.

The *model loader* is responsible for loading models from different sources, such as **Amazon S3**. When a new model is loaded, the model loader notifies the model manager about the availability of the new model, and the model manager will decide what the next step should be (such as unloading the previous version and loading the new version).

TensorFlow Serving can be extended to support non-TensorFlow models. For example, models trained in other frameworks can be converted to the **ONNX** format and served using TensorFlow Serving. ONNX is a common format for representing models to support interoperability across different ML frameworks.

The TorchServe serving framework

TorchServe is an open source framework for serving trained **PyTorch** models. Similar to TensorFlow Serving, TorchServe provides a REST API for serving models with its built-in web server. With core features such as multi-model serving, model versioning, server-side request batching, and built-in monitoring, TorchServe can serve production workloads at scale. There is also no need to write custom code to host PyTorch models with TorchServe. TorchServe comes with a built-in web server for hosting the model. The following figure (*Figure 7.5*) shows the architecture components of the TorchServe framework:

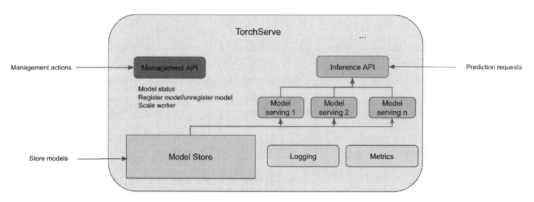

Figure 7.5 – TorchServe architecture

The *inference API* is responsible for handling prediction requests from client applications using loaded PyTorch models. It supports the REST protocol and provides a prediction API, as well as other supporting APIs such as health check and model explanation APIs. The inference API can handle prediction requests for multiple models.

The model artifacts are packaged into a single archive file and stored in a model store within the TorchServe environment. You use a **command-line interface (CLI)** command called `torch-mode-archive` to package the model.

The TorchServe backend loads the archived models from the model store into different worker processes. These worker processes interact with the inference API to process requests and send back responses.

The management API is responsible for handling management tasks such as registering and unregistering PyTorch models, checking the model status, and scaling worker process. The management API is normally used by system administrators.

TorchServe also provides built-in support for logging and metrics. The logging component logs both access logs and processing logs. The TorchServe metrics collect a list of system metrics, such as CPU/GPU utilization and custom model metrics.

KFServing framework

TensorFlow Serving and TorchServe are standalone model serving frameworks for a specific deep learning framework. In contrast, **KFServing** is a general-purpose multi-framework model serving framework that supports different ML models. KFServing uses standalone model serving frameworks such as TensorFlow Serving and TorchServe as the backend model servers. It is part of the Kubeflow project and provides pluggable architecture for different model formats:

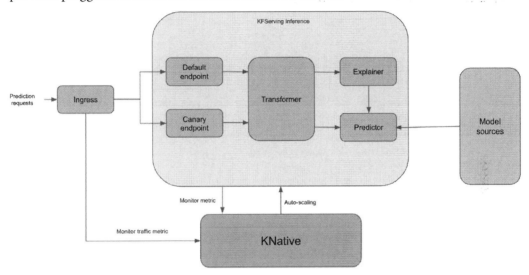

Figure 7.6 – KFServing components

As a general-purpose, multi-framework model serving solution, KFServing provides several out-of-the-box model servers (also known as predictors) for different model types, including TensorFlow, **PyTorch XGBoost**, **scikit-learn**, and ONNX. With KFServing, you can serve models using both REST and gRPC protocols. To deploy a supported model type, you simply need to define a YAML specification that points to the model artifact in a data store. You can also build your own custom containers to serve models in KFServing. The container needs to provide a model serving implementation as well as a web server. The following code shows a sample YAML specification to deploy a `tensorflow` model using KFServing:

```
apiVersion: "serving.kubeflow.org/v1alpha2"
kind: "InferenceService"
metadata:
  name: "model-name"
spec:
  default:
```

```
predictor:
  tensorflow:
    storageUri: <uri to model storage such as s3>
```

KFServing has a transformer component that allows the custom processing of the input payload before it is sent to the predictors, and also allows the transforming of the response from the predictor before it is sent back to the calling client. Sometimes, you need to provide an explanation for the model prediction, such as which features have a stronger influence on the prediction. We will cover more details on model explainability in a later chapter.

KFServing is designed for production deployment and provides a range of production deployment capabilities. Its auto-scaling feature allows the model server to scale up/down based on the amount of request traffic. With KFServing, you can deploy both the default model serving endpoint and the canary endpoint and split the traffic between the two, and specify model revisions behind the endpoint. For operational support, KFServing also has built-in functionality for monitoring (for example, monitoring request data and request latency).

Seldon Core

Seldon Core is another multi-framework model serving framework for deploying models on Kubernetes. Compared to KFServing, Seldon Core provides richer model serving features, for example, model serving inference graphs for use cases such as A/B testing and model ensembles. The following figure shows the core components of the Seldon Core framework:

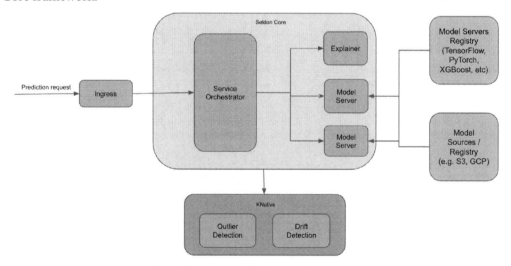

Figure 7.7 – The Seldon Core model serving framework architecture

Seldon Core provides packaged model servers for some of the common ML libraries, including the SKLearn server for scikit-learn models, the XGBoost server for XGBoost models, TensorFlow Serving for TensorFlow models, and MLflow server-based model serving. You can also build your own custom serving container for specific model serving needs and host it using Seldon Core.

The following template shows how to deploy a model using the SKLearn server using Seldon Core. You simply need to change the modelUri path to point to a saved model on a cloud object storage provider such as **Google Cloud Storage**, Amazon S3 storage, or **Azure Blob storage**. To test with an example, you can change the following modelUri value to an example provided by Seldon Core – gs://seldon-models/sklearn/iris:

```yaml
apiVersion: machinelearning.seldon.io/v1alpha2
kind: SeldonDeployment
metadata:
  name: sklearn
spec:
  name: sklearn-model
  predictors:
  - graph:
      children: []
      implementation: SKLEARN_SERVER
      modelUri: <model uri to model artifacts on the cloud
storage>
      name: classifier
    name: default
    replicas: 1
```

Seldon Core also supports an advanced workflow (also known as an inference graph) for serving models. The *inference graph* feature allows you to have a graph with different models and other components in a single inference pipeline. An inference graph can consist of several components:

- One or more ML models for the different prediction tasks

- Traffic routing management for different usage patterns, such as traffic splitting to different models for A/B testing

- A component for combining results from multiple models, such as a model ensemble component

- Components for transforming the input requests (such as performing feature engineering) or output responses (for example, returning an array format as a **JSON** format)

To build inference graph specifications in YAML, you need the following key components in the `seldondeployment` YAML file:

- A list of predictors, with each predictor having its own `componentSpecs` section that specifies details such as container images

- A graph that describes how the components are linked together for each `componentSpecs` section

The following sample template shows the inference graph for a custom canary deployment to split the traffic into two different versions of a model:

```yaml
apiVersion: machinelearning.seldon.io/v1alpha2
kind: SeldonDeployment
metadata:
  name: canary-deployment
spec:
  name: canary-deployment
  predictors:
  - componentSpecs:
    - spec:
        containers:
        - name: classifier
          image: <container uri to model version 1>
    graph:
      children: []
      endpoint:
        type: REST
      name: classifier
      type: MODEL
    name: main
    replicas: 1
    traffic: 75
  - componentSpecs:
    - spec:
```

```
        containers:
          - name: classifier
            image: <container uri to model version 2>
      graph:
        children: []
        endpoint:
          type: REST
        name: classifier
        type: MODEL
    name: canary
    replicas: 1
      traffic: 25
```

Once a deployment manifest is applied, the Seldon Core operator is responsible for creating all the resources needed to serve an ML model. Specifically, the operator will create resources defined in the manifest, add orchestrators to the Pods to manage the orchestration of the inference graph, and configure the traffic using ingress gateways such as Istio.

Automating ML pipeline workflows

To automate the core ML platform components we have covered so far, we need to build pipelines that can orchestrate different steps using these components. Automation not only increases efficiency and productivity – it also helps enforce consistency, enable reproducibility, and reduce human errors. There are several open source technologies that can be used for automating ML workflows. In this section, we will take a look at Apache Airflow and Kubeflow Pipelines.

Apache Airflow

Apache Airflow is an open source software package for programmatically authoring, scheduling, and monitoring multi-step workflows. It is a general-purpose workflow orchestration tool that can be used to define workflows for a wide range of tasks, including ML tasks. First, let's review some core Airflow concepts:

- **Directed Acyclic Graph** (**DAG**): A DAG defines independent tasks that are executed independently in a pipeline. The sequences of the execution can be visualized like a graph.

- **Tasks**: Tasks are basic units of execution in Airflow. Tasks have dependencies between them during executions.

- **Operators**: Operators are DAG components that describe a single task in the pipeline. An operator implements the task execution logic. Airflow provides a list of operators for common tasks, such as a Python operator for running Python code, or an Amazon S3 operator to interact with the S3 service. Tasks are created when operators are instantiated.

- **Scheduling**: A DAG can run on demand or on a predetermined schedule.

Airflow can run on a single machine or in a cluster. It can also be deployed on the Kubernetes infrastructure. The following figure shows a multi-node Airflow deployment:

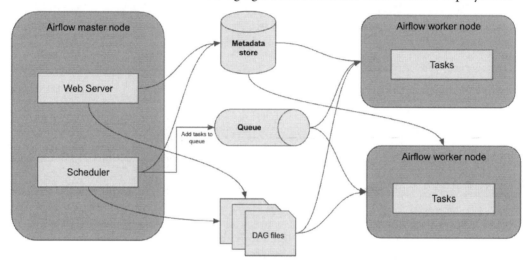

Figure 7.8 – Apache Airflow architecture

The *master node* mainly runs the *web server* and *scheduler*. The scheduler is responsible for scheduling the execution of the DAGs. It sends tasks to a queue, and the worker nodes retrieve the tasks from the queue and run them. The metadata store is used to store the metadata of the Airflow cluster and processes, such as task instance details or user data.

You can author the Airflow DAGs using Python. The following sample code shows how to author a basic Airflow DAG in Python with two bash operators in a sequence:

```
from airflow import DAG
from airflow.operators.bash_operator import BashOperator
from datetime import datetime, timedelta


default_args = {
    'owner': myname,
}
```

```
dag = DAG('test', default_args=default_args, schedule_
interval=timedelta(days=1))

t1 = BashOperator(
    task_id='print_date',
    bash_command='date',
    dag=dag)

t2 = BashOperator(
    task_id='sleep',
    bash_command='sleep 5',
    retries=3,
    dag=dag)

t2.set_upstream(t1)
```

Airflow can connect to many different sources and has built-in operators for many external services, such as **AWS EMR** and **Amazon SageMaker**. It has been widely adopted by many enterprises in production environments.

Kubeflow Pipelines

Kubeflow Pipelines is a Kubeflow component, and it is purpose-built for authoring and orchestrating end-to-end ML workflows on Kubernetes. First, let's review some core concepts of Kubeflow Pipelines:

- **Pipeline**: A pipeline describes an ML workflow, all the components in the workflow, and how the components are related to each other in the pipeline.

- **Pipeline components**: A pipeline component performs a task in the pipeline. An example of a pipeline component could be a data processing component or model training component.

- **Experiment**: An experiment organizes different trial runs (model training) for an ML project so you can easily inspect and compare the different runs and their results.

- **Step**: The execution of one component in a pipeline is called a step.

- **Run trigger**: You use a run trigger to kick off the execution of a pipeline. A run trigger can be a periodic trigger (for example, to run every 2 hours), or a scheduled trigger (for example, run at a specific date and time).

- **Output artifacts**: Output artifacts are the outputs from the pipeline components. Examples of output artifacts could be model training metrics or visualizations of datasets.

Kubeflow Pipelines is installed as part of the Kubeflow installation. It comes with its own UI, which is part of the overall Kubeflow dashboard UI. The Pipelines service manages the pipelines and their run status and stores them in a metadata database. There is an orchestration and workflow controller that manages the actual execution of the pipelines and the components. The following figure (*Figure 7.9*) shows the core architecture components in a Kubeflow pipeline:

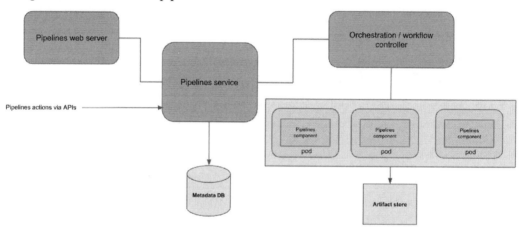

Figure 7.9 – Kubeflow Pipelines architecture

You author the pipeline using the pipeline SDK in Python. To create and run a pipeline, follow these steps:

1. Create a pipeline definition using the Kubeflow SDK. The pipeline definition specifies a list of components and how they are joined together in a graph.

2. Compile the definition into a static YAML specification to be executed by the Kubeflow Pipelines service.

3. Register the specification with the Kubeflow Pipelines service and call the pipeline to run from the static definition.

4. The Kubeflow Pipelines service calls the API server to create resources to run the pipeline.

5. Orchestration controllers execute various containers to complete the pipeline run.

Ok, we have now covered a number of open source tools for building ML platforms. Now, let's put them into practice and use these tools to build a basic ML platform.

Hands-on exercise – building a data science architecture using open source technologies

In this hands-on exercise, you will build an ML platform using several open source ML platform software. There are three main parts to this hands-on exercise:

1. Installing Kubeflow and setting up a Kubeflow notebook
2. Tracking experiments, managing models, and deploying models
3. Automating the ML steps with Kubeflow Pipelines

Alright, let's get started with the first part – installing Kubeflow on the Amazon EKS cluster.

Part 1 – Installing Kubeflow

You will continue to use the **Amazon (EKS)** infrastructure you created earlier and install Kubeflow on top of it. To start, let's complete the following steps:

1. **Launch AWS CloudShell**: Log in to your AWS account, select the Oregon region, and launch AWS CloudShell again.
2. **Install the kfctl utility**: The `kfctl` utility is a command-line utility for installing and managing Kubeflow. Run the following commands one by one in the CloudShell shell environment to install `kfctl`:

```
sudo yum search tar
```

```
curl --silent --location "https://github.com/kubeflow/
kfctl/releases/download/v1.2.0/kfctl_v1.2.0-0-gbc038f9_
linux.tar.gz" | tar xz -C /tmp
```

```
chmod +x /tmp/kfctl
```

```
sudo mv /tmp/kfctl ./bin/kfctl
```

3. **Add environment variables**: Add environment variables to allow easier command executions later. You will need to provide the Amazon EKS cluster name. You can look up the EKS cluster name in the AWS Management Console:

```
export CONFIG_URI="https://raw.githubusercontent.
com/kubeflow/manifests/v1.2-branch/kfdef/kfctl_aws.
v1.2.0.yaml"
```

```
export AWS_CLUSTER_NAME=<cluster name>
mkdir ${AWS_CLUSTER_NAME} && cd ${AWS_CLUSTER_NAME}
```

4. **Download the installation template**: The `kfctl_aws.yaml` file contains specifications for setting up Kubeflow. Let's download it and modify it with the cluster details using the following command:

```
wget -O kfctl_aws.yaml $CONFIG_URI
```

```
vim kfctl_aws.yaml
```

After the **Vim** text editor is open, look for the **Region** parameter, and update the value with the correct region. For example, if your AWS region is **Oregon**, the value should be **us-west-2**. As open source is fast changing, it is possible that this instruction might no longer be applicable as EKS and Kubeflow evolve.

You will also find a `username` and `password` pair in the `yaml` file. The default user name should be `admin@kubeflow.org`, and the default password should be `12341234`. Change these to something else to be more secure. Take a note of the `username` and `password` values, as you will need them later to access the Kubeflow UI.

5. **Install Kubeflow**: Now, we are ready to install Kubeflow using the `kfctl` utility. Run the following command to start installing Kubeflow (this is going to take 3-5 minutes to complete):

```
kfctl apply -V -f kfctl_aws.yaml
```

When the installation is complete, explore what has been installed by running the `kubectl get namespaces` command. You will notice a few namespaces have been created:

- **Kubeflow**: You will find all the Kubeflow-related Pods running in this namespace.

- **Auth**: The Dex authentication Pod runs in this namespace.

- **Istio-system**: All Istio-related components, such as **Istio Pilot** and **Istio Citadel**, run in this namespace.

6. **Launch the Kubeflow dashboard**: Look up the Kubeflow dashboard URL using the following command:

```
kubectl get ingress -n istio-system
```

You should see something similar to the following screenshot returned. The URL under the ADDRESS header is the URL for the Kubeflow dashboard:

Figure 7.10 – Kubeflow dashboard URL

Open up a browser window and copy and paste the dashboard URL to launch the dashboard. When prompted, enter the username and password from *Step 4* to log into the dashboard.

You will be prompted to select the workspace. Keep the default admin name and follow the onscreen instructions to complete installation. You will see the following screen after the dashboard has launched:

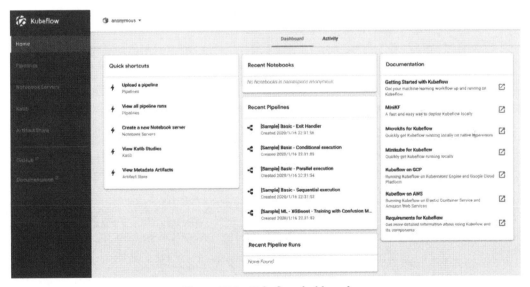

Figure 7.11 - Kubeflow dashboard

The Kubeflow dashboard allows you to navigate to different Kubeflow components from this single interface. We will use this dashboard to configure and manage notebooks and tracking pipelines.

7. **Scale up the cluster**: To run Kubeflow applications such as notebooks and pipelines, we will need a bigger cluster. Let's scale the cluster to add more Kubernetes worker nodes. The worker nodes are associated with nodegroups, and we will need the `nodegroup` name to scale it up. You can look up the name of `nodegroup` by running the following command:

```
eksctl get nodegroup --cluster=<name of cluster>
```

   Now, let's scale the nodegroup to 4 nodes from the `two` existing nodes by running the following command:

```
eksctl scale nodegroup --cluster=<name of cluster>
--nodes=4 --name=<nodegroup name> --nodes-max=4
```

   The scaling process will take a few minutes. When the process is complete, run the `kubectl get nodes` command to confirm you now have 4 worker nodes. You should see four servers listed in the output.

8. **Create a new Jupyter notebook**: You have now successfully set up Kubeflow on the EKS cluster. Next, let's use Kubeflow to set up a Jupyter notebook environment for code authoring and model building:

   I. On the Kubeflow dashboard home page, select **Notebook Server** and click on **+ NEW SERVER**.

   II. Give the server a name and select a custom image from the dropdown. Select an image that has `CPU with Tensorflow 2.x` in its name. Change the **CPU** number to 1 and **Memory** size to 3GB for a more powerful environment.

   III. Leave everything else as default, and click on **Launch** at the bottom to launch the notebook. It will take a few minutes for the notebook to be ready.

9. **Using the Jupyter notebook**: Let's see what we can do with the newly launched Jupyter notebook. Follow these steps to train a simple model in the Jupyter notebook:

   I. Upload the `churn.csv` file you used earlier from your local machine into the Jupyter notebook.

   II. Select **File | New | Notebook** to create a new notebook. When prompted, select **Python 3** as the **Kernel** type. Upload the `churn.csv` file to the folder using the upload button (the up arrow icon).

III. Enter the following code blocks into different cells and see the execution results for each step. This is the same exercise we did in *Chapter 3, Machine Learning Algorithms*:

```
! pip3 install matplotlib
import pandas as pd
churn_data = pd.read_csv("churn.csv")
churn_data.head()
```

```
# The following command calculates the various statistics
for the features.
churn_data.describe()
```

```
# The following command displays the histograms for the
different features.
# You can replace the column names to plot the histograms
for other features
churn_data.hist(['CreditScore', 'Age', 'Balance'])
```

```
# The following command calculate the correlations among
features
churn_data.corr()
```

```
from sklearn.preprocessing import OrdinalEncoder
encoder = OrdinalEncoder()
churn_data['Geography_code'] = encoder.fit_
transform(churn_data[['Geography']])
churn_data['Gender_code'] = encoder.fit_transform(churn_
data[['Gender']])
churn_data.drop(columns =
['Geography','Gender','RowNumber','Surname'],
inplace=True)
```

```
# we import the train_test_split class for data split
from sklearn.model_selection import train_test_split
# Split the dataset into training (80%) and testing
(20%).
churn_train, churn_test = train_test_split(churn_data,
test_size=0.2)
```

```
# Split the features from the target variable "Exited" as
it is required for model training
# and validation later.
churn_train_X = churn_train.loc[:, churn_train.columns !=
'Exited']
churn_train_y = churn_train['Exited']


churn_test_X = churn_test.loc[:, churn_test.columns !=
'Exited']
churn_test_y = churn_test['Exited']


# We will use the Random Forest algorithm to train the
model
from sklearn.ensemble import RandomForestClassifier
bank_churn_clf = RandomForestClassifier(max_depth=2,
random_state=0)
bank_churn_clf.fit(churn_train_X, churn_train_y)


# We use the accuracy_score class of the sklearn library
to calculate the accuracy.
from sklearn.metrics import accuracy_score
# We use the trained model to generate predictions using
the test dataset
churn_prediction_y = bank_churn_clf.predict(churn_test_X)
# We measure the accuracy using the accuracy_score class.
accuracy_score(churn_test_y, churn_prediction_y)
```

Congratulations! You have now successfully trained an ML model using the Kubeflow Jupyter notebook server. In Part 2, let's get hands-on with how to track experiments, manage models, and deploy models.

Part 2 – tracking experiments and models, and deploying models

To train an ML model, you will likely need to run the training many times with different algorithms, hyperparameters, and data features. Soon, you'll realize that it's becoming quite difficult to keep track of everything you have done. As we discussed earlier, MLflow and Kubeflow have experiment tracking features. MLflow tracking can be implemented anywhere in the training scripts from different data science environments (such as Kubeflow notebooks or your local machine), while Kubeflow tracks everything in the context of Kubeflow Pipelines. In this part of the exercise, we'll use MLflow for experiment tracking and model management. Specifically, we will build the experiment tracking and model management architecture shown in the following figure (*Figure 7.12*):

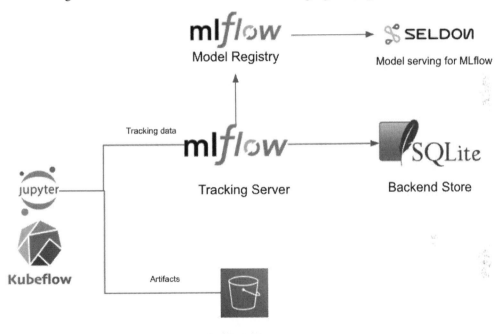

Figure 7.12 – Tracking an experiment and model, deploying the model

To get started, let's set up a central MLflow tracking server so different data science environments can all use it for tracking. Complete the following steps to start:

1. **Launch an EC2 instance**: We will install the MLflow tracking server on an EC2 instance. You can also install an MLflow tracking server as a container running on EKS. Launch an EC2 instance in the same AWS region you have been using. If you don't know how to start an EC2 instance, follow the instructions at https://aws.amazon.com/ec2/getting-started/.

Create an AWS access key pair and add the AWS access key pair info to the EC2 server using the `aws configure` command. If you don't know how to create an AWS access key pair, follow the instructions at `https://docs.aws.amazon.com/powershell/latest/userguide/pstools-appendix-sign-up.html`. Make sure the AWS credential has read/write permissions to S3, as the MLflow server will need to use S3 as the store for artifacts.

2. **Install the MLflow packages**: After the instance is ready, connect to the EC2 instance using the EC2 **Instance Connect** feature in the AWS console. MLflow can be easily installed as Python packages. Run the following commands in the EC2 terminal window to install the MLflow packages:

```
sudo yum update
sudo yum install python3
sudo pip3 install mlflow
sudo pip3 install boto3
```

3. **Install a database**: MLflow requires a database for storing metadata. In this step, you will install a database as the backend for storing all the tracking data. There are many different database options, such as `postgresql` and `sqlite`. For simplicity, we will install a `sqlite` database as the backend:

```
sudo yum install sqlite
```

4. **Set up the tracking server**: Now, we are ready to configure the `mlflow` server. First, create a directory called `mlflowsvr` for storing `sqlite` database files on the EC2 server – you can use the `mkdir` Linux command to create the directory. Next, create an S3 bucket called `mlflow-tracking-<your initials>` for storing the artifacts. After you have created the directory and S3 bucket, run the following command to configure and start the tracking server:

```
mlflow server --backend-store-uri sqlite:///mlflowsvr/
mlsa.db \
--default-artifact-root s3://mlflow-tracking --host
0.0.0.0 -p 5000
```

5. **Access the tracking server site**: To access the site, you will need to open up the security group for the EC2 server to allow port `5000`. Check the AWS instructions on how to modify the security group rules if you are not familiar with them. By default, only port `22` is open.

To access the `mlflow` tracking server site, look up the public DNS name for the EC2 and enter it into the browser window. The address should look something like the following example:

`http://<EC2 public DNS url>:5000.`

Please note, the MLfLow tracking server does not have built-in security, so the tracking server is publicly accessible. You should stop/terminate this tracking server when it is not in use. For secured access to the tracking server, you can set up a secure reverse proxy server in front of the tracking server, which is out of scope for this book.

6. **Use MLflow tracking from the Kubeflow notebook**: Now that we are ready to use the tracking server to track experiments, launch the Jupyter notebook you created earlier from your Kubeflow dashboard and select **Terminal** under the **New** dropdown on the screen to open up a Terminal console window. Inside the Terminal window, run the following code block to install the **AWS Command Line Interface (CLI)** and configure the AWS CLI environment variables. Provide the AWS access key pair values when prompted by running the `aws configure` command. The MLflow client will use these credentials to upload artifacts to the S3 bucket for the MLflow tracking server:

```
pip3 install awscli
aws configure
```

Next, create a new notebook by selecting `file->new>notebook`, and insert the next example code block shown. Replace `<<tracking server uri>>` with your own tracking server uniform resource indentifier (`URI`), and run the code. This code block will install the `mlflow` client library on the Jupyter notebook, and it sets up experiment tracking with the `mlflow.set_experiment()` function, turns on automatic tracking with the `mlflow.sklearn.autolog()` function, and finally, registers the trained model with the `mlflow.sklearn.log_model()` function:

```
! pip3 install mlflow


import pandas as pd
import mlflow
from sklearn.ensemble import RandomForestClassifier
from sklearn.model_selection import train_test_split
from sklearn.preprocessing import OrdinalEncoder

```

```
churn_data = pd.read_csv("churn.csv")


encoder = OrdinalEncoder()

churn_data['Geography_code'] = encoder.fit_
transform(churn_data[['Geography']])

churn_data['Gender_code'] = encoder.fit_transform(churn_
data[['Gender']])

churn_data.drop(columns =
['Geography','Gender','RowNumber','Surname'],
inplace=True)


# Split the dataset into training (80%) and testing
(20%).

churn_train, churn_test = train_test_split(churn_data,
test_size=0.2)


# Split the features from the target variable "Exited" as
it is required for model training

churn_train_X = churn_train.loc[:, churn_train.columns !=
'Exited']

churn_train_y = churn_train['Exited']


churn_test_X = churn_test.loc[:, churn_test.columns !=
'Exited']

churn_test_y = churn_test['Exited']


#setting mlflow tracking server

tracking_uri = <tracking server uri>

mlflow.set_tracking_uri(tracking_uri)


mlflow.set_experiment('customer churn')

mlflow.sklearn.autolog()


with mlflow.start_run():

    bank_churn_clf = RandomForestClassifier(max_depth=2,
random_state=0)

    bank_churn_clf.fit(churn_train_X, churn_train_y)

    mlflow.sklearn.log_model(sk_model=bank_churn_
```

```
clf, artifact_path="sklearn-model", registered_model_
name="churn-model")
```

Now, go back to the tracking server site and refresh the page. Under the **Experiment** tab, you should see a new experiment called **customer churn**. Click on the **customer churn** link to see the run detail, and then click on the **Model** tab. You will see a model called **churn model**.

Now, run the same code again in the Jupyter notebook. You will now see a new run, and a new version of the model is created.

7. **Deploy the model to Seldon Core**: You have successfully trained an ML model and registered the model in the MLflow model registry. Next, let's deploy this model using the Seldon Core model serving framework.

    Let's download the model artifacts from the model registry and save them to a deployment bucket in S3. To do this, first, create a new S3 bucket called `model-deployment-<your initial>`. We will be using Seldon Core's SKLearn server package to host the model, and it expects the model name to be `model.joblib`. Run the following code block to download the model artifacts from the model registry, copy the `model.pkl` file to another directory, and name it `model.joblib`:

```
import mlflow.sklearn

import shutil

model_name = "churn-model"

model_version = <version>


sk_model = mlflow.sklearn.load_model(f"models:/{model_
name}/{model_version}")

mlflow.sklearn.save_model(sk_model, f"{model_name}_
{model_version}")


src = f"{model_name}_{model_version}/model.pkl"

des = f"skserver_{model_name}_{model_version}/model.
joblib"


shutil.copyfile(src, des)
```

Next, run the following code block to upload the model artifacts to the target S3 bucket:

```python
import boto3
import os


targetbucket = "model-deployment-<your initial>"
prefix = f"mlflow-models/{model_name}_{model_version}"


def upload_objects(src_path, bucketname):
    s3 = boto3.resource('s3')
    my_bucket = s3.Bucket(bucketname)

    for path, dirs, files in os.walk(src_path):
        dirs[:] = [d for d in dirs if not
d.startswith('.')]

        path = path.replace("\\","/")
        directory_name = prefix + path.replace(src_
path,"")
        for file in files:
            my_bucket.upload_file(os.path.join(path,
file), directory_name + "/" + file)


local_dir = f"skserver_{model_name}_{model_version}
upload_objects(local_dir, targetbucket)
```

The Seldon Core deployment will need access to the S3 bucket to download the model. To enable access, we create a `secret` object to store the AWS credential that we can use to inject into the **Seldon Core** containers. Let's create the secret using the following `.yaml` file and run `kubectl apply` on the file to set up the secret. Replace the values for `AWS_ACCESS_KEY_ID` and `AWS_SECRET_ACCESS_KEY` with your own AWS access key pair that has the right access to the S3 bucket for the models. Run the following code block in CloudShell to create the file and then run the `kubectl apply -f aws_secret.yaml` command in CloudShell to deploy the secret:

```
cat << EOF > aws_secret.yaml
apiVersion: v1
kind: Secret
```

```
metadata:
  name: aws-secret
type: Opaque
data:
  AWS_ACCESS_KEY_ID: <<your aws access key>>
  AWS_SECRET_ACCESS_KEY: <<you aws secret access key>>
EOF
```

We will use the Seldon Core SKLearn server to host the model. To do this, we need to create a deployment `.yaml` file, as shown in the next code block. Replace the `<<S3 uri of model file>>` placeholder with the S3 `uri` of the model artifacts we just uploaded. The S3 `uri` should be something like `s3://model-deployment<your initials>/mlflow-models/sklearn-model/`. The `envSecretRefName: aws-secret` line tells the deployment to create environment variables using the information stored in the secret. Run the code block in the CloudShell to create the `.yaml` file:

```
cat << EOF > bank_churn.yaml
apiVersion: machinelearning.seldon.io/v1alpha2
kind: SeldonDeployment
metadata:
  name: bank-churn
spec:
  name: bank-churn
  predictors:
    - graph:
        children: []
        implementation: SKLEARN_SERVER
        modelUri: <<S3 uri of model file>>
        envSecretRefName: aws-secret
        name: classifier
      name: default
      replicas: 1
EOF
```

After the file is created, run `kubectl apply -f bank_churn.yaml` to deploy the model.

To check the status of the deployment, run the following commands. The first command installs the utility for displaying strings in JSON format, and the second command queries the status:

```
sudo yum -y install jq gettext bash-completion moreutils
```
```
kubectl get sdep bank-churn -o json | jq .status
```

You can also directly check any logs inside of the running container for their status by using the following command:

```
kubectl logs <pod name> -c <container name>
```

Let's test the new Seldon Core endpoint inside the cluster. To do this, we will run a Pod inside the cluster and shell into it to test the endpoint. Create the template in CloudShell with the following code block. This template will create a Pod with a container running the **Ubuntu** operating system:

```
cat << EOF > ubuntu.yaml
apiVersion: v1
kind: Pod
metadata:
  name: ubuntu
  labels:
    app: ubuntu
spec:
  containers:
  - name: ubuntu
    image: ubuntu:latest
    command: ["/bin/sleep", "3650d"]
    imagePullPolicy: IfNotPresent
  restartPolicy: Always
EOF
```

Run `kubectl apply -f ubuntu.yaml` to deploy the Pod. After the Pod is running, run `kubectl exec --stdin --tty ubuntu -- /bin/bash` to access the Ubuntu shell. Then, run the following command inside the Ubuntu shell to install the `curl` utility:

```
apt update
```
```
apt upgrade
```
```
apt install curl
```

Now, run the following curl command to call the endpoint:

```
curl -X POST http://bank-churn-default.default:
8000/api/v1.0/predictions \
    -d '{ "data": { "ndarray":
[[123,544,37,2,79731,1,1,1,57558,1,1]] } }' \
    -H "Content-Type: application/json"
```

You should see a response similar to the following, which represents the probabilities for the output labels (0 and 1):

```
{"data":{"names":["t:0","t:1"],"ndarray":
[[0.8558529455725855,0.1441470544274145]]},"meta":{}}
```

The following figure (*Figure 7.13*) shows the data flow for the inference call we just made:

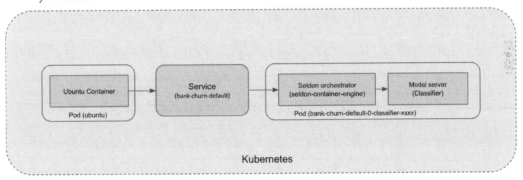

Figure 7.13 – An model inference data flow with Seldon Core hosted models

In *Figure 7.13*, the Ubuntu container is where the curl http command is initiated. The HTTP call hits the bank-churn-default service, which acts as the abstraction layer for the bank-churn-default-0-classifier-xxxx Pod. And the Pod runs the Seldon orchestrator container and the Model server container that hosts the trained model.

Congratulations! You have now successfully configured an MLflow tracking server and used it from a Jupyter notebook to centrally manage all your experiments, and you've deployed your model using the Seldon Core SKLearn server. Next, we will dive into how to automate everything with an automation pipeline.

Part 3 – Automating with an ML pipeline

An ML process involves multiple steps, including data preparation, feature engineering, model training, and model deployment. After a data scientist completes all the experiments and model-building tasks, the whole process should be automated using an ML pipeline. There are various architecture and technology options to consider when you design a pipeline. In this exercise, we will use the Kubeflow Pipelines platform to orchestrate the steps. Before we start, we will need to add some configurations to allow the Kubeflow notebook to access the Kubeflow Pipelines service.

Giving permission to the namespace service account to access the Istio service

The admin Kubernetes namespace is used by the Kubeflow notebook, and it comes with a number of service accounts, such as default, default-viewer, and default-editor. When a notebook runs, it will assume the default-editor service account. The Kubernetes Istio is a service mesh network that controls how microservices in a Kubernetes cluster interact with each other. For the service accounts in the admin namespace to access the Kubeflow pipeline component to create and run an ML pipeline, a servicerolebinding object needs to be created in the Kubeflow namespace between the default-editor service account and ServiceRole (ml-pipeline-services) object. Run the following code in the CloudShell terminal to create a .yaml definition file. Note that admin in the code is the admin namespace for the notebook environment:

```
cat << EOF > notebook_rbac.yaml
apiVersion: rbac.istio.io/v1alpha1
kind: ServiceRoleBinding
metadata:
  name: bind-ml-pipeline-nb-admin
  namespace: kubeflow
spec:
  roleRef:
    kind: ServiceRole
    name: ml-pipeline-services
  subjects:
  - properties:
      source.principal: cluster.local/ns/admin/sa/default-editor
EOF
```

Then, run the following command to apply the configuration to the Kubernetes environment:

```
kubectl apply -f notebook_rbac.yaml
```

The Envoy is the Istio proxy that handles all the inbound and outbound traffic of the service mesh. When the notebook communicates with the `ml-pipeline` service through the service mesh, the header information needs to be forwarded the `ml-pipeline` service to establish the user identity from the notebook. The following `.yaml` file enables that. Run the following in the CloudShell shell environment to create the file:

```
cat << EOF > notebook_filter.yaml
apiVersion: networking.istio.io/v1alpha3
kind: EnvoyFilter
metadata:
  name: add-header
  namespace: admin
spec:
  configPatches:
  - applyTo: VIRTUAL_HOST
    match:
      context: SIDECAR_OUTBOUND
      routeConfiguration:
        vhost:
          name: ml-pipeline.kubeflow.svc.cluster.local:8888
          route:
            name: default
    patch:
      operation: MERGE
      value:
        request_headers_to_add:
        - append: true
          header:
            key: kubeflow-userid
            value: admin@kubeflow.org
  workloadSelector:
    labels:
```

```
        notebook-name: david
EOF
```

After the file is created, run the following code to set up the header filter in the `admin` namespace:

```
kubectl apply -f notebook_filter.yaml
```

Great! Now, let's create a pipeline that does the following:

- Processes data saved in the data lake, creates a training dataset, and saves it in a training bucket

- Runs a model training job

- Deploys the model using the Seldon Core model serving component

We will use Kubeflow Pipelines to track the overall pipeline status, and we will continue to track experiment details and manage models in the MLflow model registry. Specifically, we are going to build the following architecture:

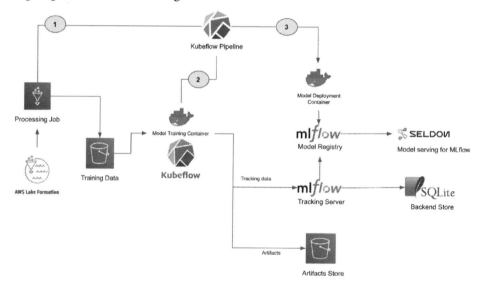

Figure 7.14 – Automation pipeline with Kubeflow Pipelines

You will create a new notebook for this portion of the exercise. On your Jupyter notebook screen, select **Python 3** under the **New** dropdown on the screen to create a new blank notebook. You will install the Kubeflow Pipelines package in the new notebook by running the following command in a cell:

```
!python3 -m pip install kfp --upgrade --user
```

Now, we are ready to assemble a pipeline, which consists of three main steps:

1. Data processing
2. Model training
3. Model deployment

The following code imports libraries, including **Kubeflow Pipelines SDK package (KFP)**, into the notebook. We will use a base Docker image (`tensorflow/tensorflow:2.0.0b0-py3`) to execute each step (Kubeflow component) in the pipeline. Copy and run the following code block in a cell to import the libraries:

```
import kfp
import kfp.dsl as dsl
from kfp import compiler
from kfp import components
from kfp.aws import use_aws_secret


BASE_IMAGE = 'tensorflow/tensorflow:2.0.0b0-py3'
```

Next, let's define the first component in the workflow – the data processing component. You will see a `@dsl.python_component` decorator. This decorator allows you to set metadata associated with components. The `process_data()` function is the function we will run to execute this data processing step. In this function, we will call the GLUE job that we defined in *Chapter 4, Data Management for Machine Learning*, to process the `bank churn` dataset. As mentioned earlier, there are several ways to create the Kubeflow components. For simplicity, we are creating a Python function operator component that allows us to run a Python function (such as `process_data()`) directly instead of building a custom container. The `components.func_to_container_op()` function takes the `process_data()` function and adds it to the base container. Run the following code block to create the `process_data_op` Kubeflow component:

```
@dsl.python_component(
    name='data_process_op',
    description='process data',
    base_image=BASE_IMAGE  # you can define the base image
here, or when you build in the next step.
)
def process_data(glue_job_name: str, region: str ) -> str:
    import os
    import boto3
```

```
import time

print ('start data processing')

# kick off the Glue Job to process data
client = boto3.client('glue', region_name= region)
job_id = client.start_job_run(JobName = glue_job_name)

#wait for the job to complete
job_state = "RUNNING"
while job_state != "SUCCEEDED":
    time.sleep(60)
    status = client.get_job_run(JobName = glue_job_name,
RunId = job_id['JobRunId'])
    job_state = status['JobRun']['JobRunState']

print ('data processing completed')
return f"GLUE job id: {job_id['JobRunId']}"

process_data_op = components.func_to_container_op(
    process_data,
    base_image=BASE_IMAGE,
    packages_to_install =['boto3']
)
```

Next, let's create a model training component. Similar to what we have done before, we will need to install some packages. Here, we will integrate the model training component with MLflow to track the experiment metrics and model artifacts. Also, remember to replace <<your mlflow tracking server url>> with your own mlflow tracking server URL:

```
@dsl.python_component(
    name='model_training_op',
    description='model training step',
    base_image=BASE_IMAGE  # you can define the base image
here, or when you build in the next step.
)
def train_model(bucket: str, key: str, region: str, previous_
```

```
output: str ) -> str :
    import os


    import boto3
    import mlflow
    import pandas as pd
    from sklearn.ensemble import RandomForestClassifier
    from sklearn.model_selection import train_test_split


    s3 = boto3.client('s3', region_name= region)
    response = s3.list_objects (Bucket = bucket, Prefix = key)


    key = response['Contents'][0]['Key']
    s3.download_file ('datalake-demo-dyping', key, "churn.csv")


    churn_data = pd.read_csv('churn.csv')


    # Split the dataset into training (80%) and testing (20%).
    churn_train, churn_test = train_test_split(churn_data,
test_size=0.2)


    churn_train_X = churn_train.loc[:, churn_train.columns !=
'exited']
    churn_train_y = churn_train['exited']


    churn_test_X = churn_test.loc[:, churn_test.columns !=
'exited']
    churn_test_y = churn_test['exited']


    tracking_uri = <<your mlflow tracking server url>>


    mlflow.set_tracking_uri(tracking_uri)
    mlflow.set_experiment('Churn Experiment 3')


    with mlflow.start_run(run_name="churn_run_2") as run:
        bank_churn_clf = RandomForestClassifier(max_depth=2,
random_state=0)
```

```
        mlflow.sklearn.autolog()
        bank_churn_clf.fit(churn_train_X, churn_train_y)
        mlflow.sklearn.log_model(sk_model=bank_churn_clf,
artifact_path="sklearn-model", registered_model_name="churn-
model")


    print (f"MLflow run id: {run.info.run_id}")
    return f"MLflow run id: {run.info.run_id}"


train_model_op = components.func_to_container_op(
    train_model,
    base_image=BASE_IMAGE,
    packages_to_install =['boto3', 'mlflow', 'scikit-learn',
'matplotlib'],
)
```

The preceding training step will register the model in the MLflow model registry. We will need to download a target model version and upload it to the S3 bucket for the deployment step. Add the following code block to the notebook, which will create a download_model_op component. Remember to replace model-deployment-<your initials> with your own bucket name, and replace <<your mlflow tracking server>> with your own tracking server:

```
@dsl.python_component(
    name='model_download_op',
    description='model training step',
    base_image=BASE_IMAGE  # you can define the base image
here, or when you build in the next step.
)
def download_model(model_version: int, previous_output: str )
-> str :
    import mlflow
    import os
    import shutil
    import boto3


    model_name = "churn-model"
    model_version = model_version
```

```
tracking_uri = <<your mlflow tracking server>>

mlflow.set_tracking_uri(tracking_uri)
mlflow.set_experiment('Churn Experiment 3')

sk_model = mlflow.sklearn.load_model(f"models:/{model_
name}/{model_version}")

mlflow.sklearn.save_model(sk_model, f"{model_name}_{model_
version}")

os.mkdir(f"skserver_{model_name}_release")


src = f"{model_name}_{model_version}/model.pkl"
des = f"skserver_{model_name}_release/model.joblib"

shutil.copyfile(src, des)

targetbucket = "model-deployment-<your initials>"
prefix = f"mlflow-models/{model_name}_release"

def upload_objects(src_path, bucketname):
    s3 = boto3.resource('s3')
    my_bucket = s3.Bucket(bucketname)

    for path, dirs, files in os.walk(src_path):
        dirs[:] = [d for d in dirs if not
d.startswith('.')]

        path = path.replace("\\","/")
        directory_name = prefix + path.replace(src_path,"")
        for file in files:
            my_bucket.upload_file(os.path.join(path, file),
directory_name + "/" + file)

upload_objects (des, targetbucket)
```

```
        print (f"target bucket: {targetbucket}, prefix: {prefix} ")
        return f"target bucket: {targetbucket}, prefix: {prefix} "


model_download_op = components.func_to_container_op(
    download_model,
    base_image=BASE_IMAGE,
    packages_to_install =['boto3', 'mlflow', 'scikit-learn'],
)
```

Now, we're ready to construct the pipeline definition. You construct the pipeline definition by using the @dsl.pipeline decorator and then defining a function that specifies the flow of the pipeline. To run the pipeline, we will need to add some extra Kubernetes permissions to the service account (default-editor) associated with the pipeline in order to deploy the model to the cluster. The right way to do this is to create a new role with proper permissions. For simplicity, we will reuse the existing cluster-admin role, which has all the rights we need to deploy the model. To associate the service account (default-editor) with cluster-admin, we will create clusterrolebinding. Run the following code block in your CloudShell shell environment to create a .yaml file for the clusterrolebinding object, and then run kubectl apply -f sa-cluster-binding.yaml to establish the binding:

```
cat << EOF > sa-cluster-binding.yaml
apiVersion: rbac.authorization.k8s.io/v1
kind: ClusterRoleBinding
metadata:
  name: default-editor-binding
  namespace: admin
subjects:
- kind: ServiceAccount
  name: default-editor
  namespace: admin
roleRef:
  kind: ClusterRole
  name: cluster-admin
  apiGroup: rbac.authorization.k8s.io
EOF
```

Next, we need to create a Seldon Core deployment file for the pipeline to use. Create a new file in your Jupyter Notebook environment called `bank_churn_deployment.yaml`, copy the following code to it, and save. Make sure to replace `<<S3 uri of model file>>` before you save the file:

```
apiVersion: machinelearning.seldon.io/v1alpha2
kind: SeldonDeployment
metadata:
  name: bank-churn
spec:
  name: bank-churn
  predictors:
    - graph:
        children: []
        implementation: SKLEARN_SERVER
        modelUri: <<S3 uri of model file>>
        envSecretRefName: aws-secret
        name: classifier
      name: default
      replicas: 1
EOF
```

Alright, we are now ready to construct the pipeline by running the following code block. Note that we will use AWS credentials in some of the steps. To securely manage the AWS credentials and pass them to the component, we need to create a new secret in the `admin` namespace before we build the pipeline. Run the following script in the CloudShell terminal, and then run `kubectl apply - f aws_secret_admin.yaml`. Remember to replace `<<your AWS access key>>` and `<<your AWS secret key>>` with your own keys:

```
cat << EOF > aws_secret_admin.yaml
apiVersion: v1
kind: Secret
metadata:
  name: aws-secret
  namespace: admin
type: Opaque
data:
```

```
  AWS_ACCESS_KEY_ID: <<your AWS access key>>
  AWS_SECRET_ACCESS_KEY: <<your AWS secret key>>
EOF
```

Now, construct the pipeline definition by running the following code block in a Jupyter notebook cell. We will have four steps in this workflow:

- precess_data_task

- model_training_task

- model_download_task

- seldondeploy

For simplicity, we added the default values to the pipeline. Remember to replace <<aws region>> with your region:

```
@dsl.pipeline(
  name='bank churn pipeline',
  description='Train bank churn model'
)
def preprocess_train_deploy(
        bucket: str = 'datalake-demo-dyping',
        glue_job_name: str = 'customer-churn-processing',
        region: str = <<aws region>>,
        tag: str = '4',
        model: str = 'bank_churn_model',
        model_version: int = 1,
):
    precess_data_task = process_data_op(glue_job_name, region).
apply(use_aws_secret('aws-secret', 'AWS_ACCESS_KEY_ID', 'AWS_
SECRET_ACCESS_KEY', 'us-west-1'))


    model_training_task = train_model_op(bucket,'ml-customer-
churn/data/', region, precess_data_task.output).apply(use_aws_
secret())


    model_download_task = model_download_op(model_version,
model_training_task.output).apply(use_aws_secret())
```

```
    seldon_config = yaml.load(open("bank_churn_deployment.
yaml"))
    deploy_op = dsl.ResourceOp(
        name="seldondeploy",
        k8s_resource=seldon_config,
        action = "apply",
        attribute_outputs={"name": "{.metadata.name}"})


    deploy_op.after(model_download_task)
```

The pipeline definition needs to be registered with the Kubeflow Pipelines service. To do this, we need to compile the preceding definition and save it into a file. Run the following code block in a new cell to compile the definition into a file:

```
import kfp.compiler as compiler


pipeline_filename = 'bank_churn_pipeline.tar.gz'
compiler.Compiler().compile(preprocess_train_deploy, pipeline_
filename)
```

Now, we are ready to register and run the pipeline by creating an experiment (which is used to organize all the end-to-end workflow runs for the different experiments) and run the pipeline using the `run_pipeline()` function. Note that we are also using MLflow to track the details for the model training step of the workflow:

```
client = kfp.Client()
experiment = client.create_experiment(name='data_experiment',
namespace='admin')


arguments = {'model_version':1}
pipeline_func = preprocess_train_deploy
run_name = pipeline_func.__name__ + '_run'
run_result = client.run_pipeline(experiment.id, run_name,
pipeline_filename, arguments)
```

To monitor the status of the pipeline execution, you can switch to the **Kubeflow Dashboard** screen, select **Pipelines**, select **Experiments**, expand the section for your pipeline, and click on the link under the **Run name** column. You should see a graph similar to the following figure, which represents the execution graph of your pipeline:

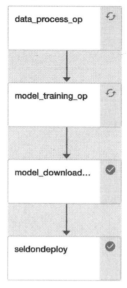

Figure 7.15 – Kubeflow Pipelines workflow execution

Congratulations, you have successfully created a simple ML platform that gives us the ability to process data, train a model, and deploy a model. You also got to build a simple ML pipeline to automate the ML steps in the pipeline, which is the key to faster and more consistent model deployment.

Summary

In this chapter, you learned about the core architecture components of a typical ML platform and their capabilities. We also discussed various open source technologies such as Kubeflow, MLflow, TensorFlow Serving, Seldon Core, Apache Airflow, and Kubeflow Pipelines. You have also built a data science environment using Kubeflow notebooks, tracked experiments and models using MLflow, and deployed your model using Seldon Core. And finally, you learned how to automate multiple ML workflow steps using Kubeflow Pipelines, including data processing, model training, and model deployment. While these open source technologies provide features for building potentially sophisticated ML platforms, it still takes significant engineering effort and know-how to build and maintain such environments, especially for large-scale ML platforms. In the next chapter, we will start looking into fully managed, purpose-built ML solutions for building and operating ML environments.

8

Building a Data Science Environment Using AWS ML Services

While some organizations choose to build **machine learning** (**ML**) platforms on their own using open source technologies, many other organizations prefer to use fully managed ML services as the foundation for their ML platforms. In this chapter, we will focus on the fully managed ML services offered by AWS. Specifically, you will learn about **Amazon SageMaker**, a fully managed ML service, and other related services for building a data science environment for data scientists. We will cover specific SageMaker components such as **SageMaker Notebook**, **SageMaker Studio**, **SageMaker Training Service**, and **SageMaker Hosting Service**. We will also discuss the architecture pattern for building a data science environment, and we will provide a hands-on exercise in building a data science environment.

After completing this chapter, you will be familiar with **Amazon SageMaker, AWS CodeCommit**, and **Amazon ECR** and be able to use these services to build a data science environment, which you can then use to build, train, and deploy ML models.

Specifically, we will be covering the following topics:

- Data science environment architecture using SageMaker

- Hands-on exercise – building a data science environment using AWS services

Technical requirements

In this chapter, you will need access to an AWS account and have the following AWS services for the hands-on lab:

- Amazon S3

- Amazon SageMaker

- AWS CodeCommit

- Amazon ECR

You will also need to download the dataset from `https://www.kaggle.com/ ankurzing/sentiment-analysis-for-financial-news`.

The sample source code used in this chapter can be found at `https://github. com/PacktPublishing/The-Machine-Learning-Solutions-Architect- Handbook/tree/main/Chapter08`.

Data science environment architecture using SageMaker

Data scientists use data science environments to iterate different data science experiments with different datasets and algorithms. They need tools such as Jupyter Notebook for code authoring and execution, data processing engines for large data processing and feature engineering, and model training services for large-scale model training. The data science environment needs to provide utilities that can help you manage and track different experimentation runs. To manage artifacts such as source code and Docker images, the data scientists also need a code repository and Docker container repository.

Amazon SageMaker provides end-to-end ML capabilities that cover data preparation and data labeling, model training and tuning, model deployment, and model monitoring. It also provides other supporting features such as experiment tracking, a model registry, a feature store, and pipelines. The following diagram illustrates a basic data science environment architecture that's using Amazon SageMaker and other supporting services:

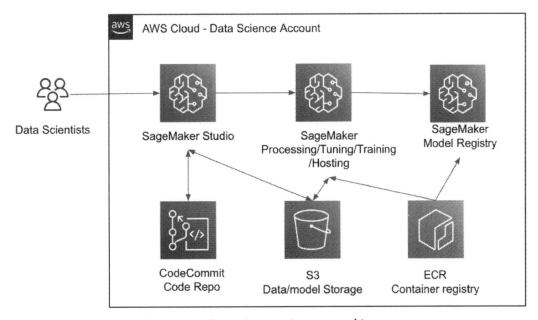

Figure 8.1 – Data science environment architecture

Now, let's take a closer look at some of these core components.

SageMaker Studio

SageMaker Studio is the data science **integrated development environment (IDE)** for SageMaker. It provides core features such as hosted notebooks for running experiments, as well as access to different backend services such as data wrangling, model training, and model hosting services from a single user interface. It is the main interface for data scientists to interact with most of SageMaker's functionality. It also provides a Python SDK for interacting with its backend services programmatically from Python notebooks or scripts. The following diagram shows the key components of SageMaker Studio:

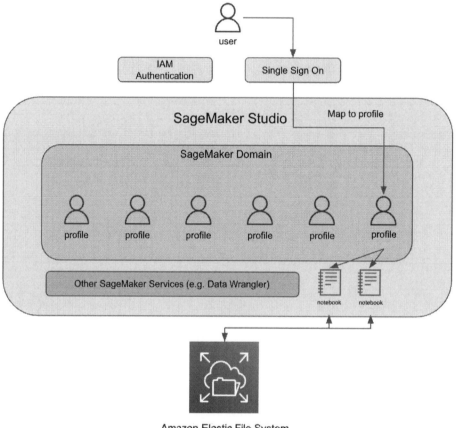

Figure 8.2 – SageMaker Studio architecture

To access the Studio environment, a user can either authenticate via AWS Management Console first (that is, via IAM mode) and then navigate to the SageMaker management console to access Studio, or they can authenticate via the Studio environment's **single sign-on** (**SSO**) interface without the need for AWS Management Console access.

SageMaker Studio uses a concept called a domain to segregate different user environments. A domain is a collection of user profiles, where each profile provides specifications such as AWS IAM roles to use for Jupyter Notebook, notebook sharing configuration, and network settings for connecting to AWS. Once a user has been authenticated, the user is mapped to a user profile to launch the actual Studio environment. Once inside the Studio environment, the user can create new notebooks using different ML kernels, such as Python, TensorFlow, or PyTorch. From inside Studio, the user will also have access to other SageMaker functionality such as Data Wrangler for data preparation, SageMaker Experiments for experiment tracking, SageMaker AutoPilot for automated ML model training, SageMaker Feature Store for feature management, and SageMaker Endpoints for hosting trained ML models.

For each SageMaker domain, an Amazon **Elastic File System** (**EFS**) volume is created and attached to the domain. This EFS volume is used as data storage for all the user data in the domain. Each user profile is mapped to a directory in the EFS volume.

The notebooks that are created in Studio will be backed by EC2 servers. SageMaker provides a wide range of CPU and GPU instances for notebooks. Users have the option to choose different EC2 server types based on their needs.

SageMaker Processing

SageMaker Processing provides a separate infrastructure for large-scale data processing such as data cleaning and feature engineering for large datasets. It can be accessed directly from a notebook environment via the SageMaker Python SDK or Boto3 SDK. SageMaker Processing uses Docker container images to run data processing jobs. Several built-in containers, such as scikit-learn containers and Spark containers, are provided out of the box. You also have the option to use your custom containers for processing. The following diagram shows the SageMaker Processing architecture:

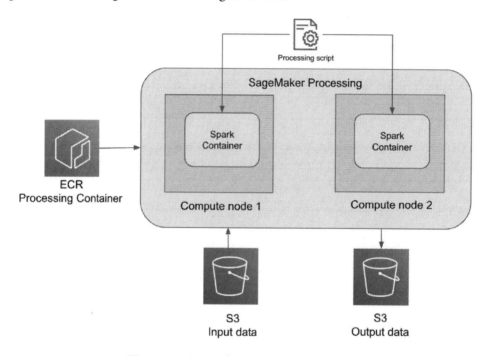

Figure 8.3 – SageMaker Processing architecture

When a SageMaker Processing job is initiated, the processing container is pulled from Amazon ECR and loaded into the EC2 compute cluster. The data in S3 is copied over to the storage attached to the compute nodes for the data processing scripts to access and process. Once the processing procedure is completed, the output data is copied back to the S3 output location.

SageMaker Training Service

SageMaker Training Service provides a separate infrastructure for model training. SageMaker provides three main methods for model training:

- SageMaker provides a list of built-in containerized algorithms for model training. With the built-in algorithm, you only need to provide training data stored in S3 and infrastructure specifications.

- SageMaker provides a list of managed framework containers such as containers for scikit-learn, TensorFlow, and PyTorch. With a managed framework container, in addition to providing data sources and infrastructure specifications, you also need to provide a training script that runs the model training loop.

- SageMaker allows you to bring your own custom container for model training. This container needs to contain the model training scripts, as well as all the dependencies required to run the training loop.

The following diagram shows the architecture of SageMaker Training Service:

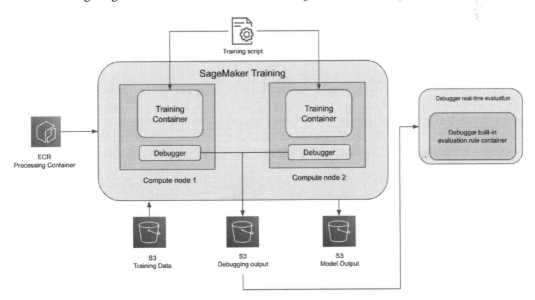

Figure 8.4 – SageMaker Training Service architecture

You can use the AWS Boto3 SDK or the SageMaker Python SDK to kick off a training job. To run the training job, you need to provide configuration details such as the training Docker image's URL, training script location, framework version, training dataset, and model output location, as well as infrastructure details such as the compute's instance type and number, as well as networking details.

By default, SageMaker tracks all training jobs and their associated metadata, such as algorithms, input training dataset URLs, hyperparameters, and model output locations. Training jobs also emit system metrics and algorithm metrics to AWS CloudWatch for monitoring. Training logs are also sent to CloudWatch logs for inspection and analysis needs.

SageMaker training jobs also allow you to integrate with the SageMaker debugger service. The debugger service allows the training job to capture additional details, such as system metrics (for example, CPU/GPU memory, network, and I/O metrics), deep learning framework metrics (for example, model training metrics at different neural network layers), and model training tensors (for example, model parameters) and save them to S3. Real-time debugger evaluation rules can be configured to monitor these stats and send out alerts when they meet a certain threshold. Some examples of the built-in evaluation rules are vanishing gradients and model overfitting.

SageMaker Tuning

To optimize the model's performance, you also need to try different hyperparameters, such as a learning rate for gradient descent and model training. An algorithm can contain a large number of hyperparameters, and tuning them manually would be a highly labor-intensive task. The SageMaker Tuning service works with SageMaker training jobs to tune model training hyperparameters automatically.

The SageMaker Tuning service supports two types of hyperparameter tuning strategies:

- **Random search**: This is where a random combination of values for the hyperparameters is used to train a model.

- **Bayesian search**: This is where the hyperparameter search is treated like a regression problem, where the inputs for regression are the values of the hyperparameters and the output is the model's performance metric once the model has been trained using the input values. The Tuning service uses the values that have been collected from the training jobs to predict the next set of values that would produce model improvement.

The SageMaker Tuning service works with SageMaker training jobs to optimize the hyperparameters. It works by sending different input hyperparameter values to the training jobs and picking the hyperparameter values that return the best model metrics.

SageMaker Experiments

You can organize and track your experiments using SageMaker Experiments. SageMaker Experiments has two core concepts:

- **Trial**: A trial is a collection of training steps involved in a trial run. This can include trial components such as processing, training, and evaluation. You can enrich trials and trial components with a set of metadata, such as dataset sources, hyperparameters, and model training metrics.

- **Experiment**: An experiment is a collection of trials, so you can group all the trials related to an experiment to easily compare different trial runs.

Now, let's look at SageMaker Hosting.

SageMaker Hosting

As a data scientist builds and experiments with different models, sometimes, there is a need to host the model behind an API so that it can be used by downstream applications for integration testing. SageMaker Hosting provides such capabilities. They are listed as follows:

- **AWS CodeCommit**: AWS CodeCommit is a fully managed code repository for source code version control. It is similar to any Git-based repository and integrates with SageMaker Studio UI to allow data scientists to clone code repositories in AWS CodeCommit, as well as pull and push files from and to the repository. For the data science environment, you can also use other code repository services such as GitHub and Bitbucket.

  AWS CodeCommit provides three different ways for connections: HTTPS, which allows a Git client to connect to the repository via the HTTPS protocol; SSH, which allows a Git client to connect to the repository via the SSH protocol; and HTTPS, which is the protocol you should use with the **Git-remote-codecommit** (**GRC**) utility. This utility extends Git to pull and push code from AWS CodeCommit.

- **Amazon ECR**: Amazon ECR is a fully-managed Docker container repository and registry service. SageMaker uses container images for data processing, model training, and model hosting. These images can be stored in Amazon ECR for management and access.

With that, we have discussed the core architecture components of a data science environment in AWS. Next, we will provide a hands-on exercise where you will configure a data science environment and perform some data science experiments and model building.

Hands-on exercise – building a data science environment using AWS services

In this hands-on exercise, you will create a data science environment using SageMaker with AWS CodeCommit as the source control.

Problem statement

As an ML Solutions Architect, you have been tasked with building a data science environment on AWS for the data scientists in the Equity Research department. The data scientists in the Equity Research department have several NLP problems, such as detecting the sentiment of financial phrases. Once you have created the environment for the data scientists, you also need to build a proof of concept to show the data scientists how to build and train an NLP model using the environment.

Dataset

The data scientists have indicated that they like to use the BERT model to solve sentiment analysis problems, and they plan to use the financial phrase dataset to establish some initial benchmarks for the model: `https://www.kaggle.com/ankurzing/sentiment-analysis-for-financial-news`.

Lab instructions

Follow these steps to create a data science environment using SageMaker with AWS CodeCommit as the source control.

Setting up SageMaker Studio

Follow these steps to set up a SageMaker Studio environment:

1. To create a SageMaker Studio environment, we need to set up a domain and a user profile in the respective AWS region. Navigate to the SageMaker management console once you've logged into AWS Management Console and click on the **Amazon SageMaker Studio** link on the left.

2. On the right-hand side of the screen, choose the **Quick Start** option. The **Quick Start** option will use IAM mode for authentication. You can keep the default username or change it to something else. For the execution role dropdown, choose the **Create a new role** option, keep all the default options on the pop-up screen as-is, and create the role. The execution role provides permission to access different resources, such as S3 buckets, and will be associated with Studio notebooks, which we will create later.

3. Lastly, click on the **Create** button to set up the domain and user. It will take a few minutes for the domain to be set up.

Additionally, the following resources are also created behind the scenes:

- **An S3 bucket for the domain**: The name of the domain should look something like `sagemaker-studio-<AWS account number>-XXXX`. This bucket can be used for storing datasets and model artifacts.

- **Elastic File System volume**: This volume is used by the Studio domain for storing user data. If you navigate to the EFS management console, you should see that a new filesystem has been created.

Once the setup is completed, you should see the following screen:

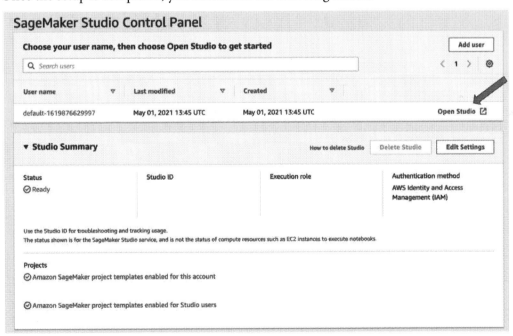

Figure 8.5 – Studio setup screen

To start the Studio environment for the newly created user, click on the Launch app dropdown and select Studio. It will take a few minutes for the Studio environment to appear. Once everything is ready, you will see a screen similar to the following:

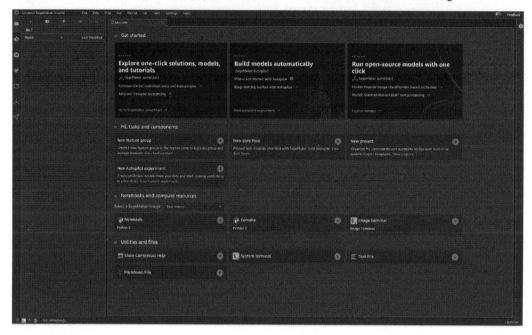

Figure 8.6 – Studio UI

Now that we have configured the Studio environment, let's set up an Amazon CodeCommit repository for source code version control.

Setting up CodeCommit

Navigate to the AWS CodeCommit management console, click on the **Repositories** link in the left pane, and then click **Create repositories** to start creating a CodeCommit repository. Provide a name for the repository and select **Create**.

Now that we've created a new repository, let's configure the newly created Studio environment to use this new repository. There are several approaches we can take to set up authentication credentials to access the CodeCommit repository:

- **IAM user credential**: To do this, create a new IAM user and attach the **AWSCodeCommitPowerUser** policy to it for simplicity. Download the AWS credential to your local machine and look up the IAM credentials in the file. Next, open a Terminal in Studio by selecting **File** > **New** > **Terminal** from the menu dropdown. Once the new Terminal window is open, run the AWS Config command to set up the IAM credential.

- **Studio Notebook execution role**: You can also attach the **AWSCodeCommitPowerUser** policy to the Studio notebook execution role you created in the previous section. To do this, look up the SageMaker Execution role under the Studio username you are using under the Studio control panel. Then, use the AWS IAM service to attach the policy to the role.

You can use either of the preceding approaches to configure the authentication for CodeCommit. Once you have done this, you can clone the CodeCommit repository we created earlier. To do this, select the **Git** menu dropdown in the Studio UI pick the **Clone a Repository** option (see the following screenshot), and paste the HTTPS URL for the repository. You can copy the HTTPS URL next to the repository name in the CodeCommit management console:

Figure 8.7 – Clone a Repository

Once you've done this, you should see a new folder in the folder view. Now that we have created a data science environment, let's use it to perform some experiments and build an ML model.

Training the BERT model in the Jupyter Notebook

In this part of the hands-on exercise, we will train a financial sentiment analysis NLP model using the BERT transformer, which we learned about in *Chapter 3, Machine Learning Algorithms*. To get started, double-click on the newly cloned folder in the folder view and create a new notebook to author our code by selecting **File** > **New** > **Notebook** from the menu dropdown in the folder. When prompted to select a kernel, pick **Python 3 (PyTorch 1.6 Python 3.6 GPU Optimized)**. You can rename the file so that it has a more meaningful name by selecting **File** > **Rename Notebook** from the menu.

We will use the financial news sentiment dataset for model training. Download the dataset from Kaggle at `https://www.kaggle.com/ankurzing/sentiment-analysis-for-financial-news`. Note that you will need a Kaggle account to download it. Once it's been downloaded, you should see an `archive.zip` file.

Next, let's upload the `archive.zip` file to the Studio notebook. Create a new folder called `data` in the same folder where the new notebook is located and upload it to the `data` directory using the **File Upload** utility (the up arrow icon) in Studio UI or drag it into the `data` folder. You can unzip the ZIP file using the unzip utility in a Terminal window. Please note that the Amazon Linux environment does not come with the `unzip` utility by default. To install this utility, run `sudo yum install unzip` in the Terminal window. You should see several files inside the folder. You will see a file called `all_data.csv` inside the `data` folder.

Now, let's install some additional packages for our exercise. Run the following code block inside the notebook cell to install the transformer package. The transformer package provides a list of pre-trained transformers such as BERT. You will use these transformers to fine-tune an ML task. Note that some of the code block samples are not complete. You can find the complete code samples at `https://github.com/PacktPublishing/The-Machine-Learning-Solutions-Architect-Handbook/blob/main/Chapter08/bert-financial-sentiment.ipynb`:

```
!pip install transformers
!pip install ipywidgets
```

Restart the kernel of the notebook after installing `ipywidgets`. Next, import some libraries into the notebook and set up the logger for logging purposes:

```
import logging
import os
import sys
import numpy as np
import pandas as pd
import torch
from torch.utils.data import DataLoader, TensorDataset
from transformers import AdamW, BertForSequenceClassification, BertTokenizer
from sklearn.preprocessing import OrdinalEncoder
from sklearn.model_selection import train_test_split
from types import SimpleNamespace
logger = logging.getLogger(__name__)
```

```
logger.setLevel(logging.DEBUG)
logger.addHandler(logging.StreamHandler(sys.stdout))
```

Now, we are ready to load the `data` file and process it. The following code block loads the `data` file and splits the data into train and test datasets. We will select the first two columns from the file and name them `sentiment` and `article`. The `sentiment` column is the label column. It contains three different unique values (`negative`, `neutral`, and `positive`). Since they are string values, we will convert them into integers (0,1,2) using `OrdinalEncoder` from the scikit-learn library. We also need to determine the max length of the article column. The max length is used to prepare the input for the transformer since the transformer requires a fixed length:

```
filepath = './data/all-data.tsv'
data = pd.read_csv(filepath, encoding="ISO-8859-1",
    header=None, usecols=[0, 1],
    names=["sentiment", "article"])


ord_enc = OrdinalEncoder()
data["sentiment"] = ord_enc.fit_transform(data[["sentiment"]])
data = data.astype({'sentiment':'int'})


train, test = train_test_split(data)
train.to_csv("./data/train.csv", index=False)
test.to_csv("./data/test.csv", index=False)


MAX_LEN = data.article.str.len().max()   # this is the max
length of the sentence
```

Next, we will build a list of utility functions to support the data loading and model training. We need to feed data to the transformer model in batches. The following `get_data_loader()` function loads the dataset into the PyTorch `DataLoader` class with a specified batch size. Note that we also encode the articles into tokens with the `BertTokenizer` class:

```
def get_data_loader(batch_size, training_dir, filename):
    logger.info("Get data loader")
    tokenizer = BertTokenizer.from_pretrained("bert-base-
uncased", do_lower_case=True)
    dataset = pd.read_csv(os.path.join(training_dir, filename))
```

```
    articles = dataset.article.values
    sentiments = dataset.sentiment.values     input_ids = []
    for sent in articles:
        encoded_articles = tokenizer.encode(sent, add_special_
tokens=True)
        input_ids.append(encoded_articles)
...
    return tensor_dataloader
```

The following `train()` function will run the training loop using the
`BertForSequenceClassification` class. We will use the pre-trained BERT model
for fine-tuning, instead of training from scratch. We will feed one batch of data to the
BERT model at a time. Note that we will also check if there is a GPU device on the server.
If there is one, we will use the `cuda` device for GPU training, instead of `cpu` for CPU
training. We need to manually move the data and BERT model to the same target device
using the `.to(device)` function so that the training can happen on the target device
with the data residing in memory on the same device. The optimizer we're using here is
AdamW, which is a variant of the gradient descent optimization algorithm. The training
loop will run through the number of epochs specified. One epoch runs through the entire
training dataset once:

```
def train(args):
    use_cuda = args.num_gpus > 0
    device = torch.device("cuda" if use_cuda else "cpu")
    # set the seed for generating random numbers
    torch.manual_seed(args.seed)
    if use_cuda:
        torch.cuda.manual_seed(args.seed)
    train_loader = get_data_loader(args.batch_size, args.data_
dir, args.train_file)
    test_loader = get_data_loader(args.test_batch_size, args.
data_dir, args.test_file)
    model = BertForSequenceClassification.from_pretrained(
        "bert-base-uncased",
        num_labels=args.num_labels,
        output_attentions=False,
        output_hidden_states=False,  )
...
    return model
```

We also want to test the model's performance using a separate test dataset during training. To do this, we will implement the following `test()` function, which is called by the `train()` function:

```
def test(model, test_loader, device):
    def get_correct_count(preds, labels):
        pred_flat = np.argmax(preds, axis=1).flatten()
        labels_flat = labels.flatten()
        return np.sum(pred_flat == labels_flat), len(labels_
flat)

    model.eval()
    _, eval_accuracy = 0, 0
    total_correct = 0
    total_count = 0
...
    logger.info("Test set: Accuracy: %f\n", total_correct/
total_count)
```

Now, we have all the functions needed to load and process data, run the training loop, and measure the model metrics using a test dataset. With that, we can kick off the training process. We will use the `args` variable to set up various values, such as batch size, data location, and learning rate, to be used by the training loop and the testing loop:

```
args = SimpleNamespace(num_labels=3, batch_size=16, test_batch_
size=10, epochs=3, lr=2e-5, seed=1,log_interval =50, model_dir
= "model/", data_dir="data/", num_gpus=1, train_file = "train.
csv", test_file="test.csv")
model = train(args)
```

Once you have run the preceding code, you should see training stats for each batch and epoch. The model will also be saved in the specified directory.

Next, let's see how the trained model can be used for making predictions directly. To do this, we must implement several utility functions. The following `input_fn()` function takes input in JSON format and outputs an input vector that represents the string input and its associated mask. The output will be sent to the model for prediction:

```
def input_fn(request_body, request_content_type):
    if request_content_type == "application/json":
```

```
            data = json.loads(request_body)
        if isinstance(data, str):
            data = [data]
        elif isinstance(data, list) and len(data) > 0 and
isinstance(data[0], str):
            pass
        else:
            raise ValueError("Unsupported input type. Input
type can be a string or a non-empty list. \
                    I got {}".format(data))

        tokenizer = BertTokenizer.from_pretrained("bert-base-
uncased", do_lower_case=True)

        input_ids = [tokenizer.encode(x, add_special_
tokens=True) for x in data]

        # pad shorter sentence
        padded =   torch.zeros(len(input_ids), MAX_LEN)
        for i, p in enumerate(input_ids):
            padded[i, :len(p)] = torch.tensor(p)

        # create mask
        mask = (padded != 0)

        return padded.long(), mask.long()
    raise ValueError("Unsupported content type: {}".
format(request_content_type))
```

The following `predict_fn()` function takes `input_data` returned by `input_fn()` and uses the trained model to generate the prediction. Note that we will also use a GPU if a GPU device is available on the server:

```
def predict_fn(input_data, model):
    device = torch.device("cuda" if torch.cuda.is_available()
else "cpu")
    model.to(device)
    model.eval()
```

```
    input_id, input_mask = input_data
    input_id = input_id.to(device)
    input_mask = input_mask.to(device)
    with torch.no_grad():
        y = model(input_id, attention_mask=input_mask)[0]
    return y
```

Now, run the following code to generate a prediction. Replace the value of the article with different financial text to see the result:

```
import json
print("sentiment label : " + str(np.argmax(preds)))
article = "Operating profit outpaced the industry average"
request_body = json.dumps(article)
enc_data, mask = input_fn(request_body, 'application/json')
output = predict_fn((enc_data, mask), model)
preds = output.detach().cpu().numpy()
print("sentiment label : " + str(np.argmax(preds)))
```

Now, let us look at an alternative way to train the BERT model.

Training the BERT model with SageMaker Training Service

In the previous section, you trained the BERT model directly inside a GPU-based Jupyter Notebook. Instead of provisioning a GPU-based notebook instance, you can provision a less costly CPU-based instance and send the model training task to SageMaker Training Service. To use SageMaker Training Service, you need to make some minor changes to the training script and create a separate launcher script to kick off the training. As we discussed in the *SageMaker Training Service* section, there are three main approaches to training a model in SageMaker. Since SageMaker provides a managed container for PyTorch, we will use the managed container approach to train the model. With this approach, you will need to provide the following inputs:

- A training script as the entry point, as well as dependencies

- An IAM role to be used by the training job

- Infrastructures such as the instance type and number

- A data (training/validation/testing) location in S3

- A model output location in S3
- Hyperparameters for training the model

When a training job is started, SageMaker Training Service will perform the following tasks in sequence:

1. Launch the EC2 instances needed for the training job.
2. Download the data from S3 to the training host.
3. Download the appropriate managed container from the SageMaker ECR registry and run the container.
4. Copy the training script and dependencies to the training container.
5. Run the training script and pass the hyperparameters as command-line arguments to the training script. The training script will load the training/validation/testing data from specific directories in the container, run the training loop, and save the model to a specific directory in the container. Several environment variables will be set in the container to provide configuration details, such as directories for the data and model output, to the training script.
6. Once the training script exits with success, SageMaker Training Service will copy the saved model artifacts from the container to the model output location in S3.

Now, let's create the following training script, name it `train.py`, and save it in a new directory called `code`. Note that the training script is almost the same as the code in *Training the BERT model in the Jupyter Notebook* section. We have also added an `if __name__ == "__main__":` section at the end. This section contains the code for reading the values of the command-line arguments and the values of the system environment variables such as SageMaker's data directory (`SM_CHANNEL_TRAINING`), the model output directory (`SM_MODEL_DIR`), and the number of GPUs (`SM_NUM_GPUS`) available on the host. Note that the following code sample is not complete. You can find the complete code sample at `https://github.com/PacktPublishing/The-Machine-Learning-Solutions-Architect-Handbook/blob/main/Chapter08/code/train.py`:

```
import argparse
import logging
import os
import sys
import numpy as np
import pandas as pd
import torch
```

```
from torch.utils.data import DataLoader, TensorDataset
from transformers import AdamW, BertForSequenceClassification,
BertTokenizer
logger = logging.getLogger(__name__)
logger.setLevel(logging.DEBUG)
logger.addHandler(logging.StreamHandler(sys.stdout))
...


    train(parser.parse_args())
```

The preceding script requires library packages that are not available in the managed training container. You can install custom library packages using the requirement.txt file. Create a requirement.txt file with the following code and save it in the code directory:

```
transformers==2.3.0
```

Next, let's create a launcher notebook for kicking off the training job using SageMaker Training Service. The launcher notebook will do the following:

- Upload the training and test dataset to the S3 bucket and folders.
- Set up SageMaker PyTorch Estimator using the SageMaker SDK to configure the training job.
- Kick off the SageMaker training job.

Create a new notebook called bert-financial-sentiment-launcher.ipynb in the folder where the code folder is located and copy the following code block into the notebook one cell at a time. When you're prompted to choose a kernel, pick the **Python 3 (Data Science)** kernel.

The following code specifies the S3 bucket to be used for saving the training and testing dataset, as well as the model artifacts. You can use the bucket that was created earlier in *Setting up SageMaker Studio* section, when the Studio domain was configured. The training and test dataset we created earlier will be uploaded to the bucket. The get_execution_role() function returns the IAM role associated with the notebook, which we will use to run the training job later:

```
import os
import numpy as np
import pandas as pd
import sagemaker
```

```
sagemaker_session = sagemaker.Session()
bucket = <bucket name>
prefix = "sagemaker/pytorch-bert-financetext"
role = sagemaker.get_execution_role()

inputs_train = sagemaker_session.upload_data("./data/train.
csv", bucket=bucket, key_prefix=prefix)
inputs_test = sagemaker_session.upload_data("./data/test.csv",
bucket=bucket, key_prefix=prefix)
```

Finally, we must set up the SageMaker PyTorch estimator and kick off the training job. Note that you can also specify the PyTorch framework version and Python version to set up the container. For simplicity, we are passing the name of the training file and test file, as well as max length, as hyperparameters. The `train.py` file can also be modified to look them up dynamically:

```
from sagemaker.pytorch import PyTorch
output_path = f"s3://{bucket}/{prefix}"

estimator = PyTorch(
    entry_point="train.py",
    source_dir="code",
    role=role,
    framework_version="1.6",
    py_version="py3",
    instance_count=1,
    instance_type="ml.p3.2xlarge",
    output_path=output_path,
    hyperparameters={
        "epochs": 4,
        "lr" : 5e-5,
        "num_labels": 3,
        "train_file": "train.csv",
        "test_file" : "test.csv",
        "MAX_LEN" : 315,
        "batch-size" : 16,
        "test-batch-size" : 10
```

```
        }
)
estimator.fit({"training": inputs_train, "testing": inputs_
test})
```

Once the training job has been completed, you can go to the SageMaker management console to access the training job's details and metadata. Training jobs also send outputs to CloudWatch logs and CloudWatch metrics. You can navigate to these logs by clicking on the respective links on the training job detail page.

Deploying the model

In this step, we will deploy the trained model to a SageMaker RESTful endpoint so that it can be integrated with downstream applications. We will use the managed PyTorch serving container to host the model. With the managed PyTorch serving container, you can provide an interference script to process the request data before it is sent to the model for inference, as well as control how to call the model for inference. Let's create a new script called inference.py in the code folder that contains the following code block. As you have probably noticed, we have used the same functions that we used in *Training the BERT model in the Jupyter Notebook* section for the predictions. Note that you need to use the same function signatures for these two functions as SageMaker will be looking for the exact function name and parameter lists. You can find the complete source code at https://github.com/PacktPublishing/The-Machine-Learning-Solutions-Architect-Handbook/blob/main/Chapter08/code/inference.py:

```
import logging
import os
import sys
import json
import numpy as np
import pandas as pd
import torch
from torch.utils.data import DataLoader, TensorDataset
from transformers import BertForSequenceClassification,
BertTokenizer
...
def model_fn(model_dir):
    ...
    loaded_model = BertForSequenceClassification.from_
```

```
pretrained(model_dir)
    return loaded_model.to(device)


def input_fn(request_body, request_content_type):

    ...
def predict_fn(input_data, model):
    device = torch.device("cuda" if torch.cuda.is_available()
else "cpu")
    model.to(device)
    model.eval()
    ...
    return y
```

Next, we need to modify the `bert-financial-sentiment-launcher.ipynb` file to create the endpoint. You can deploy trained models from the SageMaker `estimator` class directly. Here, however, we want to show you how to deploy a model that's been trained previously, as this is the most likely deployment scenario:

```
from sagemaker.pytorch.model import PyTorchModel
model_data = estimator.model_data
pytorch_model = PyTorchModel(model_data=model_data,
                             role=role,
                             framework_version="1.6",
                             source_dir="code",
                             py_version="py3",
                             entry_point="inference.py")

predictor = pytorch_model.deploy(initial_instance_count=1,
instance_type="ml.m4.xlarge")
```

After the model has been deployed, we can call the model endpoint to generate some predictions:

```
predictor.serializer = sagemaker.serializers.JSONSerializer()
predictor.deserializer = sagemaker.deserializers.
JSONDeserializer()
result = predictor.predict("The market is doing better than
last year")
print("predicted class: ", np.argmax(result, axis=1))
```

Try out different phrases and see if the model predicts the sentiment correctly. You can also access the endpoint's details by navigating to the SageMaker management console and clicking on the endpoint.

To avoid any ongoing costs for the endpoint, let's delete it. Run the following command in a new cell to delete the endpoint:

```
predictor.delete_endpoint()
```

With that, you have finished building the model and finalized your source code. Now, let's persist the source code to the CodeCommit repository.

Saving the source code to the CodeCommit repository

There are several steps involved in committing a changed file to a source code repository:

1. Stage the files for source code control.

2. Commit the changes and provide a change summary and description.

3. Push the changes to the code repository.

Now, let's save a file to the CodeCommit repository. Click on the **Git** icon on the left pane in the Studio environment. You should see a list of files under the **untracked** section. For testing purposes, let's push a single file to the repository for now. Hover over a file until the + sign shows up on the right. Click on the + sign to start tracking the changes and stage the file. To commit the change to the repository, enter a short sentence in the summary text box toward the bottom of the left pane and click on **Commit**. Enter a name and email when prompted. Click on the **Git** icon at the top to push the changes to the repository. To verify this, navigate to the CodeCommit repository and see if a new file has been uploaded.

Congratulations – you have finished building a basic data science environment and used it to train and deploy an NLP model to detect its sentiment. If you don't want to keep this environment to avoid any associated costs, make sure that you shut down any instances of the SageMaker Studio notebooks.

Summary

In this chapter, we discussed how a data science environment can provide a scalable infrastructure for experimentation, model training, and model deployment for testing purposes. You learned about the core architecture components for building a fully managed data science environment using AWS services such as Amazon SageMaker, Amazon ECR, AWS CodeCommit, and Amazon S3. You also practiced setting up a data science environment and trained and deployed an NLP model using both SageMaker Studio Notebook and SageMaker Training Service. At this point, you should be able to talk about the key components of a data science environment, as well as how to build one using AWS services and use it for model building, training, and deployment. In the next chapter, we will talk about how to build an enterprise ML platform for scale through automation.

9
Building an Enterprise ML Architecture with AWS ML Services

To support a large number of fast-moving **machine learning** (**ML**) initiatives, many organizations often decide to build enterprise ML platforms capable of supporting the full ML life cycle, as well as a wide range of usage patterns, which also needs to be automated and scalable. As a practitioner, I have often been asked to provide architecture guidance on how to build enterprise ML platforms. In this chapter, we will discuss the core requirements for enterprise ML platform design and implementation. We will cover topics such as workflow automation, infrastructure scalability, and system monitoring. You will learn about architecture patterns for building technology solutions that automate the end-to-end ML workflow and deployment at scale. We will also dive deep into other core enterprise ML architecture components such as model training, model hosting, the feature store, and the model registry at enterprise scale.

Specifically, we will cover the following topics:

- Key requirements for an ML platform
- Enterprise ML architecture pattern
- Adopting **ML Operations (MLOps)** for an ML workflow
- Hands-on exercise – building an MLOps pipeline on AWS

Governance and security is another important topic for enterprise ML, which we will cover in greater detail in *Chapter 11, ML Governance, Bias, Explainability, and Privacy*. To get started, let's discuss the key requirements for an enterprise ML platform.

Technical requirements

We will continue to use the AWS environment for the hands-on portion of this chapter. All the source code mentioned in this chapter can be found at `https://github.com/PacktPublishing/The-Machine-Learning-Solutions-Architect-Handbook/tree/main/Chapter09`.

Key requirements for an enterprise ML platform

To deliver the business values for ML at scale, organizations need to be able to experiment quickly with different scientific approaches, ML technologies, and datasets at scale. Once the ML models have been trained and validated, they need to be deployed to production with minimal friction. While there are similarities between a traditional enterprise software system and an ML platform, such as scalability and security, an enterprise ML platform poses many unique challenges, such as integrating with the data platform and high-performance computing infrastructure for large-scale model training. Now, let's talk about some specific enterprise ML platform requirements:

- **Support for the end-to-end ML life cycle**: An enterprise ML platform needs to support both data science experimentation and production-grade operations/deployments. In *Chapter 8, Building a Data Science Environment Using AWS ML Services*, we learned about the key architecture components that are needed to build a data science experimentation environment. To enable production-grade operations and deployment, an enterprise ML platform also needs to have architecture components for large-scale model training, model management, feature management, and model hosting with high availability and scalability.

- **Support for continuous integration (CI), continuous training (CT), and continuous deployment (CD)**: An enterprise ML platform provides CI capabilities beyond just testing and validating code and components – it also provides such capabilities for data and models. The CD capability for ML is also more than just deploying a single piece of software; it is the combination of ML models and inference engines. CT is unique to ML, whereby a model is monitored continuously, and automated model retraining can be triggered when data drift or model drift is detected, or training data is changed. **Data drift** is a change in data whereby the characteristics of the data in production are statistically different from the model training data. **Model drift** is a change in model performance whereby the model performance degrades from the performance that was achieved during the model training stage.

- **MLOps support**: An enterprise ML platform provides capabilities for monitoring the statuses, errors, and metrics of different pipeline workflows, processing/training jobs, and model serving engines. It also monitors infrastructure-level stats and resource usages. The automated alert mechanism is also a key component of MLOps. Where possible, automated failure recovery mechanisms should be implemented.

- **Support for different languages and ML frameworks**: An enterprise ML platform allows data scientists and ML engineers to work on different ML problems using the programming language and ML libraries of their choice. It needs to support popular languages such as Python and R, as well as ML packages such as TensorFlow, PyTorch, and scikit-learn.

- **Computing hardware resource management**: Depending on model training and inference needs and cost considerations, an enterprise ML platform needs to support different types of compute hardware, such as CPUs and GPUs. Where applicable, it should also support specialized ML hardware such as AWS's inferentia chip.

- **Integration with other third-party systems and software**: An enterprise ML platform seldomly works in isolation. It needs to provide integration capabilities with other third-party software or platforms, such as workflow orchestration tools, container registries, and code repositories.

- **Authentication and authorization**: An enterprise ML platform needs to provide different levels of authentication and authorization control to govern secure access to data, artifacts, and ML platform resources. This authentication and authorization can be a built-in capability of the ML platform or it can be provided by an external authentication and authorization service.

- **Data encryption**: For regulated industries, such as financial services and healthcare, data encryption is a key requirement. An enterprise ML platform needs to provide capabilities for encrypting data at rest and in transit, often with customer-managed encryptions keys.

- **Artifacts management**: An enterprise ML platform processes datasets and produces different artifacts at the different phases of the ML life cycle. To establish reproducibility and meet governance and compliance requirements, an enterprise ML platform needs to be able to track, manage, and version-control these artifacts.

With that, we have talked about the key requirements of an enterprise ML platform. Next, let's discuss how AWS ML and DevOps services, such as SageMaker, CodePipeline, and Step Functions, can be used to build an enterprise-grade ML platform.

Enterprise ML architecture pattern overview

Building an enterprise ML platform on AWS starts with creating different environments to enable different data science and operations functions. The following diagram shows the core environments that normally make up an enterprise ML platform. From an isolation perspective, in the context of the AWS cloud, each environment in the following diagram is a separate AWS account:

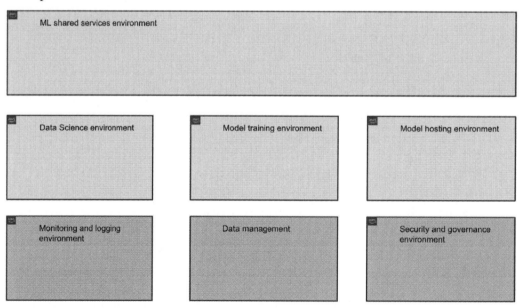

Figure 9.1 – Enterprise ML architecture environments

As we discussed in *Chapter 8, Building a Data Science Environment Using AWS ML Services*, data scientists use the data science environment for experimentation, model building, and tuning. Once these experiments are completed, the data scientists commit their work to the proper code and data repositories. The next step is to train and tune the ML models in a controlled and automated environment using the algorithms, data, and training scripts that were created by the data scientists. This controlled and automated model training process will help ensure consistency, reproducibility, and traceability for model building at scale. The following are the core functionalities and technology options provided by the training, hosting, and shared services environments:

- The model training environment manages the full life cycle of model training, from computing and storage infrastructure resource provisioning to training job monitoring and model persistence. From a technology option perspective, you can build out your training infrastructure using proprietary or open source technology, or you can choose a fully managed ML service, such as the SageMaker training service.

- The model hosting environment is used for serving the trained models behind web service endpoints or in batch inference mode. Model hosting environments can have services such as the SageMaker hosting service, Kubernetes/Kubeflow container-based model serving, Lambda, or EC2-based model serving running different model inference engines. Other supporting services such as the online feature store and API management service can also run in the model hosting environment.

- The shared services environment hosts common services tooling such as workflow orchestration tools, CI/CD tools, code repositories, Docker image repositories, and private library package tools. A central model registry can also run in the shared services environment for model registration and model life cycle management. Service provisioning capabilities, such as creating resources in different environments through **Infrastructure as Code (IaC)** or APIs, also run out of this environment. Any service ticketing tools, such as ServiceNow, and service provisioning tools, such as Service Catalog, can also be hosted in this environment.

In addition to the core ML environments, there are other dependent environments, such as security, governance, monitoring, and logging, that are required in the enterprise ML platform:

- The security and governance environment centrally manages authentication services, user credentials, and data encryption keys. Security audit and reporting processes also run in this environment. Native AWS services, such as AWS IAM, AWS KMS, and AWS Config, can be used for various security and governance functions.

- The monitoring and logging environment centrally aggregates monitoring and logging data from other environments for further processing and reporting. Custom dashboarding and alerting mechanisms are normally developed to provide easy access to key metrics and alerts from the underlying monitoring and logging data.

With that, you have had an overview of the core building blocks of an enterprise ML platform. Next, let's dive deep into several core areas. Note that there are different patterns and services we can follow to build an ML platform on AWS. In this chapter, we will cover one of the enterprise patterns.

Model training environment

Within an enterprise, a model training environment is a controlled environment with well-defined processes and policies on how it is used and who can use them. Normally, it should be an automated environment that's managed by an MLOps team, though it can be self-service enabled for direct usage by data scientists.

Automated model training and tuning are the core capabilities of the model training environment. To support a broad range of use cases, a model training environment needs to support different ML and **deep learning** frameworks, training patterns (such as single-node and distributed training), and hardware (different CPUs and GPUs).

The model training environment manages the life cycle of the model training process. This can include authentication and authorization, infrastructure provisioning, data movement, data preprocessing, ML library deployment, training loop management and monitoring, model persistence and registry, training job management, and lineage tracking. From a security perspective, the training environment needs to provide security capabilities for different isolation requirements, such as network isolation, job isolation, and artifacts isolation. To assist with operational support, a model training environment also needs to be able to training status logging, metrics reporting, and training job monitoring and alerting.

Next, let's learn how the SageMaker training service can be used in a controlled model training environment in an enterprise setting.

Model training engine

The SageMaker training service provides built-in modeling training capabilities for a range of ML/DL libraries. In addition, you can bring your own Docker containers for customized model training needs. The following are a subset of supported options for the SageMaker Python SDK:

- **Training TensorFlow models**: SageMaker provides a built-in training container for TensorFlow models. The following code sample shows how to train a TensorFlow model using the built-in container through the TensorFlow estimator API:

```
from sagemaker.tensorflow import TensorFlow
tf_estimator = TensorFlow(
    entry_point="<Training script name>",
    role= "<AWS IAM role>",
    instance_count=<Number of instances),
    instance_type="<Instance type>",
    framework_version="<TensorFlow version>",
    py_version="<Python version>",)
tf_estimator.fit("<Training data location>")
```

- **Training PyTorch models**: SageMaker provides a built-in training container for the PyTorch model. The following code sample shows how to train a PyTorch model using the PyTorch estimator:

```
from sagemaker.pytorch import PyTorch
pytorch_estimator = PyTorch(
    entry_point="<Training script name>",
    role= "<AWS IAM role>",
    instance_count=<Number of instances),
    instance_type="<Instance type>",
    framework_version="<PyTorch version>",
    py_version="<Python version>",)
pytorch_estimator.fit("<Training data location>")
```

- **Training XGBoost models**: XGBoost training is also supported via a built-in container. The following code shows the syntax for training a XGBoost model using the XGBoost estimator:

```
from sagemaker.xgboost.estimator import XGBoost
xgb_estimator = XGBoost(
```

```
entry_point=" <Training script name>",
hyperparameters=<List of hyperparameters>,
role=<AWS IAM role>,
instance_count=<Number of instances>,
instance_type="<Instance type>",
framework_version="<Xgboost version>")
xgb_estimator.fit("<train data location>")
```

- **Training scikit-learn models**: The following code sample shows how to train a scikit-learn model using the built-in container:

```
from sagemaker.sklearn.estimator import SKLearn
sklearn_estimator = SKLearn(
  entry_point=" <Training script name>",
  hyperparameters=<List of hyperparameters>,
  role=<AWS IAM role>,
  instance_count=<Number of instances>,
  instance_type="<Instance type>",
    framework_version="<sklearn version>")
Sklearn_estimator.fit("<training data>")
```

- **Training models using custom containers**: You can also build a custom training container and use the SageMaker training service for model training. See the following code for an example:

```
from sagemaker.estimator import Estimator
custom_estimator = Estimator (
  Custom_training_img,
  role=<AWS IAM role>,
  instance_count=<Number of instances>,
  instance_type="<Instance type>")
custom_estimator.fit("<training data location>")
```

In addition to using the SageMaker Python SDK to kick off training, you can also use the boto3 library and SageMaker CLI commands to start training jobs.

Automation support

The SageMaker training service is exposed through a set of APIs and can be automated by integrating with external applications or workflow tools, such as Airflow and AWS Step Functions. For example, it can be one of the steps in an Airflow-based pipeline for an end-to-end ML workflow. Some workflow tools, such as Airflow and AWS Step Functions, also provide SageMaker-specific connectors to interact with the SageMaker training service more seamlessly. The SageMaker training service also provides Kubernetes operators, so it can be integrated and automated as part of the Kubernetes application flow. The following sample code shows how to kick off a training job using the low-level API via the AWS `boto3` SDK:

```
import boto3
client = boto3.client('sagemaker')
response = client.create_training_job(
    TrainingJobName='<job name>',
    HyperParameters={<list of parameters and value>},
    AlgorithmSpecification={...},
    RoleArn='<AWS IAM Role>',
    InputDataConfig=[...],
    OutputDataConfig={...},
    ResourceConfig={...},
    ...
}
```

Regarding using Airflow as the workflow tool, the following sample shows how to use the Airflow SageMaker operator as part of the workflow definition. Here, `train_config` contains training configuration details, such as the training estimator, training instance type and number, and training data location:

```
import airflow
from airflow import DAG
from airflow.contrib.operators.sagemaker_training_operator
import SageMakerTrainingOperator
default_args = {
    'owner': 'myflow',
    'start_date': '2021-01-01'
}
dag = DAG('tensorflow_training', default_args=default_args,
          schedule_interval='@once')
```

```
train_op = SageMakerTrainingOperator(
    task_id='tf_training',
    config=train_config,
    wait_for_completion=True,
    dag=dag)
```

SageMaker also has a built-in workflow automation tool called **SageMaker Pipelines**. A training step can be created using the SageMaker **TrainingStep** API and become part of the larger SageMaker Pipelines workflow.

Model training life cycle management

SageMaker training manages the life cycle of the model training process. It uses AWS IAM as the mechanism to authenticate and authorize access to its functions. Once authorized, it provides the desired infrastructure, deploys the software stacks for the different model training requirements, moves the data from sources to training nodes, and kicks off the training job. Once the training job has been completed, the model artifacts are saved into an S3 output bucket and the infrastructure is torn down. For lineage tracing, model training metadata such as source datasets, model training containers, hyperparameters, and model output locations are captured. Any logging from the training job runs is saved in CloudWatch Logs, and system metrics such as CPU and GPU utilization are captured in the CloudWatch metrics.

Depending on the overall end-to-end ML platform architecture, a model training environment can also host services for data preprocessing, model validation, and model training postprocessing, as those are important steps in an end-to-end ML flow. There are multiple technology options available for this, such as the SageMaker Processing service and AWS Lambda.

Model hosting environment deep dive

An enterprise-grade model hosting environment needs to support a broad range of ML frameworks in a secure, performant, and scalable way. It should come with a list of pre-built inference engines that can serve common models out of the box behind a **RESTful API** or via the **gRPC protocol**. It also needs to provide flexibility to host custom-built inference engines for unique requirements. Users should also have access to different hardware devices, such as CPU, GPU, and purpose-built chips, for the different inference needs.

Some model inference patterns demand more complex inference graphs, such as traffic split, request transformations, or model ensemble support. A model hosting environment can provide this capability as an out-of-the-box feature or provide technology options for building custom inference graphs. Other common model hosting capabilities include **concept drift detection** and **model performance drift detection**. Concept drift occurs when the statistical characteristics of the production data deviate from the data that's used for model training. An example of concept drift is the mean and standard deviation of a feature changing significantly in production from that of the training dataset.

Components in a model hosting environment can participate in an automation workflow through its API, scripting, or IaC deployment (such as AWS CloudFormation). For example, a RESTful endpoint can be deployed using a CloudFormation template or by invoking its API as part of an automated workflow.

From a security perspective, the model hosting environment needs to provide authentication and authorization control to manage access to both the **control plane** (management functions) and **data plane** (model endpoints). The accesses and operations that are performed against the hosting environments should be logged for auditing purposes. For operations support, a hosting environment needs to enable status logging and system monitoring to support system observability and problem troubleshooting.

The SageMaker hosting service is a fully managed model hosting service. Similar to KFServing and Seldon Core, which we reviewed earlier in this book, the SageMaker hosting service is also a multi-framework model serving service. Next, let's take a closer look at its various capabilities for enterprise-grade model hosting.

Inference engine

SageMaker provides built-in inference engines for multiple ML frameworks, including scikit-learn, XGBoost, TensorFlow, PyTorch, and Spark ML. SageMaker supplies these built-in inference engines as Docker containers. To stand up an API endpoint to serve a model, you just need to provide the model artifacts and infrastructure configuration. The following is a list of model serving options:

- **Serving TensorFlow models**: SageMaker uses TensorFlow Serving as the inference engine for TensorFlow models. The following code sample shows how to deploy a TensorFlow Serving model using the SageMaker hosting service:

```
from sagemaker.tensorflow.serving import Model
tensorflow_model = Model(
    model_data=<S3 location of the Spark ML model
artifacts>,
    role=<AWS IAM role>,
```

```
      framework_version=<tensorflow version>
)
tensorflow_model.deploy(
   initial_instance_count=<instance count>, instance_
type=<instance type>
)
```

- **Serving PyTorch models**: SageMaker hosting uses TorchServe under the hood to serve PyTorch models. The following code sample shows how to deploy a PyTorch model:

```
from sagemaker.pytorch.model import PyTorchModel

pytorch_model = PyTorchModel(
    model_data=<S3 location of the PyTorch model
artifacts>,
    role=<AWS IAM role>,
    framework_version=<PyTorch version>
)
pytorch_model.deploy(
    initial_instance_count=<instance count>, instance_
type=<instance type>
)
```

- **Serving Spark ML models**: For Spark ML-based models, SageMaker uses MLeap as the backend to serve Spark ML models. These Spark ML models need to be serialized into MLeap format. The following code sample shows how to deploy a Spark ML model using the SageMaker hosting service:

```
import sagemaker
from sagemaker.sparkml.model import SparkMLModel
sparkml_model = SparkMLModel(
    model_data=<S3 location of the Spark ML model
artifacts>,
    role=<AWS IAM role>,
    sagemaker_session=sagemaker.Session(),
    name=<Model name>,
    env={"SAGEMAKER_SPARKML_SCHEMA": <schema_json>}
)
```

```
sparkml_model.deploy(
    initial_instance_count=<instance count>, instance_
type=<instance type>
)
```

- **Serving XGboost models**: SageMaker provides an XGBoost model server for serving trained XGBoost models. Under the hood, it uses Nginx, Gunicorn, and Flask as part of the model serving architecture. The entry Python script loads the trained XGBoost model and can optionally perform pre- and post-data processing:

```
from sagemaker.xgboost.model import XGBoostModel
xgboost_model = XGBoostModel(
    model_data=<S3 location of the Xgboost ML model
artifacts>,
    role=<AWS IAM role>,
    entry_point=<entry python script>,
    framework_version=<xgboost version>
)
xgboost_model.deploy(
    instance_type=<instance type>,
    initial_instance_count=<instance count>
)
```

- **Serving scikit-learn models**: SageMaker provides a built-in serving container for serving scikit-learn-based models. The technology stack is similar to the one for the Xgboost model server:

```
from sagemaker.sklearn.model import SKLearnModel
sklearn_model = SKLearnModel(
    model_data=<S3 location of the Xgboost ML model
artifacts>,
    role=<AWS IAM role>,
    entry_point=<entry python script>,
    framework_version=<scikit-learn version>
)
sklearn_model.deploy(instance_type=<instance type>,
    initial_instance_count=<instance count>)
```

- **Serving models with custom containers**: For custom-created inference containers, you can follow similar syntax to deploy the model. The main difference is that a custom inference container image's uri needs to be provided. You can find detailed documentation on building a custom inference container at `https://docs.aws.amazon.com/sagemaker/latest/dg/adapt-inference-container.html`:

```
from sagemaker.model import Model
custom_model = Model(
    Image_uri = <custom model inference container image uri>,
    model_data=<S3 location of the ML model artifacts>,
    role=<AWS IAM role>,
    framework_version=<scikit-learn version>
)
custom_model.deploy(instance_type=<instance type>,
    initial_instance_count=<instance count>)
```

SageMaker hosting provides an inference pipeline feature that allows you to create a linear sequence of containers (up to 15) to perform custom data processing before and after invoking a model for predictions. SageMaker hosting can support traffic splits between multiple versions of a model for A/B testing.

SageMaker hosting can be provisioned using an AWS CloudFormation template. There is also support for the AWS CLI for scripting automation, and it can be integrated into custom applications via its API. The following are some code samples for different endpoint deployment automation methods:

- The following is a CloudFormation code sample for SageMaker endpoint deployment. You can find the complete code at `https://github.com/PacktPublishing/The-Machine-Learning-Solutions-Architect-Handbook/blob/main/Chapter09/sagemaker_hosting.yaml`:

```
Description: "Model hosting cloudformation template"
Resources:
  Endpoint:
    Type: "AWS::SageMaker::Endpoint"
    Properties:
      EndpointConfigName:
        !GetAtt EndpointConfig.EndpointConfigName
  EndpointConfig:
```

```
      Type: "AWS::SageMaker::EndpointConfig"
      Properties:
        ProductionVariants:
          - InitialInstanceCount: 1
            InitialVariantWeight: 1.0
            InstanceType: ml.t2.large
            ModelName: !GetAtt Model.ModelName
            VariantName: !GetAtt Model.ModelName
    Model:
      Type: "AWS::SageMaker::Model"
      Properties:
        PrimaryContainer:
          Image: <container uri>
          ExecutionRoleArn: !GetAtt ExecutionRole.Arn
  ...
```

- The following is an AWS CLI sample for SageMaker endpoint deployment:

```
Aws sagemaker create-model --model-name <value>
--execution-role-arn <value>

aws sagemaker Create-endpoint-config --endpoint-config-
name <value> --production-variants <value>

aws sagemaker Create-endpoint --endpoint-name <value>
--endpoint-config-name <value>
```

If the built-in inference engines do not meet your requirements, you can also bring your own Docker container to serve your ML models.

Authentication and security control

The SageMaker hosting service uses AWS IAM as the mechanism to control access to its control plane APIs (for example, an API for creating an endpoint) and data plane APIs (for example, an API for invoking a hosted model endpoint). If you need to support other authentication methods for the data plane API, such as **OpenID Connect (OIDC)**, you can put a proxy service as the frontend to manage user authentication. A common pattern is to use AWS API Gateway to frontend the SageMaker API for custom authentication management, as well as other API management features such as metering and throttling management.

Monitoring and logging

SageMaker provides out-of-the-box monitoring and logging capabilities to assist with support operations. It monitors both system resource metrics (for example, CPU/GPU utilization) and model invocation metrics (for example, the number of invocations, model latencies, and failures). These monitoring metrics and any model processing logs are captured by AWS CloudWatch metrics and CloudWatch Logs.

Adopting MLOps for ML workflows

Similar to the DevOps practice, which has been widely adopted for the traditional software development and deployment process, the MLOps practice is intended to streamline the building and deployment processes of ML pipelines and improve the collaborations between data scientists/ML engineers, data engineering, and the operations team. Specifically, an MLOps practice is intended to deliver the following main benefits in an end-to-end ML life cycle:

- **Process consistency**: The MLOps practice aims to create consistency in the ML model building and deployment process. A consistent process improves the efficiency of the ML workflow and ensures a high degree of certainty in the input and output of the ML workflow.

- **Tooling and process reusability**: One of the core objectives of the MLOps practice is to create reusable technology tooling and templates for faster adoption and deployment of new ML use cases. These can include common tools such as code and library repositories, package and image building tools, pipeline orchestration tools, the model registry, as well as common infrastructure for model training and model deployment. From a reusable template perspective, these can include common reusable scripts for Docker image builds, workflow orchestration definitions, and CloudFormation scripts for model building and model deployment.

- **Model building reproducibility**: ML is highly iterative and can involve a large number of experimentations and model training runs using different datasets, algorithms, and hyperparameters. An MLOps process needs to capture all the data inputs, source code, and artifacts that are used to build an ML model and establish model lineage from this input data, code, and artifacts for the final models. This is important for both experiment tracking as well as governance and control purposes.

- **Delivery scalability**: An MLOps process and the associated tooling enable a large number of ML pipelines to run in parallel for high delivery throughputs. Different ML project teams can use the standard MLOps processes and common tools independently without creating conflicts from a resource contention, environment isolation, and governance perspective.

- **Process and operations audibility**: MLOps enables greater audibility into the process and the audibility of ML pipelines. This includes capturing the details of machine pipeline executions, dependencies, and lineage across different steps, job execution statuses, model training and deployment details, approval tracking, and actions that are performed by human operators.

Now that we are familiar with the intended goals and benefits of the MLOps practice, let's look at the specific operational process and concrete technology architecture of MLOps on AWS.

Components of the MLOps architecture

One of the most important MLOps concepts is the automation pipeline, which executes a sequence of tasks, such as data processing, model training, and model deployment. This pipeline can be a linear sequence of steps or a more complex DAG with parallel execution for multiple tasks. An MLOps architecture also has several repositories for storing different assets and metadata as part of pipeline executions. The following diagram shows the core components and tasks involved in an MLOps operation:

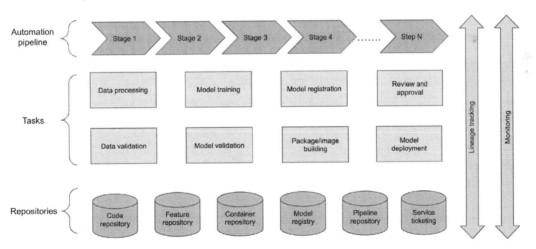

Figure 9.2 – MLOps components

A **code repository** in an MLOps architecture not only serves as a source code control mechanism for data scientists and engineers – it is also the triggering mechanism to kick off different pipeline executions. For example, when a data scientist checks an updated training script into the code repository, a model training pipeline execution can be triggered.

A **feature repository** stores reusable ML features and can be the target of a data processing/feature engineering job. The features from the feature repository can be a part of the training datasets where applicable. The feature repository is also used as a part of the model inference request.

A **container repository** stores the container images that are used for data processing tasks, model training jobs, and model inference engines. It is usually the target of the container building pipeline.

A **model registry** keeps an inventory of trained models, along with all the metadata associated with the model, such as its algorithm, hyperparameters, model metrics, and training dataset location. It also maintains the status of the model life cycle, such as its deployment approval status.

A **pipeline repository** maintains the definition of automation pipelines and the statuses of different pipeline job executions.

In an enterprise setting, a task ticket also needs to be created when different tasks, such as model deployment, are performed, so that these actions can be tracked in a common enterprise ticketing management system. To support audit requirements, the lineage of different pipeline tasks and their associated artifacts need to be tracked.

Another critical component of the MLOps architecture is **monitoring**. In general, you want to monitor items such as the pipeline's execution status, model training status, and model endpoint status. Model endpoint monitoring can also include system/ resource performance monitoring, model statistical metrics monitoring, drift and outlier monitoring, and model explainability monitoring. Alerts can be triggered on certain execution statuses to invoke human or automation actions that are needed.

AWS provides multiple technology options for implementing an MLOps architecture. The following diagram shows where these technology services fit in an enterprise MLOps architecture:

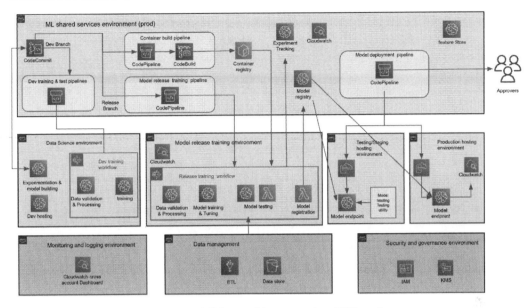

Figure 9.3 – MLOps architecture using AWS services

As we mentioned earlier, the shared service environment hosts common tools for pipeline management and execution, as well as common repositories such as code repositories and model registries.

Here, we use AWS CodePipeline to orchestrate the overall CI/CD pipeline. AWS CodePipeline is a continuous delivery service that integrates natively with different code repositories such as AWS CodeCommit and Bitbucket. It can source files from the code repository and make them available to downstream tasks such as building containers using the AWS CodeBuild service, or training models in the model training environment. You can create different pipelines to meet different needs. A pipeline can be triggered on-demand via an API or the CodePipeline management console, or it can be triggered by code changes in a code repository. Depending on your requirements, you can create different pipelines. In the proceeding diagram, we can see four example pipelines:

- A container build pipeline for building different container images.

- A model training pipeline for training a model for release.

- A model deployment pipeline for deploying trained models to production.

- A development, training, and testing pipeline for model training and deployment testing in a data science environment.

A code repository is one of the most essential components in an MLOps environment. It is not only used by data scientists/ML engineers and other engineers to persist code artifacts, but it also serves as a triggering mechanism for a CI/CD pipeline. This means that when a data scientist/ML engineer commits a code change, it can automatically kick off a CI/CD pipeline. For example, if the data scientist makes a change to the model training script and wants to test the automated training pipeline in the development environment, he/she can commit the code to a development branch to kick off a model training pipeline in the dev environment. When it is ready for production release deployment, the data scientist can commit/merge the code to a release branch to kick off the production release pipelines.

In this MLOps architecture, we use AWS **Elastic Container Registry (ECR)** as the central container registry service. ECR is used to store containers for data processing, model training, and model inference. You can tag the container images to indicate different life cycle statuses, such as development or production.

The **SageMaker model registry** is used as the central model repository. The central model repository can reside in the shared service environment, so it can be accessed by different projects. All the models that go through the formal training and deployment cycles should be managed and tracked in the central model repository.

SageMaker Feature Store provides a common feature repository for reusable features to be used by different projects. It can reside in the shared services environment or be part of the data platform. Features are normally pre-calculated in a data management environment and sent to SageMaker Feature Store for offline model training in the model training environment, as well as online inferences by the different model hosting environments.

SageMaker Experiments is used to track experiments and trials. The metadata and artifacts that are generated by the different components in a pipeline execution can be tracked in SageMaker Experiments. For example, the processing step in a pipeline can contain metadata such as the locations of input data and processed data, while the model training step can contain metadata such as the algorithm and hyperparameters for training, model metrics, and the location of the model artifact. This metadata can be used to compare the different runs of model training, and they can also be used to establish model lineage.

Monitoring and logging

The ML platform presents some unique challenges in terms of monitoring. In addition to monitoring common software system-related metrics and statuses, such as infrastructure utilization and processing status, an ML platform also needs to monitor model and data-specific metrics and performances. Also, unlike traditional system-level monitoring, which is fairly straightforward to understand, the opaqueness of ML models makes it inherently difficult to understand the system. Now, let's take a closer look at the three main areas of monitoring for an ML platform.

Model training monitoring

Model training monitoring provides visibility into the training progress and helps identify training bottlenecks and error conditions during the training process. It enables operational processes such as training job progress reporting and response, model training performance progress evaluation and response, training problem troubleshooting, and data and model bias detection and model interpretability and response. Specifically, we want to monitor the following key metrics and conditions during model training:

- **General system and resource utilization and error metrics**: These provide visibility into how the infrastructure resources (such as CPU, GPU, disk I/O, and memory) are utilized for model training. These can help with making decisions on provisioning infrastructure for the different model training needs.

- **Training job events and status**: This provides visibility into the progress of a training job, such as job starting, running, completion, and failure details.

- **Model training metrics**: These are model training metrics such as loss curve and accuracy reports to help you understand the model's performance.

- **Bias detection metrics and model explainability reporting**: These metrics help you understand if there is any bias in the training datasets or machine learning models. Model explainability can also be monitored and reported to help you understand high-importance features versus low-importance features.

- **Model training bottlenecks and training issues**: These provide visibility into training issues such as vanishing gradients, poor weights initialization, and overfitting to help determine the required data, algorithmic, and training configuration changes. Metrics such as CPU and I/O bottlenecks, uneven load balancing, and low GPU utilization can help determine infrastructure configuration changes for more efficient model training.

There are multiple native AWS services for building out a model training architecture on AWS. The following diagram shows an example architecture for building a monitoring solution for a SageMaker-based model training environment:

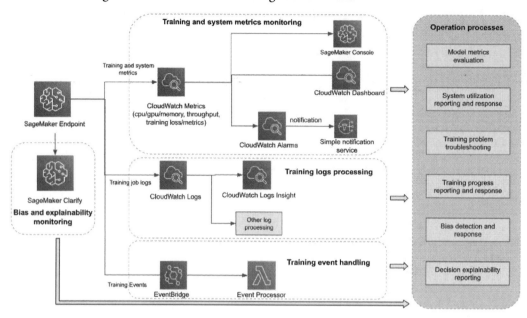

Figure 9.4 – Model training monitoring architecture

This architecture lets you monitor training and system metrics and perform log capture and processing, training event capture and processing, and model training bias and explainability reporting. It helps enable operation processes, such as training progress and status reporting, model metric evaluation, system resource utilization reporting and response, training problem troubleshooting, bias detection, and model decision explainability.

During model training, SageMaker can emit model training metrics, such as training loss and accuracy, to AWS CloudWatch to help with model training evaluation. AWS CloudWatch is the AWS monitoring and observability service. It collects metrics and logs from other AWS services and provides dashboards for visualizing and analyzing these metrics and logs. System utilization metrics (such as CPU/GPU/memory utilization) are also reported to CloudWatch for analysis to help you understand any infrastructure constraints or under-utilization. CloudWatch alarms can be created for a single metric or composite metrics to automate notifications or responses. For example, you can create alarms on low CPU/GPU utilization to help proactively identify sub-optimal hardware configuration for the training job. And when an alarm is triggered, it can send automated notifications (such as SMS and emails) to support for review via AWS **Simple Notification Service (SNS)**.

You can use CloudWatch Logs to collect, monitor, and analyze the logs that are emitted by your training jobs. You can use these captured logs to understand the progress of your training jobs and identify errors and patterns to help troubleshoot any model training problems. For example, the CloudWatch Logs logs might contain errors such as insufficient GPU memory to run model training or permission issues when accessing specific resources to help you troubleshoot model training problems. By default, CloudWatch Logs provides a UI tool called *CloudWatch Logs Insights* for interactively analyzing logs using a purpose-built query language. Alternatively, these logs can also be forwarded to an Elasticsearch cluster for analysis and querying. These logs can be aggregated in a designated logging and monitoring account to centrally manage log access and analysis.

SageMaker training jobs can also send events, such as a training job status changing from running to complete. You can create automated notification and response mechanisms based on these different events. For example, you can send out notifications to data scientists when a training job is either completed successfully or failed, along with a failure reason. You can also automate responses to these failures to the different statuses, such as model retraining on a particular failure condition.

The **SageMaker Clarify** component can detect data and model bias and provide model explainability reporting on the trained model. You can access bias and model explainability reports inside the SageMaker Studio UI or SageMaker APIs.

The **SageMaker Debugger** component can detect model training issues such as non-converging conditions, resource utilization bottlenecks, overfitting, vanishing gradients, or conditions where the gradients become too small for efficient parameter updates. Alerts can be sent when training anomalies are found.

Model endpoint monitoring

Model endpoint monitoring provides visibility into the performance of the modeling serving infrastructure, as well as model-specific metrics such as data drift, model drift, and inference explainability. The following are some of the key metrics for model endpoint monitoring:

- **General system and resource utilization and error metrics**: These provide visibility into how the infrastructure resources (such as CPU, GPU, and memory) are utilized for model servicing. These can help with making decisions on provisioning infrastructure for the different model serving needs.

- **Data statistics monitoring metrics**: The statistical nature of data could change over time, which can result in degraded ML model performance from the original benchmarks. These metrics can include basic statistics deviations such as mean and standard changes, as well as data distribution changes.

- **Model quality monitoring metrics**: These model quality metrics provide visibility into model performance deviation from the original benchmark. These metrics can include regression metrics (such as MAE and RMSE) and classification metrics (such as confusion matrix, F1, precision, recall, and accuracy).

- **Model inference explainability**: This provides model explainability on a per prediction basis to help you understand what features had the most influence on the decision that was made by the prediction.

- **Model bias monitoring metrics**: Similar to bias detection for training, the bias metrics help us understand model bias at inference time.

The model monitoring architecture relies on many of the same AWS services, including CloudWatch, EventBridge, and SNS. The following diagram shows an architecture pattern for a SageMaker-based model monitoring solution:

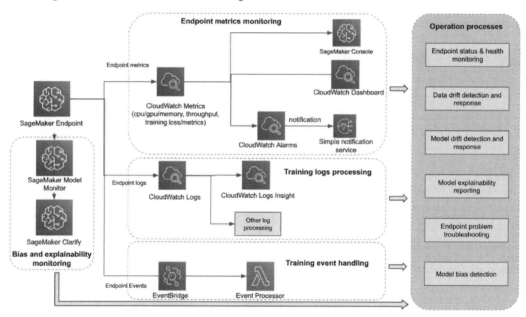

Figure 9.5 – Model endpoint monitoring architecture

This architecture works similarly to the model training architecture. **CloudWatch metrics** capture endpoint metrics such as CPU/GPU utilization and model invocation metrics (number of invocations and errors) and model latencies. These metrics help with operations such as hardware optimization and endpoint scaling.

CloudWatch Logs captures logs that are emitted by the model serving endpoint to help us understand the status and troubleshoot technical problems.

Similarly, endpoint events, such as the status changing from **Creating** to **InService**, can help you build automated notification pipelines to kick off corrective actions or provide status updates.

In addition to system and status-related monitoring, this architecture also supports data and model-specific monitoring through a combination of SageMaker Model Monitor and SageMaker Clarify. Specifically, SageMaker Model Monitor can help you monitor data drift and model quality.

For data drift, SageMaker Monitor can use the training dataset to create baseline statistics metrics such as standard deviation, mean, max, min, and data distribution for the dataset features. It uses these metrics and other data characteristics, such as data types and completeness, to establish constraints. Then, it captures the input data in the production environment, calculates the metrics, compares them with the baseline metrics/constraints, and reports baseline drifts. Model Monitor can also report data quality issues such as incorrect data types and missing values. Data drift metrics can be sent to CloudWatch metrics for visualization and analysis, and CloudWatch Alarms can be configured to trigger a notification or automated response when a metric crosses a predefined threshold.

For model quality monitoring, it creates baseline metrics (such as MAE for regression and accuracy for classification) using the baseline dataset, which contains both predictions and true labels. Then, it captures the predictions in production, ingests ground truth labels, and merges the ground truth with the predictions to calculate various regression and classification metrics before comparing those with the baseline metrics. Similar to data drift metrics, model quality metrics can be sent to CloudWatch Metrics for analysis and visualization, and CloudWatch Alarms can be configured for automated notifications and/or responses. The following diagram shows how SageMaker Model Monitor works:

Model Deployment and Monitoring for Drift

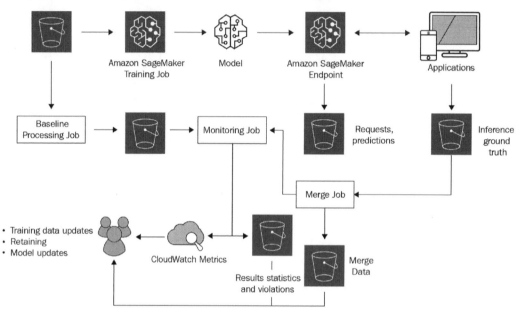

Figure 9.6 – SageMaker Model Monitor process flow

For bias detection, SageMaker Clarify can monitor bias metrics for deployed models continuously and raises alerts through CloudWatch when a metric crosses a threshold. We will cover bias detection in detail in *Chapter 11, ML Governance, Bias, Explainability, and Privacy.*

ML pipeline monitoring

The ML pipeline's execution needs to be monitored for statuses and errors, so corrective actions can be taken as needed. During a pipeline execution, there are pipeline-level statuses/events as well as stage-level and action-level statuses/events. You can use these events and statuses to understand the progress of each pipeline and stage and get alerted when something is wrong. The following diagram shows how AWS CodePipeline, CodeBuild, and CodeCommit can work with CloudWatch, CloudWatch Logs, and EventBridge for general status monitoring and reporting, as well as problem troubleshooting:

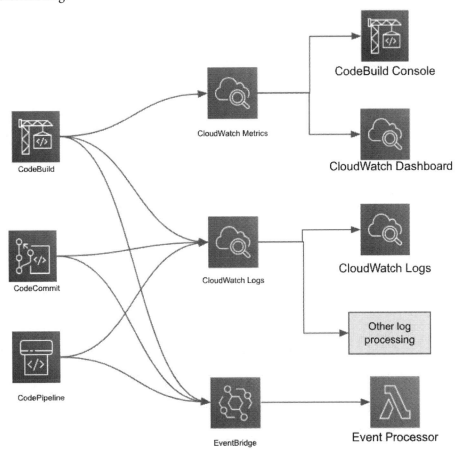

Figure 9.7 – ML CI/CD pipeline monitoring architecture

CodeBuild can send metrics, such as `SuceededBuilds`, `FailedBuilds`, and `Duration` metrics. These CodeBuild metrics can be accessed through both the CodeBuild console and the CloudWatch dashboard.

CodeBuild, CodeCommit, and CodePipeline can all emit events to EventBridge to report detailed status changes and trigger custom event processing, such as notifications, or log the events to another data repository for event archiving. All three services can send detailed logs to CloudWatch Logs to support operations such as troubleshooting or detailed error reporting.

Step Functions also provides a list of monitoring metrics to CloudWatch, such as execution metrics (such as execution failure, success, abort, and timeout) and activity metrics (such as activity started, scheduled, and succeeded). You can view these metrics in the management console and set a threshold to set up alerts.

Service provisioning management

Another key component of enterprise-scale ML platform management is **service provisioning management**. For large-scale service provisioning and deployment, an automated and controlled process should be adopted. Here, we will focus on provisioning the ML platform itself, not provisioning AWS accounts and networking, which should be established as the base environment for ML platform provisioning in advance. For ML platform provisioning, there are the following two main provisioning tasks:

- **Data science environment provisioning**: Provisioning the data science environment for data scientists mainly includes provisioning data science and data management tools, storage for experimentation, as well as access entitlement for data sources and pre-built ML automation pipelines.

- **ML automation pipeline provisioning**: ML automation pipelines need to be provisioned in advance for data scientists and MLOps engineers to use them to automate different tasks such as container build, model training, and model deployment.

There are multiple technical approaches to automating service provisioning on AWS, such as using provisioning shell scripts, CloudFormation scripts, and AWS Service Catalog. With shell scripts, you can sequentially call the different AWS CLI commands in a script to provision different components, such as creating a SageMaker notebook. CloudFormation is the IaC service for infrastructure deployment on AWS. With CloudFormation, you create templates that describe the desired resources and dependencies that can be launched as a single stack. When the template is executed, all the resources and dependencies specified in the stack will be deployed automatically. The following code shows the template for deploying a SageMaker Studio domain:

```
Type: AWS::SageMaker::Domain
Properties:
  AppNetworkAccessType: String
```

```
AuthMode: String
DefaultUserSettings:
   UserSettings
DomainName: String
KmsKeyId: String
SubnetIds:
   - String
Tags:
   - Tag
VpcId: String
```

AWS Service Catalog allows you to create different IT products to be deployed on AWS. These IT products can include SageMakenotebooks, a CodeCommit repository, and CodePipeline workflow definitions. AWS Service Catalog uses CloudFormation templates to describe IT products. With Service Catalog, administrators create IT products with CloudFormation templates, organize these products by product portfolio, and entitle end users with access. The end users then access the products from the Service Catalog product portfolio. The following diagram shows the flow of creating a Service Catalog product and launching the product from the Service Catalog service:

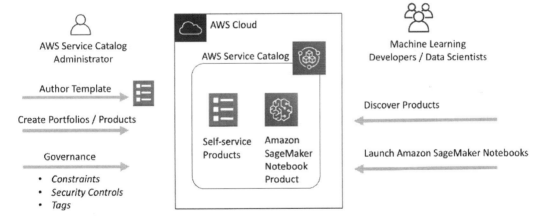

Figure 9.8 – Service Catalog workflow

For large-scale and governed IT product management, Service Catalog is the recommended approach. Service Catalog supports multiple deployment options, including single AWS account deployments and hub-and-spoke cross-account deployments. A hub-and-spoke deployment allows you to centrally manage all the products and make them available in different accounts. In our enterprise ML reference architecture, we use the hub-and-spoke architecture to support the provisioning of data science environments and ML pipelines, as shown in the following diagram:

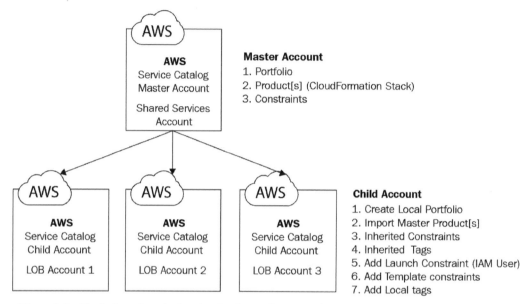

Figure 9.9 – The hub-and-spoke Service Catalog architecture for enterprise ML product management

In the preceding architecture, we set up the central portfolio in the shared services account. All the products, such as creating new Studio domains, new Studio user profiles, CodePipeline definitions, and training pipeline definitions, are centrally managed in the central hub account. Some products are shared with the different data science accounts to create data science environments for data scientists and teams. Some other products are shared with model training accounts for standing up ML training pipelines.

With that, we have talked about the core components of an enterprise-grade ML platform. Next, let's get hands-on and build a pipeline to automate model training and deployment.

Hands-on exercise – building an MLOps pipeline on AWS

In this hands-on exercise, you will get hands on with building a simplified version of the enterprise MLOps pipeline. For simplicity, we will not be using the multi-account architecture for the enterprise pattern. Instead, we will build several core functions in a single AWS account. The following diagram shows what you will be building:

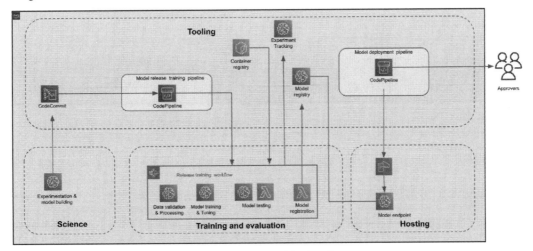

Figure 9.10 – Architecture of the hands-on exercise

At a high level, you will create two pipelines using CloudFormation: one for model training and one for model deployment.

Creating a CloudFormation template for the ML training pipeline

In this section, we will create two CloudFormation templates that do the following:

- The first template creates AWS Step Functions for an ML model training workflow that performs data processing, model training, and model registration. This will be a component of the training pipeline.

- The second template creates a CodePipeline ML model training pipeline definition with two stages:

  I.   A **source stage**, which listens to changes in a CodeCommit repository to kick off the execution of the Step Functions workflow that we created

  II. A **deployment stage**, which kicks off the execution of the ML model training workflow

Now, let's get started with the CloudFormation template for the Step Functions workflow:

1. Create a Step Functions workflow execution role called `AmazonSageMaker-StepFunctionsWorkflowExecutionRole`. Then, create and attach the following IAM policy to it. This role will be used by the Step Functions workflow to provide permission to invoke the various SageMaker APIs. Take note of the ARN of the newly created IAM role as you will need it for the next step. You can find the complete code sample at `https://github.com/PacktPublishing/The-Machine-Learning-Solutions-Architect-Handbook/blob/main/Chapter09/AmazonSageMaker-StepFunctionsWorkflowExecutionRole-policy.json`:

```
{
    "Version": "2012-10-17",
    "Statement": [
        {
            "Effect": "Allow",
            "Action": [
                "sagemaker:CreateModel",
                "sagemaker:DeleteEndpointConfig",
                "sagemaker:DescribeTrainingJob",
                "sagemaker:CreateEndpoint",
                "sagemaker:StopTrainingJob",
                "sagemaker:CreateTrainingJob",
                "sagemaker:UpdateEndpoint",
                "sagemaker:CreateEndpointConfig",
                "sagemaker:DeleteEndpoint"
            ],
            "Resource": [
                "arn:aws:sagemaker:*:*:*"
            ]
```

```
        },
    ...
    }
```

2. Copy and save the following code block to a file locally and name it `training_workflow.yaml`. You can find the complete file at `https://github.com/PacktPublishing/The-Machine-Learning-Solutions-Architect-Handbook/blob/main/Chapter09/training_workflow.yaml`. This CloudFormation template will create a Step Functions state machine with a training step and model registration step. The training step will train the same BERT model we trained in *Chapter 8, Building a Data Science Environment Using AWS ML Services*. For simplicity, we will reuse the same source data and training script as well to demonstrate the MLOps concepts we have learned about in this chapter. Note that we are using CloudFormation here to demonstrate managing IaC. Data scientists also have the option to use the Step Functions Data Science SDK to create the pipeline using a Python script:

```
AWSTemplateFormatVersion: 2010-09-09
Description: 'AWS Step Functions sample project for
training a model and save the model'
Parameters:
    StepFunctionExecutionRoleArn:
        Type: String
        Description: Enter the role for Step Function
Workflow execution
        ConstraintDescription: requires a valid arn value
        AllowedPattern: 'arn:aws:iam::\w+:role/.*'
Resources:
  TrainingStateMachine2:
    Type: AWS::StepFunctions::StateMachine
    Properties:
      RoleArn: !Ref StepFunctionExecutionRoleArn
      DefinitionString: !Sub |
        {
            "StartAt": "SageMaker Training Step",
            "States": {
                "SageMaker Training Step": {
```

```
                         "Resource":
   "arn:aws:states:::sagemaker:createTrainingJob.sync",
   ...
```

3. Launch the newly created cloud template in the CloudFormation console. Make sure that you provide a value for the **StepFunctionExecutionRoleArn** field when prompted. This is the ARN you took down from the last step. Once the CloudFormation execution is completed, go to the **Step Functions** console to test it.

4. Test the workflow in the **Step Functions** console to make sure it works. Navigate to the newly created **Step Functions state machine** and click on **Start Execution** to kick off the execution. When you're prompted for any input, copy and paste the following JSON as input for the execution. These are the input values that will be used by the Step Functions workflow. Make sure that you replace the actual values with the values for your environment. For the AWS hosting account information for the training images, you can look up the account number at https://github. com/aws/deep-learning-containers/blob/master/available_ images.md:

```
{
    "TrainingImage": "<aws hosting account>.dkr.ecr.<aws
region>.amazonaws.com/pytorch-training:1.3.1-gpu-py3",
    "S3OutputPath": "s3://<your s3 bucket name>/sagemaker/
pytorch-bert-financetext",
    "SageMakerRoleArn": "arn:aws:iam::<your aws
account>:role/service-role/<your sagemaker execution
role>",
    "S3UriTraining": "s3://<your AWS S3 bucket>/sagemaker/
pytorch-bert-financetext/train.csv",
    "S3UriTesting": "s3://<your AWS S3 bucket>/sagemaker/
pytorch-bert-financetext/test.csv",
    "InferenceImage": " aws hosting account>.dkr.ecr. <aws
region>.amazonaws.com/pytorch-inference:1.3.1-cpu-py3",
    "SAGEMAKER_PROGRAM": "train.py",
    "SAGEMAKER_SUBMIT_DIRECTORY": "s3:// <your AWS S3
bucket> /berttraining/source/sourcedir.tar.gz",
    "SAGEMAKER_REGION": "<your aws region>"
}
```

5. Check the processing status in the **Step Functions** console and make sure that the model has been trained and registered correctly. Once everything is completed, save the input JSON in *Step 4* to a file called `sf_start_params.json`. Launch the SageMaker Studio environment you created in *Chapter 8, Building a Data Science Environment Using AWS ML Services*, navigate to the folder where you had cloned the `CodeCommit` repository, and upload the `sf_start_params.json` file into it. Commit the change to the code repository and verify it is in the repository. We will use this file in the `CodeCommit` repository for the next section of the lab.

Now, we are ready to create the CloudFormation template for the CodePipeline training pipeline. This pipeline will listen to changes to a `CodeCommit` repository and invoke the Step Functions workflow we just created:

1. Copy and save the following code block to a file called `mlpipeline.yaml`. This is the template for building the training pipeline. You can find the complete file at `https://github.com/PacktPublishing/The-Machine-Learning-Solutions-Architect-Handbook/blob/main/Chapter09/mlpipeline.yaml`:

```
Parameters:
  BranchName:
    Description: CodeCommit branch name
    Type: String
    Default: master
  RepositoryName:
    Description: CodeCommit repository name
    Type: String
    Default: MLSA-repo
  ProjectName:
    Description: ML project name
    Type: String
    Default: FinanceSentiment
  MlOpsStepFunctionArn:
    Description: Step Function Arn
    Type: String
    Default: arn:aws:states:ca-central-
1:300165273893:stateMachine:TrainingStateMachine2-
89fJblFkOh7b
```

```
Resources:
  CodePipelineArtifactStoreBucket:
    Type: 'AWS::S3::Bucket'
    DeletionPolicy: Delete
  Pipeline:
    Type: 'AWS::CodePipeline::Pipeline'
  ...
```

2. Similarly, let's launch this cloud template in the CloudFormation console to create the pipeline definition for execution. Once the CloudFormation template has been executed, navigate to the CodePipeline management console to verify that it has been created. The CloudFormation execution will also execute the newly created pipeline automatically, so you should see that it already ran once. You can test it again by clicking on the **Release changes** button in the **SageMaker management** console.

We want to be able to kick off the CodePipeline execution when a change is made (such as a code commit) in the CodeCommit repository. To enable this, we need to create a CloudWatch event that monitors this change and kicks off the pipeline. Let's get started:

1. Add the following code block to the mlpipeline.yaml file, just before the **Outputs** section, and save the file as mlpipeline_1.yaml. You can find the complete file at https://github.com/PacktPublishing/The-Machine-Learning-Solutions-Architect-Handbook/blob/main/Chapter09/mlpipeline_1.yaml:

```
AmazonCloudWatchEventRole:
    Type: 'AWS::IAM::Role'
    Properties:
      AssumeRolePolicyDocument:
        Version: 2012-10-17
        Statement:
          - Effect: Allow
            Principal:
              Service:
                - events.amazonaws.com
            Action: 'sts:AssumeRole'
      Path: /
      Policies:
```

```
            - PolicyName: cwe-pipeline-execution
              PolicyDocument:

    ...
```

2. Now, run this CloudFormation template to create a new pipeline. You can delete the previously created pipeline by deleting the CloudFormation stack. This will run the pipeline again automatically. Wait until the pipeline's execution is complete before you start the next step.

3. Now, let's test the automatic execution of the pipeline by committing a change to the code repository. Find a file in your cloned code repository directory. Create a new file called `pipelinetest.txt` and commit the change to the code repository. Navigate to the CodePipeline console; you should see the `codecommit-events-pipeline` pipeline starting to run.

Congratulations! you have successfully used CloudFormation to build a CodePipeline-based ML training pipeline that automatically runs when there is a file change in a CodeCommit repository. Next, let's build the ML deployment pipeline for the model.

Creating a CloudFormation template for the ML deployment pipeline

To start creating a deployment, perform the following steps:

1. Copy the following code block to create a file called `mldeployment.yaml`. This CloudFormation template will deploy a model using the SageMaker hosting service. Make sure that you enter the correct model name for your environment:

```
Description: Basic Hosting of registered model
Parameters:
ModelName:
Description: Model Name
Type: String
Default: <mode name>
Resources:
Endpoint:
Type: AWS::SageMaker::Endpoint
Properties:
EndpointConfigName: !GetAtt EndpointConfig.
EndpointConfigName
```

```
EndpointConfig:
  Type: AWS::SageMaker::EndpointConfig
  Properties:
    ProductionVariants:
      InitialInstanceCount: 1
      InitialVariantWeight: 1.0
      InstanceType: ml.m4.xlarge
      ModelName: !Ref ModelName
      VariantName: !Ref ModelName
Outputs:
  EndpointId:
    Value: !Ref Endpoint
  EndpointName:
    Value: !GetAtt Endpoint.EndpointName
```

2. Create a CloudFormation stack using this file and verify that a SageMaker endpoint has been created. Now, upload the `mldeployment.yaml` file to the code repository directory and commit the change to `CodeCommit`. Note that this file will be used by the CodePipeline deployment pipeline, which we will create in the following steps.

3. Before we create the deployment pipeline, we need a template config file for passing parameters to the deployment template when it is executed. Here, we need to pass the model name to the pipeline. Copy the following code block, save it to a file called `mldeployment.json`, upload it to the code repository directory in Studio, and commit the change to `codecommit`:

```
{
  "Parameters" : {
    "ModelName" : <name of the financial sentiment model
    you have trained>
  }
}
```

4. Now, we can create a CodePipeline pipeline CloudFormation template for automatic model deployment. This pipeline has two main stages:

I. The first stage fetches source code (such as the configuration file we just created and the `mldeployment.yaml` template) from a `CodeCommit` repository.

II. The second stage creates a CloudFormation change set (**a change set** is the difference between a new template and an existing CloudFormation stack) for the `mldeployment.yaml` file we created earlier. It adds a manual approval step and then deploys the CloudFormation template's `mldeployment.yaml` file.

This CloudFormation template also creates supporting resources, including an S3 bucket for storing the CodePipeline artifacts, an IAM role for CodePipeline to run with, and another IAM role for CloudFormation to use to create the stack for `mldeployment.yaml`.

5. Copy the following code block and save the file as `mldeployment-pipeline.yaml`. You can find the complete code sample at `https://github.com/PacktPublishing/The-Machine-Learning-Solutions-Architect-Handbook/blob/main/Chapter09/mldeployment-pipeline.yaml`:

```
Parameters:
  BranchName:
    Description: CodeCommit branch name
    Type: String
    Default: master
  RepositoryName:
    Description: CodeCommit repository name
    Type: String
    Default: MLSA-repo
  ProjectName:
    Description: ML project name
    Type: String
    Default: FinanceSentiment
  CodePipelineSNSTopic:
    Description: SNS topic for NotificationArn
    Default: arn:aws:sns:ca-central-1:300165273893:CodePi
pelineSNSTopicApproval
    Type: String
  ProdStackConfig:
```

```
         Default: mldeploymentconfig.json
         Description: The configuration file name for the
production WordPress stack
         Type: String
   ProdStackName:
         Default: FinanceSentimentMLStack1
         Description: A name for the production WordPress
stack
         Type: String
   TemplateFileName:
         Default: mldeployment.yaml
         Description: The file name of the WordPress template
         Type: String
   ChangeSetName:
         Default: FinanceSentimentchangeset
         Description: A name for the production stack change
set
         Type: String
Resources:
   CodePipelineArtifactStoreBucket:
      Type: 'AWS::S3::Bucket'
      DeletionPolicy: Delete
   Pipeline:
. . . . .
```

6. Now, let's launch the newly created `mldeployment-pipeline.yaml` template in the **CloudFormation** console to create the deployment pipeline, and then run the pipeline from the **CodePipeline** console.

Congratulations! You have successfully created and run a CodePipeline deployment pipeline to deploy a model from the SageMaker model registry.

Summary

In this chapter, we discussed the key requirements for building an enterprise ML platform to meet needs such as end-to-end ML life cycle support, process automation, and separating different environments. We also talked about architecture patterns and how to build an enterprise ML platform on AWS using AWS services. We discussed the core capabilities of different ML environments, including training, hosting, and shared services. You should now have a good understanding of what an enterprise ML platform could look like, as well as the key considerations for building one using AWS services. You have also developed some hands-on experience in building the components of the MLOps architecture and automating model training and deployment. In the next chapter, we will discuss advanced ML engineering by covering large-scale distributed training and the core concepts for achieving low-latency inference.

10

Advanced ML Engineering

Congratulations on making it so far. By now, you should have developed a good understanding of the core fundamental skills that a **machine learning** (**ML**) solutions architect needs to work effectively across different phases of the ML life cycle. In this chapter, we will dive deep into several advanced ML topics. Specifically, we will cover various distributed model training options for large models and large datasets. We will also discuss the various technical approaches for reducing model inference latency. We will close this chapter with a hands-on lab on distributed model training.

Specifically, we will cover the following topics in this chapter:

- Training large-scale models with distributed training
- Achieving low latency model inference
- Hands-on lab – running distributed model training with PyTorch

Technical requirements

You will need access to your AWS environment for the hands-on portion of this chapter. All the code samples are located at `https://github.com/PacktPublishing/The-Machine-Learning-Solutions-Architect-Handbook/blob/main/Chapter10`.

Training large-scale models with distributed training

As ML algorithms continue to become more complex and the data that's available for ML gets increasingly large, model training can become a big bottleneck in the ML life cycle. Training models with large datasets on a single machine/device can become too slow or is simply not possible when the model is too large to fit into the memory of a single device. The following diagram shows how quickly language models have evolved in recent years and the growth in terms of model size:

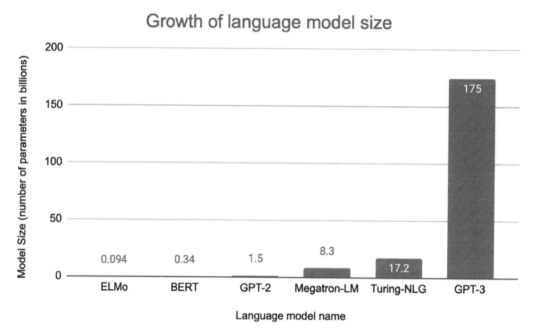

Figure 10.1 – The growth of language models

To solve the challenges of training large models with large data, we can turn to distributed training. Distributed training allows you to train models across multiple devices on a single node or across multiple nodes so that you can split up the data or model across these devices and nodes for model training. There are two main types of distributed training: **data parallelism** and **model parallelism**. Before we get into the details of distributed training, let's quickly review how a neural network trains again:

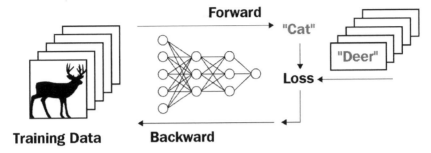

Figure 10.2 – Deep neural network training

The preceding diagram shows how an **artificial neural network** (**ANN**) trains. The training data is fed to the ANN in a forward pass. The loss (the difference between the predicted value and the true value) is calculated at the end of the forward pass, and the backward pass calculates the gradients for all the parameters. These parameters are updated with new values for the next step until the loss is minimized.

In the next section, we'll look at distributed model training using data parallelism.

Distributed model training using data parallelism

Data parallel distributed training allows you to split a large training dataset into smaller subsets and train the smaller subsets in different devices and nodes in parallel. This allows you to run multiple training processes in parallel on the available devices to speed up training. To use data parallel distributed training, the underlying ML frameworks and/or algorithms will need to support it.

As we discussed earlier, one key task in training **deep learning** (**DL**) models is to calculate the gradients concerning the loss function for every batch of the data, and then update the model parameters with gradient information to minimize the loss gradually. Instead of running the gradient calculations and parameter updates in a single device, the basic concept behind data parallel distributed training is to run multiple training processes using the same algorithm in parallel, with each process using a different subset of the training dataset. The following diagram shows the main concept behind data parallelism training:

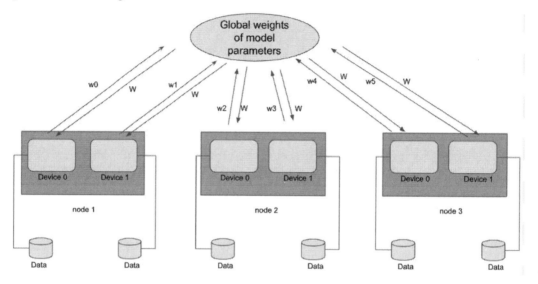

Figure 10.3 – Data parallelism concept

In the preceding diagram, there are three nodes in a cluster participating in a distributed data parallelism training job, with each node having two devices. The partial gradients that are calculated by each device are represented by **w0 ~ w5** for each of the devices on the nodes, while **W** is the value for a global parameter for the model. Specifically, data parallel distributed training has the following main steps:

1. Each device (CPU or GPU) in every node loads a copy of the same algorithm and a subset of the training data.

2. Each device runs a training loop to calculate the gradients (**w0~w5**) to optimize its loss function and exchange the gradients with other devices in the cluster at each training step.

3. The gradients from all the devices are aggregated and the common model parameters (**W**) are calculated using aggregated gradients.

4. Each device pulls down the newly calculated common model parameters (**W**) and continues with the next step of model training.

5. *Steps 2* to *4* are repeated until the model training is completed.

In a distributed training setting, efficiently exchanging gradients and parameters across processes is one of the most important aspects of ML system engineering design. Several distributed training topologies have been developed over the years to optimize communications across different training processes. In this chapter, we will discuss two of the most widely adopted topologies for data parallel distributed training.

Parameter server overview

The parameter server (**PS**) is a topology built on the concept of server nodes and worker nodes. The worker nodes are responsible for running the training loops and calculating the gradients, while the server nodes are responsible for aggregating the gradients and calculating the globally shared parameters. The following diagram shows the architecture of a PS:

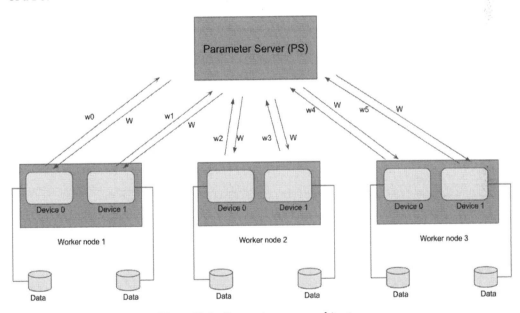

Figure 10.4 – Parameter server architecture

Here, the server node is called the PS, and it is usually implemented as a key value or vector store for storing gradients and parameters. As the number of model parameters to manage can become very large, there could also be multiple server nodes for managing the global parameters and gradient aggregations. In a multi-parameter server configuration, there is also a server manager that manages and coordinates all the server nodes to ensure consistency.

In this architecture, the worker nodes only communicate with the PS nodes to exchange gradients and parameters, and not with each other. In a multi-server node environment, each server node also communicates with every other server node to replicate parameters for reliability and scalability. The gradients and parameters are exchanged so that updates can be implemented synchronously and asynchronously. The synchronously gradient update strategy blocks the devices from processing the next mini-batch of data until the gradients from all the devices have been synchronized. This means that each update has to wait for the slowest device to complete. This can slow down training and make the training process less robust in terms of device failure. On the positive side, synchronous updates do not have to worry about stale gradients, which can lead to higher model accuracy. Asynchronous updates do not need to wait for all the devices to be synchronized before processing the next mini-batch of data, though this might lead to reduced accuracy.

Implementing the PS in frameworks

PS distributed training is natively supported by several DL frameworks, such as TensorFlow. Specifically, TensorFlow supports PS-based distributed training natively with its `ParameterServerStrategy` API. The following code sample shows how to instantiate the `ParameterServerStrategy` API for TensorFlow:

```
strategy = tf.distribute.experimental.ParameterServerStrategy(
    cluster_resolver)
```

In this code sample, the `cluster_resolver` parameter helps discover and resolve the IP addresses of workers.

`ParameterServerStrategy` can be used directly with the `model.fit()` function of Keras or a custom training loop by wrapping the model with the `strategy.scope()` syntax. See the following sample syntax on how to use `scope()` to wrap a model for distributed training:

```
with strategy.scope()
    model = <model architecture definition>
```

In addition to PS implementation, which is natively supported within DL libraries, there are also general-purpose PS training frameworks, such as BytePS from ByteDance and Herring from Amazon, which work with different DL frameworks. SageMaker uses Herring under the hood for data parallel distributed training through its SageMaker Distributed Training library. One of the shortcomings of the parameter-server strategy is the inefficient use of network bandwidth. The Herring library addresses this shortcoming by combining AWS **Elastic Fabric Adapter** (**EFA**) and the parameter sharding technique, which makes use of network bandwidth to achieve faster distributed training. EFA takes advantage of cloud resources and their characteristics, such as multi-path backbones, to improve network communication efficiency. You can find out more about Herring at `https://www.amazon.science/publications/herring-rethinking-the-parameter-server-at-scale-for-the-cloud`.

AllReduce overview

While the PS architecture is easy to understand and set up, it does come with several challenges. For example, the PS architecture requires additional nodes for the parameter servers, and it is also hard to determine the right ratio between server nodes and worker nodes to ensure the server nodes do not become bottlenecks.

The AllReduce topology tries to improve some of the limitations of parameter servers by eliminating the server nodes and distributing all the gradient aggregation and global parameter updates to all the workers, hence why it's called **AllReduce**. The following diagram shows the topology of AllReduce:

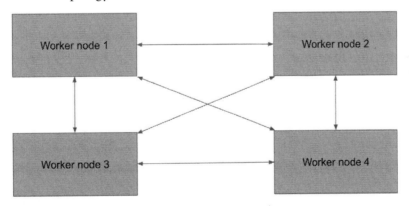

Figure 10.5 – AllReduce architecture

In an AllReduce topology, each node sends gradients of parameters to all the other nodes at each training step. Then, each node aggregates the gradients and performs the reduce function (such as `average`, `sum`, or `max`) locally before calculating the new parameters using the next training step. Since every node needs to communicate with every other node, this results in a large number of networks communicating among the nodes, and duplicate compute and storage being used as every node has a copy of all the gradients.

A more efficient AllReduce architecture is Ring AllReduce. In this architecture, each node only sends some gradients to its next neighboring node, and each node is responsible for aggregating the gradients for the global parameters that it is assigned to calculate. This architecture greatly reduces the amount of network communication in a cluster and compute overhead, so it is more efficient for model training. The following diagram shows the Ring AllReduce architecture:

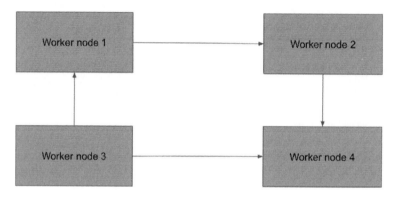

Figure 10.6 – Ring AllReduce

Implementing AllReduce and Ring AllReduce in frameworks

The AllReduce and Ring AllReduce architectures are natively supported within multiple DL frameworks, including TensorFlow and PyTorch.

TensorFlow supports AllReduce distributed training across multiple GPUs on one machine with its `tf.distribute.MirroredStrategy` API. With this strategy, each GPU has a copy of the model, and all the model parameters are mirrored across different devices. An efficient AllReduce mechanism is used to keep these parameters in sync. The following code sample shows how to instantiate the `MirroredStrategy` API:

```
strategy = tf.distribute.MirroredStrategy()
```

For multi-machine distributed training, TensorFlow uses the `tf.distribute.MultiWorkerMirroredStrategy` API. Similar to `MirroredStrategy`, `MultiWorkerMirroredStrategy` creates copies of all the parameters across all the devices on all the machines and synchronizes them with the AllReduce mechanism. The following code sample shows how to instantiate the `MultiWorkerMirroredStrategy` API:

```
strategy = tf.distribute.MultiWorkerMirroredStrategy()
```

Similar to `ParameterServerStrategy`, `MirroredStrategy` and `MultiWorkerMirroredStrategy` can work with the `keras model.fit()` function or a custom training loop. To associate a model with a training strategy, you can use the same `strategy.scope()` syntax.

PyTorch also provides native support for AllReduce-based distributed training via its `torch.nn.DataParallel` and `torch.nn.parallel.DistributedDataParallel` APIs. The `torch.nn.DataParallel` API supports single-process multi-threading across GPUs on the same machine, while `torch.nn.parallel.DistributedDataParallel` supports multi-processing across GPUs and machines. The following code sample shows how to initiate a distributed training cluster and wrap a model for distributed training using the `DistributedDataParallel` API:

```
torch.distributed.init_process_group(...)
model = torch.nn.parallel.DistributedDataParallel(model, ...)
```

Another popular implementation of the general-purpose Ring AllReduce architecture is **Horovod**, which was created by the engineers at Uber. Horovod works with multiple DL frameworks, including TensorFlow and PyTorch. You can find out more about Horovod at `https://github.com/horovod/horovod`.

Distributed model training using model parallelism

Model parallelism is still nascent in its adoption since most of the distributed training that happens today involves data parallelism that deals with large datasets. However, the applications of state-of-the-art big DL algorithms such as BERT, GPT, and T5 are driving the increasing adoption of model parallelism. The qualities of these models are known to increase with the model's size, and these large NLP models require a large amount of memory to store the model's states (which includes the model's parameters, optimizer states, and gradients) and memory for other overheads.

As such, these models can no longer fit into the memory of a single GPU. While data parallelism helps solve the large dataset challenge, it cannot help with training large models due to its large memory size requirements. Model parallelism allows you to split a single large model across multiple devices so that the total memory across multiple devices is enough to hold a copy of the model. Model parallelism also allows for a larger batch size for model training as a result of larger collective memory across multiple devices.

There are two main ways to split the model for model parallel distributed training: splitting by layers and splitting by tensors. Let's take a closer look at these two approaches.

Naïve model parallelism overview

As an artificial neural network consists of many layers, one way to split the model is to distribute the layers across multiple devices. For example, if you have an 8-layer **multi-layer perceptron network (MLP)** and two GPUs (GPU0, and GPU1), you can simply place the first four layers in GPU0 and the last four layers in GPU1. During training, the first four layers of the model are trained as you would normally train a model in a single device. When the first four layers are complete, the output from the fourth layer will be copied from GPU0 to GPU1, incurring communication overhead. After getting the output from GPU0, GPU1 continues training layers five to eight. The following diagram illustrates splitting a model by layers across multiple devices:

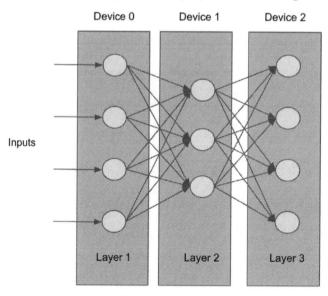

Figure 10.7 – Naïve model parallelism

Implementing model parallelism by splitting requires knowledge about the training task. It is not a trivial task to design an efficient model parallelism strategy. Here are a few heuristics that could be helpful for the layer split design:

- Place neighboring layers on the same devices to minimize communication overhead.

- Balance the workload between devices.

- Different layers have different compute and memory utilization properties.

Training an ANN model is inherently a sequential process, which means that the network layers are processed sequentially, while the backward process will only start when the forward process is completed. When you're splitting layers across multiple devices, only the device currently processing the layers on it will be busy; the other devices will be idle, wasting compute resources, which results in a waste of hardware resources. The following diagram shows processing the sequences for the forward and backward passes for one batch of data:

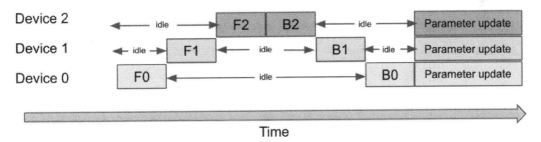

Figure 10.8 – Naïve model parallelism

In the preceding diagram, **F0**, **F1**, and **F2** are the forward passes on the different neural network layers on each device. **B2**, **B1**, and **B0** are the backward passes for the layers on each device. As you can see, when one of the devices is busy with either a forward pass or a backward pass, the other devices are idle. Next, let's look at an approach (pipeline model parallelism) that can help increase resource utilization.

Pipeline model parallelism overview

To resolve the resource idling issue, pipeline model parallelism can be implemented. This improves on naïve model parallelism so that different devices can work in parallel on the different stages of the training pipeline on a smaller chunk of data batch, commonly known as a micro-batch. The following diagram shows how pipeline model parallelism works:

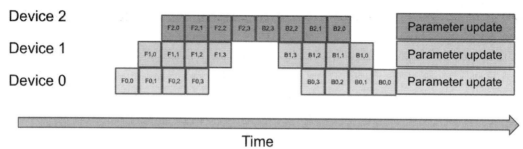

Figure 10.9 – Pipeline model parallelism

With pipeline model parallelism, instead of processing one batch of data with each full forward and backward pass, the one batch of data is broken down into smaller mini-batches. In the preceding diagram, after **Device 0** completes the forward pass for the first mini-batch, **Device 1** can start its forward pass on the output of the **Device 1** forward pass. Instead of waiting for **Device 1** and **Device 2** to complete their forward pass and backward passes, **Device 0** starts to process the next mini-batch of data. This scheduled pipeline allows for higher utilization of the hardware resources, resulting in faster model training.

There are other variations of pipeline parallelism. One example is interleaved parallelism, where a backward execution is prioritized whenever possible. This improves the utilization of the devices for end-to-end model training. The following diagram shows how an interleaved pipeline works:

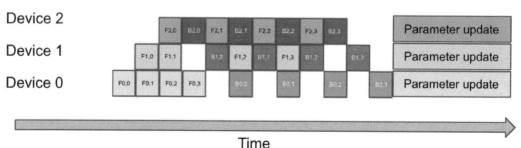

Figure 10.10 – Interleaved pipeline

Next, let's look at an overview of tensor parallelism, also known as tensor slicing.

Tensor parallelism/tensor slicing overview

As we mentioned earlier, tensor parallelism is another approach to spitting a large model to make it fit into memory. Before we dive into this, let's quickly review what a tensor is and how it is processed by an ANN.

A **tensor** is a multi-dimensional matrix of a single data type such as a 32-bit floating-point or 8-bit integer. In the forward pass of neural network training, a dot product is used on the input tensor and weight matrix tensors (the connections between the input tensors and the neurons in the hidden layer). You can find out more about dot products at `https://en.wikipedia.org/wiki/Dot_product`. The following diagram illustrates a dot product between the input vector and the weight matrix:

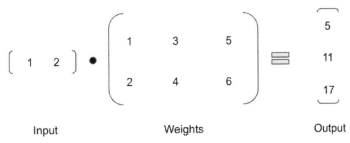

Figure 10.11 – Matrix calculation

In this matrix calculation, you get an output vector of **[5,11,17]**. If there is a single device for dot product calculation, three separate calculations will be performed sequentially to get the output vector.

But what if we break up the single weights matrix into three vectors and use a dot product separately? This can be seen in the following diagram:

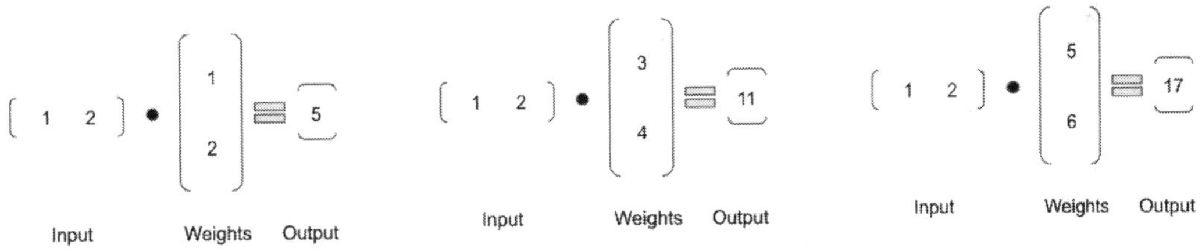

Figure 10.12 – Splitting the matrix calculation

As you can see, you would get three separate values that are the same as the individual values in the output vector in the preceding diagram. If there are three separate devices for performing dot product calculations, we can perform these three dot product calculations in parallel and combine the values into a single vector at the end if needed. This is the basic concept of why tensor parallelism works. With tensor parallelism, each device works independently without the need for any communication until the end, which is when the results need to be synchronized. This strategy allows for faster tensor processing as multiple devices can work in parallel to reduce training time and increase the utilization of computing devices.

Implementing model parallelism training

To implement model parallelism, you can manually design the parallelism strategy by deciding how to split the layers and tensors, as well as their placements, across different devices and nodes. However, it is not trivial to do this efficiently, especially for large clusters. To make the model parallelism implementation easier, several model parallelism library packages have been developed. In this section, we'll take a closer look at some of these libraries. Note that the frameworks we will discuss can support both data parallelism and model parallelism and that both techniques are often used together to train large models with large training datasets.

Megatron-LM overview

Megatron-LM is an open source distributed training framework developed by Nvidia. It supports data parallelism, tensor parallelism, and pipeline model parallelism, as well as a combination of all three for extreme-scale model training.

Megatron-LM implements micro-batch-based pipeline model parallelism to improve device utilization. It also implements periodic pipeline flushes to ensure optimizer steps are synchronized across devices. Two different pipeline schedules are supported by Megatron-LM, as follows:

- The default schedule works by completing the forward pass for all micro-batches first, before starting the backward pass for all the batches.

- The interleaved stage schedule works by running multiple different subsets of layers on a single device, instead of running just a single continuous set of layers. This can further improve the utilization of devices and reduce idle time.

Megatron-LM implements a specific tensor parallelism strategy for transformer-based models. A transformer consists mainly of self-attention blocks, followed by a two-layer MLP. For the MLP portion, Megatron-LM splits the weight matrix by columns. The matrices for the self-attention heads are also partitioned by columns. The following diagram shows how the different parts of the transformers can be split:

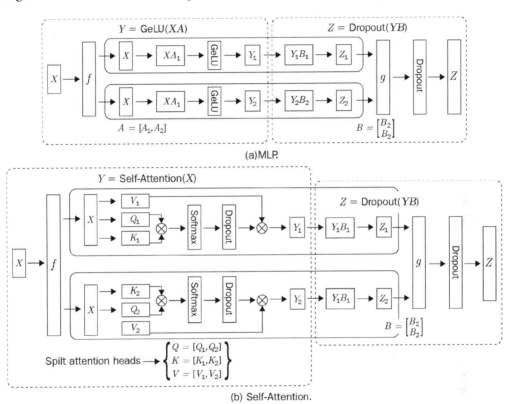

(a) MLP.

(b) Self-Attention.

Figure 10.13 – Tensor parallelism for transformers

Using data parallelism, pipeline model parallelism, and tensor parallelism together, Megatron-LM can be used to train extremely large transformer-based models (with a trillion parameters) scaled across thousands of GPUs.

Training using Megatron-LM involves the following key steps:

1. Initializing the Megatron library using the `initialize_megatron()` function.

2. Setting up the Megatron model optimizer using the `setup_model_and_optimizer()` function by wrapping the original model.

3. Training the model using the `train()` function, which takes the Megatron model and optimizer as input.

Megatron-LM has been used for many large model training projects, such as BERT, GPT, and the Biomedical domain language model. Its scalable architecture can be used to train models with trillions of parameters.

DeepSpeed overview

DeepSpeed is an open source distributed training framework developed by Microsoft. Similar to Megatron-LM, DeepSpeed also supports tensor slicing (another name for splitting tensors) parallelism, pipeline parallelism, and data parallelism.

DeepSpeed implements micro-batch-based pipeline model parallelism, where a batch is broken into micro-batches to be processed by different devices in parallel. Specifically, DeepSpeed implements interleaved pipeline parallelism to optimize resource efficiency and utilization.

Similar to Megatron-LM, DeepSpeed can use data parallelism, pipeline model parallelism, and tensor parallelism together to train extremely large deep neural networks. This is also known as DeepSpeed 3D parallelism.

One core capability of the DeepSpeed framework is its **Zero Redundancy Optimizer (ZeRO)**. ZeRO is capable of managing memory efficiently by partitioning parameters, optimizer states, and gradients across devices instead of keeping a copy in all devices. The partitions are brought together at runtime when needed. This allows ZeRO to reduce the memory footprint by eight times compared to regular data parallelism techniques. ZeRO is also capable of using CPU and GPU memory together to train large models.

The attention-based mechanism is widely adopted in DL models, such as the transformer model, to address text and image inputs. However, its ability to address long input sequences is limited due to its large memory and compute requirements. DeepSpeed helps alleviate this issue with its implementation of a sparse attention kernel – a technology that reduces the compute and memory requirements of attention computation via block-sparse computation.

One major bottleneck in large-scale distributed training is the communication overhead due to gradients sharing and updates. Communication compression, such as 1-bit compression, has been adopted as an effective mechanism to reduce communication overhead. DeepSpeed has an implementation of a 1-bit Adam optimizer, which can reduce the communication overhead by up to five times to improve the training speed. 1-bit compression works by representing each number using 1 bit, combined with error compensation, which remembers the error during gradient compression and adds the error back to next the step to compensate for the error.

To use DeepSpeed, you need to modify your training script. The following steps explain the main changes you need to make to a training script to run distributed training:

1. Use the `deepspeed.initialize()` function to wrap the model and return a DeepSpeed model engine. This model engine will be used to run a forward pass and a backward pass.

2. Use the returned DeepSpeed model engine to run the forward pass, backward pass, and step function to update the model parameters.

DeepSpeed primarily supports the PyTorch framework and requires minor code changes to adopt model training using PyTorch. DeepSpeed has been used for training models with hundreds of billions of parameters and has delivered some of the fastest model training times. You can find out more about DeepSpeed at `https://www.deepspeed.ai`.

SageMaker Distributed Training library overview

Amazon's **SageMaker Distributed Training** (SMD) library is part of the Amazon SageMaker service offering. SMD supports data parallelism (by using Herring under the hood) and interleaved pipeline model parallelism. Unlike DeepSpeed and Megatron-LM, where you need to manually decide on your model partitions, **SageMaker Model Parallel (SMP)**

has a feature for automated model splitting support.

This automated model splitting feature of SMP balances memory and communication constraints between devices to optimize performance. Automated model splitting takes place during the first training step, where a version of a model is constructed in CPU memory. The graph is analyzed, a partition decision is made, and different model partitions are loaded into different GPUs. The partition software performs framework-specific analysis for TensorFlow and PyTorch to determine the partition decision. It considers graph structures such as variable/parameter sharing, parameter sizes, and constraints to balance the number of variables and the number of operations for each device to come up with split decisions.

To use SageMaker Distributed Training, you need to make some changes to your existing training scripts and create SageMaker training jobs. There are different instructions for TensorFlow and PyTorch. The following are examples for the PyTorch framework:

1. Modify the PyTorch training script:

   - Call `smp.init()` to initialize the library.

   - Wrap the model with `smp.DistributedModel()`.

- Wrap the optimizer with `smp.DistributedOptimizer()`.

- Restrict each process to its own device through `torch.cuda.set_device(smp.local_rank())`.

- Use the wrapped model to perform a forward pass and a backward pass.

- Use the distributed optimizer to update the parameters.

2. Create a SageMaker training job using SageMaker PyTorch Estimator and enable SMP distributed training.

In this section, we reviewed the different distributed training strategies and frameworks for running distributed training. Distributed model training allows us to train extremely large models, though running inferences on large models could result in high latency due to the size of the models and other technological constraints. Next, let's discuss the various techniques we can use to achieve low latency inference.

Achieving low latency model inference

As ML models continue to grow and get deployed to different hardware devices, latency can become an issue for certain inference use cases that require low latency and high throughput inferences, such as real-time fraud detection. To reduce the overall model inference latency for a real-time application, there are different optimization considerations and techniques we can use, including model optimization, graph optimization, hardware acceleration, and inference engine optimization. In this section, we will focus on model optimization, graph optimization, and hardware optimization. But first, let's try to understand how model inference works, specifically for DL models, since that's what most of the inference optimization processes focus on.

How model inference works and opportunities for optimization

As we discussed earlier in this book, DL models are constructed as computational graphs with nodes and edges, where the nodes represent the different operations and edges represent the data flow. Examples of such operations include addition, matrix multiplication, activation (for example, Sigmoid and ReLU), and pooling. These operations perform computations on tensors as inputs and produce tensors as outputs. For example, the $c=matmul(a,b)$ operation takes a and b as input tensors and produces c as the output tensor. Deep learning frameworks, such as TensorFlow and PyTorch, have built-in operators to support different operations. The implementation of an operator is also called a kernel.

During inference time for a trained model, the DL framework's runtime will walk through the computational graph and invoke the appropriate kernels (such as add or Sigmoid) for each of the nodes in the graph. The kernel will take various inputs, such as the inference data samples, learned model parameters, and intermediate outputs, from the preceding operators and perform specific computations according to the data flow defined by the computational graph to produce the final predictions. The size of a trained model is mainly determined by the number of nodes in a graph, as well as the number of model parameters and their numerical precisions (for example, floating-point 32, floating-point 16, or integer 8).

Different hardware providers such as Nvidia and Intel also provide hardware-specific implementations of kernels for common computational graph operations. CuDNN is the library from Nvidia for optimized kernel implementations for their GPU devices, while MKL-DNN is the library from Intel for optimized kernel implementations for Intel chips. These hardware-specific implementations take advantage of the unique capabilities of the underlying hardware architecture. They can perform better than the kernels that are implemented by the DL framework implementation since the framework implementations are hardware-agnostic.

At this point, you should have a basic understanding of how inference works. Next, let's discuss some of the common optimization techniques we can use to improve model latency.

Hardware acceleration

Different hardware produces varying inference latency performance for different ML models. The list of common hardware for model inference includes the CPU, GPU, **application-specific integrated circuit** (**ASIC**), **field-programmable gate array** (**FPGA**), and edge hardware (such as Nvidia Jetson Nano). In this section, we will review the core architecture characteristics for some of these pieces of hardware and how their designs help with model inference acceleration.

Central processing units (CPUs)

A CPU is a general-purpose chip for running computer programs. It consists of four main building blocks:

- The control unit is the brain of the CPU that directs the operations of the CPU; that is, it instructs other components such as memory.

- The **arithmetic logic unit** (**ALU**) is the basic unit that performs arithmetic and logical operations, such as addition and subtraction, on the input data.

- The address generation unit is used for calculating an address to access memory.

- Memory management, which is used for all memory components such as main memory and the local cache. A CPU can also be made up of multiple cores, with each core having a control unit and ALUs.

The degree of parallel executions in a CPU mainly depends on how many cores it has. Each core normally runs a single thread at a time, except for hyper-threading (a proprietary simultaneous multi-threading implementation from Intel). The more cores it has, the higher the degree of parallel executions. A CPU is designed to handle a large set of instructions and manage the operations of many other components; it usually has high performance and a complex core, but they aren't many of them. For example, the Intel Xeon processor can have up to 56 cores.

CPUs are usually not suited for neural network-based model inference if low latency is the main requirement. Neural network inference mainly involves operations that can be parallelized at a large scale (for example, matrix multiplication). Since the total number of cores for a CPU is usually small, it cannot be parallelized at scale to meet the needs of a neural network inference. On the positive side, CPUs are more cost-effective and usually have good memory capacities for hosting larger models.

Graphical processing units (GPUs)

The design of a GPU is the opposite of the design of a CPU. Instead of having a few powerful cores, it has thousands of less powerful cores that are designed to perform a small set of instructions highly efficiently. The basic design of a GPU core is like that of a CPU. It also contains a control unit, ALU, and a local memory cache. However, the GPU control unit handles a much simpler instruction set, and the local memory is much smaller.

When the GPU processes instructions, it schedules blocks of threads, and within each block of threads, all the threads perform the same operations but on different pieces of data – a parallelization scheme called **Single Instruction Multiple Data (SIMD)**. This architecture fits nicely with how a DL model works, where many neurons perform the same operation (mainly matrix multiplication) on different pieces of data.

The Nvidia GPU architecture contains two main components:

- The global memory component

- The **streaming multiprocessor (SM)** component

An SM is analogous to a CPU and each SM has many **Computer Unified Device Architecture (CUDA)** cores, special functional units that perform different arithmetic operations. It also has a small, shared memory and cache, and many registers. A CUDA core is responsible for functions such as floating-point/integer operations, logic calculation, and branching. The thread block mentioned previously is executed by the SM. The global memory is located on the same GPU board. When you're training a ML model, both the model and the data need to be loaded into the global memory.

In a multi-GPU configuration, low latency and high throughput communication channels are available, such as the Nvidia NVLink, which provides up to 600 GB/sec bandwidth, which is almost 10x the bandwidth of PCIe4.

GPUs are well suited for low latency and high throughput neural network model inferences due to their massive number of CUDA cores for large-scale parallelism.

Application-specific integrated circuit

An application-specific integrated circuit (ASIC) is a primary alternative to a GPU. ASIC chips are purpose-designed for particular DL architectures for computation and data flow, so are faster and require less power than the GPUs. For example, Google's **Tensor Processing Unit (TPU)** has dedicated **Matrix Units (MXUs)** designed for efficient matrix computations, and AWS offers the Inferentia chip, an ASIC designed for model inference. To speed up model inference, the Amazon Inferentia chip and Google's TPU chip both use the systolic array mechanism to speed up arithmetic calculations for deep neural networks. While the general-purpose chips such as CPUs and GPUs use local registers between different ALU computations to transfer data and results, a systolic array allows you to chain multiple ALUs to reduce register access to speed up processing. The following diagram shows how data flows within a systolic array architecture versus a regular architecture that's used in CPUs and GPUs:

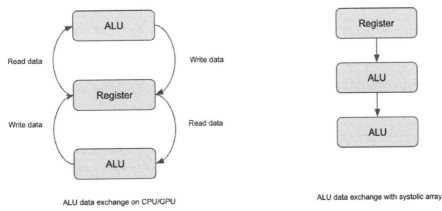

Figure 10.14 – Systolic array processing versus CPU/GPU processing

The Amazon Inferentia chip can be used directly with Amazon SageMaker for inference with improved latency. You can do this by selecting one of the supported Inferentia chips for model deployment.

Model optimization

When you're processing computational graphs for DL model inference, the size of the neural network (such as its number of layers, neurons, and so on), the number of model parameters, and the numerical precision of the model parameters directly impact the performance of model inference. The model optimization approach focuses on reducing the size of the neural network, the number of model parameters, and the numerical precisions to reduce inference latency. In general, there are two main approaches to model optimization: quantization and pruning.

Quantization

Traditionally, deep neural networks are trained with **floating-point 32 bit (FP32)**. However, for many neural networks, FP32 is not needed for the required precision.

Quantization for DL is a network compression approach that uses lower precision numbers, such as **floating-point 16 bit (FP16)** or **integer 8 bit (INT8)** instead of FP32, to represent static model parameters and perform numerical computation with dynamic data inputs/activation, all while having minimal or no impact on model performance. For example, an INT8 representation takes up four times less space than the FP32 representation, which significantly reduces the memory requirements and computational costs for neural networks, which means it can improve the overall latency for model inference.

There are different types of quantization algorithms, including uniform and non-uniform quantization algorithms. Both approaches map real values in a continuous domain to discrete lower precision values in the quantized domain. In the uniform case, the quantized values in the quantized domains are evenly spaced, whereas the non-uniform case has varying quantized values. The following diagram shows the difference between a uniform and a non-uniform quantization:

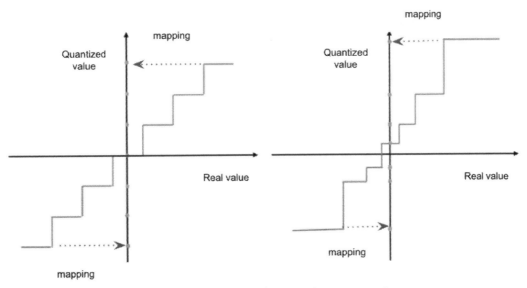

Figure 10.15 – Uniform and non-uniform quantization

Quantization can be performed both post-training and during training (quantization-aware training). Post-training quantization takes a trained model, quantizes the weights, and regenerates a quantized model. Quantization-aware training involves fine-tuning a full precision model. During training, the higher precision real numbers are reduced to lower precision numbers.

Quantization support is natively available in DL frameworks, such as PyTorch and TensorFlow. For example, PyTorch supports both forms of quantization via its `torch.quantization` package. TensorFlow supports quantization through the `tf.lite` package.

Pruning (also known as sparsity)

Pruning is another network compression technique that eliminates some of the model weights and neurons that don't impact model performance to reduce the size of the model to make inference faster. For example, weights that are close to zero or redundant can usually be removed.

Pruning techniques can be classified into static and dynamic pruning. Static pruning takes place offline before the model is deployed, while dynamic pruning is performed during runtime. Here, we will discuss some of the key concepts and approaches for static pruning.

Static pruning mainly consists of three steps:

1. Parameter selection for pruning targeting.

2. Pruning the neurons.

3. Fine-tuning or retraining if needed. Retraining may improve the model performance of the pruned neural network.

There are several approaches for selecting the parameters for static pruning, including the magnitude-based approach, the penalty-based approach, and dropout removal:

- **Magnitude-based approach**: It is widely accepted that large model weights are more important than small model weights. So, one intuitive way to select weights for pruning is to look at zero-value weights or the weights within a defined absolute threshold. The magnitude of the neural network activation layer can also be used to determine if the associated neurons can be removed.

- **Penalty-based approach**: In the penalty-based approach, the goal is to modify the loss function or add additional constraints so that some weights are forced to become zeros or near zeros. The weights that are zeros or close to zeros can then be pruned. An example of the penalty-based approach is using LASSO to shrink the weights of features.

- **Dropout removal**: Dropout layers are used in deep neural network training as regularizers to avoid overfitting data. While dropout layers are useful in training, they are not useful for inference and can be removed to reduce the number of parameters without impacting the model's performance.

DL frameworks, such as TensorFlow and PyTorch, provide APIs for pruning models. For example, you can use the `tensorflow_model_optimization` package and its `prune_low_magnitude` API for magnitude-based pruning. PyTorch provides model pruning support via its `torch.nn.utils.prune` API.

Graph and operator optimization

In addition to hardware acceleration and model optimization, there are additional optimization techniques that focus on the execution optimization of the computational graph, as well as hardware-specific operator and tensor optimization.

Graph optimization

Graph optimization focuses on reducing the number of operations that are performed in computational graphs to speed up inference. Multiple techniques are used for graph optimization, including operator fusion, dead code elimination, and constant folding.

Operator fusion combines multiple operations in a subgraph into a single operation to improve latency. In a typical execution of a subgraph with multiple operations, system memory is accessed for read/write to transfer data between operations, which is an expensive task. Operator fusion reduces the number of memory accesses, as well as optimizes the overall computations since the computations are now happening in a single kernel without the intermediate results being saved to memory. This approach also reduces the memory footprint due to a smaller number of operations being performed. The following diagram shows the concept of operator fusion:

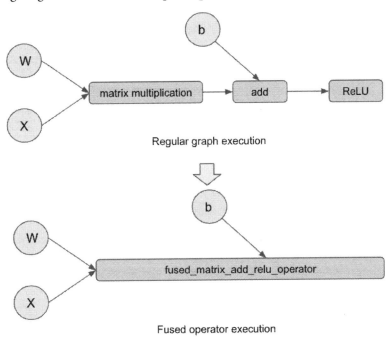

Figure 10.16 – Graph operator fusion

In the preceding diagram, the **matrix multiplication**, **add**, and **ReLU** operators are being fused into a single operator for execution in a single kernel to reduce memory access and the time needed to start multiple kernels.

Constant folding is the process of evaluating constants at compile time instead of runtime to speed up processing during runtime. For example, for the following expression, A can be assigned to a value of 300 at compile time instead of being dynamically calculated at runtime, which requires a more computational cycle: $A = 100 + 200$. Dead code elimination removes the code that does not affect the program's results. This ensures that the program doesn't waste computation on useless operations.

Operator optimization

Operator optimization (also known as tensor optimization) focuses on hardware-specific optimization for a specific model. Different hardware devices have different memory layouts and computational units and as such, hardware-specific optimization is often required to take full advantage of the hardware architecture. Multiple techniques have been developed for operator optimization for different hardware devices, including the following:

- Nested parallelism, which takes advantage of the GPU memory hierarchy and enables data reuse across threads through shared memory regions.

- Memory latency hiding, which overlaps the memory operation with computation to maximize memory and compute resources.

While graph optimization, operator optimization, and model optimization address different areas of optimizations, they are often combined to provide end-to-end optimization.

Model compilers

Manually optimizing end-to-end model performance is non-trivial. Adding the dimensions of multiple ML frameworks and a wide range of target hardware devices for optimization makes this a very challenging problem. To simplify the optimization process for different ML frameworks and different devices, several open source and commercial products have been developed. We will briefly talk about a few such packages in this section.

TensorFlow XLA

TensorFlow **Accelerated Linear Algebra** (**XLA**) is a DL compiler for TensorFlow. It compiles a TensorFlow graph into a sequence of execution kernels specifically optimized for the model. XLA transforms the original TensorFlow graph into an **intermediate representation** (**IR**) before performing several optimizations on the IR, such as operator fusion for faster computation. The output from the optimization step is then used for generating hardware-specific code that optimizes the performance of the different target hardware devices, such as CPUs and GPUs. XLA is used at Google in production for many accelerators.

PyTorch Glow

PyTorch Glow is a DL compiler for multiple DL frameworks. Similar to XLA, it also uses an IR to represent the original computational graph to perform optimizations. Unlike XLA, PyTorch Glow uses two layers of IRs. The first layer is used for performing domain-specific optimizations such as quantization, while the second IR layer is used for memory-related optimization such as memory latency hiding. After the second layer IR optimization, target device-dependent code is generated for running the models on different devices.

Apache TVM

Apache **Tensor Virtual Machine (TVM)** is an open source compiler framework for model optimization. It optimizes and compiles models built with different frameworks, such as PyTorch and TensorFlow, for different target CPUs, GPUs, and specialized hardware devices for accelerated performance. TVM supports optimization at different levels, including graph optimization and operator optimization targeting specific hardware. It also comes with a runtime for efficiently executing the compiled models.

One key feature of TVM is AutoTVM, which uses ML to search for the optimal sequences of code execution for different hardware devices. This ML-based search algorithm can significantly outperform baseline benchmarks by using vendor-provided optimization libraries such as cuDNN. This ML-based approach also enables efficient compilation scaling for a large number of hardware devices.

Amazon SageMaker Neo

Amazon SageMaker Neo is the model compiling feature in SageMaker. It mainly uses Apache TVM as the underlying compiler library. With SageMaker Neo, you take a model that's been trained in different ML/DL frameworks such as TensorFlow and PyTorch, choose the target processors such as Intel, Apple, ARM, and Nvidia, and then SageMaker Neo compiles an optimized model for the target hardware. Neo also provides a runtime library for each target platform to load and execute the compiled model. SageMaker Neo is a managed offering, so you don't need to manage the underlying infrastructure and processes for model compilation and deployment.

Inference engine optimization

One common model deployment pattern is to use open source inference engines or commercial hosting platforms for model serving. So, inference engine optimization is another approach that helps reduce model latency and inference throughput. In this section, we will talk about a few considerations. Note that there are no universal rules for inference engine optimization as they could be engine- and model-specific. It is important to test and validate different configurations for the final deployment.

Inference batching

If you have a large number of inference requests and there is no strict latency requirement on a single prediction request, then inference batching is a technique that can help reduce the total inference time for the requests. With inference batching, instead of running predictions one at a time for each request, multiple requests are batched together and sent to the inference engine. This technique reduces the total number of request round-trips, thus reducing the total inference time. Inference engines such as TensorFlow Serving and TorchServe provide built-in support for batch inference. You can find the configuration details for TorchServe and TensorFlow Serving batch inference at `https://pytorch.org/serve/batch_inference_with_ts.html` and `https://www.tensorflow.org/tfx/serving/serving_config#batching_configuration`, respectively.

Enabling parallel serving sessions

If your model hosting server has multiple compute cores, you can configure the number of parallel serving sessions to maximize the utilization of the available cores. For example, you can configure the `TENSORFLOW_INTRA_OP_PARALLELISM` setting in TensorFlow Serving based on the number of cores that can run multiple serving sessions in parallel to optimize throughput. TorchServe has settings for the number of workers per model and the number of threads for parallelization optimization.

Picking a communication protocol

Inference engines such as TensorFlow and TorchServe provide support for the gRPC protocol, which is a faster serialization format than the REST protocol. The gPRC protocol provides better overall performance but does have performance benchmarks as different models could behave differently. The REST protocol may be your preferred option based on specific requirements.

With that, you have learned about the technical approaches to large-scale training and low latency model inference. Next, let's get some hands-on experience with distributed training using SageMaker and PyTorch.

Hands-on lab – running distributed model training with PyTorch

In this hands-on lab, you will use SageMaker Training Service to run data parallel distributed training. We will use PyTorch's `torch.nn.parallel.DistributedDataParallel` API as the distributed training framework and run the training job on a small cluster. We will reuse the dataset and training scripts from the hands-on lab in *Chapter 8, Building a Data Science Environment Using AWS Services*.

All right, let's get started!

Modifying the training script

First, we need to add distributed training support to the training script. To start, create a copy of the `train.py` file, rename the file `train-dis.py`, and open the `train-dis.py` file. You will need to make changes to the following three main functions. The following steps are meant to highlight the key changes needed. To run the lab, you can download the modified `train-dis.py` file from `https://github.com/PacktPublishing/The-Machine-Learning-Solutions-Architect-Handbook/tree/main/Chapter10`.

Modifying the train() function

You need to make some changes to the `train()` function to enable distributed training. The following are the key changes that are required:

- **Process group initialization**: To enable distributed training, we need to initialize and register each training process on each device to be included in the training group. This can be achieved by calling the `torch.distributed.init_process_group()` function. This function will block until all the processes have been registered. There are a few concepts that we need to be familiar with during this initialization step:

  - **Word size**: This is the total number of processes in a distributed training group. Since we will run one process on each device (CPU or GPU), the world size is also the same as the total number of devices in a training cluster. For example, if you have two servers and each server has two GPUs, then the world size is four for this training group. The `torch.distributed.init_process_group()` function uses this information to understand how many processes to include in the distributed training job.

- **Rank**: This is the unique index that's assigned to each process in the training group. For example, the ranks for all the processes in a training group with a world size of four would be [0,1,2,3]. This unique index helps uniquely identify each process within a training group for communication.

- **Local rank**: This uniquely identifies a device in a server node. For example, if there are two devices in a server node, the local rank for two devices would be [0,1]. Local rank allows you to select a specific device to load the model and data for model training.

- **Backend**: This is the low-level communication library for exchanging and aggregating data among the different processes. PyTorch distributed training supports several communication backends, including NCCL, MPI, and Gloo. You choose a different backend based on the device and networking configuration. It uses these backends to send, receive, broadcast, or reduce data during distributed training. We are not going to get into the technical details of these backends in this book. If you are interested in how these backends work, you can easily find internet sources that cover these topics.

- **Wrap the training algorithm with PyTorch distributed library**: To use the PyTorch distributed library support for training, you need to wrap the algorithm with the PyTorch distributed training library. You can achieve this with the `torch.nn.parallel.DistributedDataParallel()` API. This allows the algorithm to participate in distributed training to exchange gradients and update global parameters.

- **Saving model using a single device**: In a multi-device server node, you only want one device to save the final model to avoid I/O conflicts. You can achieve this by selecting a device with a specific local rank ID.

Now let's take a look at the next step.

Modifying the get_data_loader() function

To ensure a different subset of training data is loaded into different devices on the server nodes, we need to configure the PyTorch DataLoader API to load data based on the rank of the training process. This can be done using the `torch.utils.data.distributed.DistributedSampler` API.

Adding multi-processing launch support for multi-device server nodes

For server nodes with multiple devices, we need to spawn several parallel processes based on the number of devices available. To enable this, we can use `torch.multiprocessing` to kick off multiple running processes on each node.

Modifying and running the launcher notebook

We are now ready to modify the launcher notebook to kick off the model training job. To start, copy the `bert-financial-sentiment-Launcher.ipynb` file from `chapter 8` and save it as `bert-financial-sentiment-dis-Launcher.ipynb`. Open the new notebook and replace the second cell's content with the following code blocks:

1. First, we initialize the Sagemaker PyTorch estimator and set the output directory for the model:

```
from sagemaker.pytorch import PyTorch
output_path = f"s3://{bucket}/{prefix}"
```

2. Now, we construct the PyTorch estimator with input parameters. We will use two instances of the `ml.g4dn.12xlarge` server, which will mean that we will be using a total of eight GPUs:

```
estimator = PyTorch(
    entry_point="train-dis.py",
    source_dir="code",
    role=role,
    framework_version="1.6",
    py_version="py3",
    instance_count=2,
    instance_type= "ml.g4dn.12xlarge",
    output_path=output_path,
    hyperparameters={
        "epochs": 10,
        "lr" : 5e-5,
        "num_labels": 3,
        "train_file": "train.csv",
        "test_file" : "test.csv",
```

```
        "MAX_LEN" : 315,
        "batch_size" : 64,
        "test_batch_size" : 10,
        "backend": "nccl"
    },
)
```

3. Finally, we kick off the training process using the `fit()` function:

```
estimator.fit({"training": inputs_train, "testing":
inputs_test})
```

You can download the revised launcher notebook at `https://github.com/PacktPublishing/The-Machine-Learning-Solutions-Architect-Handbook/blob/main/Chapter10/bert-financial-sentiment-dis-launcher.ipynb`.

Now, just execute each cell in the new notebook to kick off the distributed training. You can track the training status directly inside the notebook, and the detail status in CloudWatch Logs. You should see a total of eight processes running in parallel. Take note of the total training time and accuracy and see how they compare with the results you got from *Chapter 8, Building a Data Science Environment Using AWS ML Services*.

Congratulations! You have successfully trained a BERT model using the PyTorch distributed training library.

Summary

In this chapter, we discussed several advanced ML engineering topics, including distributed training for large-scale datasets and large models, as well as techniques and options for achieving low latency inference. Now, you should be able to talk about how data parallelism and model parallelism work, as well as the various technology options, such as the PyTorch distributed library and SageMaker Distributed Training library, for running data parallel and model parallel distribution training. You should also be able to talk about the different techniques you can use for model optimization to reduce model inference latency, as well as the model compiler tools for automated model optimization.

In the next chapter, we will talk about security and governance in ML.

11
ML Governance, Bias, Explainability, and Privacy

So far, you have successfully implemented a **machine learning** (**ML**) platform. At this point, you might be thinking that your job is done as an **ML Solutions Architect** (**ML SA**) and that the business is ready to deploy models into production. Well, it turns out that there are additional considerations. To put models into production, an organization also needs to put governance control in place to meet both the internal policy and external regulatory requirements. ML governance is usually not the responsibility of an ML SA; however, it is important for an ML SA to be familiar with the regulatory landscape and ML governance framework, especially in regulated industries, such as financial services. So, you should consider these requirements when you evaluate or build an ML solution.

In this chapter, we will provide an overview of the ML governance concept and some key components, such as model registry and model monitoring, in an ML governance framework. We will also discuss where technology solutions fit in the overall ML governance framework. After reading this chapter, you will understand why ML systems need to be designed with governance in mind, and what technologies can help address some of the governance and security requirements.

Specifically, we will be covering the following topics:

- What is ML governance and why is it needed?
- Understanding the ML governance framework
- Understanding ML bias and explainability
- Designing an ML platform for governance
- Hands-on lab – detecting ML bias, model explainability, and training privacy-preserving models

Technical requirements

You will continue to use the AWS environment you created previously for the hands-on portion of this chapter. The associated code samples can be found at `https://github.com/PacktPublishing/The-Machine-Learning-Solutions-Architect-Handbook/blob/main/Chapter11`.

What is ML governance and why is it needed?

ML governance is a set of policies, processes, and activities by which an organization manages, controls, and monitors an ML model's life cycle, dependencies, access, and performance to avoid or minimize financial risk, reputation risk, compliance risk, and legal risk.

The stakes in model risk management are high. To put this into context, let's revisit the impact of the financial crisis in 2007 and 2008 due to inadequate ML governance. Many of us probably still vividly remember the aftermath of the great recession caused by the crisis, where millions of people were impacted in terms of their jobs, investments, or both, and many of the largest financial institutions were brought to their knees and went out of business. The government had to step in to bail out many institutions such as Fannie Mae and Freddie Mac. This crisis was caused in large part by the flawed model risk management process and governance across financial organizations, where they failed to detect the risk from model failure in addressing complex derivative trading. As a result, the market was flooded with cheap credit.

To prevent and mitigate future crises like this, many regulatory bodies have issued guidelines and established formal supervisory guidance on model risk management.

The regulatory landscape around model risk management

To ensure organizations implement the proper risk management governance for model development and use, various countries and jurisdictions have established policies and guidance for the regulated industries.

In the United States, the Federal Reserve and the **Office of Controller and Currency (OCC)** have published the *Supervisory Guidance on Model Risk Management* (OCC 2011-2012 / SR 11-7). SR 11-7 has become the key regulatory guidance for model risk management in the US. This guidance establishes the main principles for model risk management and covers governance, policies and controls, model development, implementation and use, and model validation processes. In the governance and policy area, there's guidance on model inventory management, risk rating, roles, and responsibilities. In the model development and implementation area, it covers topics such as design processes, data assessment, model testing, and documentation. Finally, in the validation area, there's guidance on validation procedures, monitoring, and finding resolutions.

In Europe, **European Central Bank (ECB)** Banking Supervision launched the **Targeted Review of Internal Models (TRIM)** guideline in 2016 to guide the **model risk management framework (MRM)**. Specifically, the guideline states that an MRM needs to have a model inventory to have a holistic view of the models and their applications, a guideline for identifying and mitigating known model deficiencies, definitions of roles and responsibilities, and definitions of policies, measurement procedures, and reporting.

SR 11-7 and TRIM share several common topics and expectations, indicating that regulatory bodies in both the US and Europe have similar opinions on how MRM should be implemented. We are not going to list all the guidelines in this book. If you are interested, you can find more details on SR 11-7 and TRIMs at the following links:

- **SR 11-7**: `https://www.federalreserve.gov/supervisionreg/srletters/sr1107.htm`

- **TRIM**: `https://www.bankingsupervision.europa.eu/banking/tasks/internal_models/html/index.en.html`

Most of the major banks in the US generally have well-established MRMs and operations, partly because of the focus placed by SR 11-7.

Common causes of ML model risks

To understand how ML governance can help with model risk management, we need to understand the sources of model risks and the impact they might have. The following are some common causes that can result in potential model failures or misuse:

- **Lack of inventory and catalog**: Without a clear and accurate inventory of models running in production, an organization will not be able to explain where and how certain automated decisions are made by the underlying decision-making systems. An organization will also be unable to mitigate any erroneous decisions made by the system.

- **Lack of documentation**: Without clear lineage documentation regarding data and models, an organization will not be able to explain the behavior of a model or reproduce the model when required by auditors or regulators.

- **Defects and bias in training data**: ML models can make biased decisions as a result of training with biased datasets. This can subject an organization to potential reputational or legal risk.

- **Inconsistent data distributions**: When the distributions of training data and inference data are different, the model can make incorrect predictions in production. These data distributions can also change in production over time, which is known as data drift. Incorrect predictions made from out-of-distribution errors can result in potential financial, reputation, or legal risks.

- **Inadequate model testing and validation**: Before a model is put into production, it should be thoroughly tested and validated against established acceptance metrics. It should also be tested for robustness to identify failure points.

- **Lack of model interpretability**: For certain business applications, there are requirements for explaining how a decision is made by a model. The inability to explain the model when required can result in reputational and legal risk.

- **Inadequate change management process**: Without robust and model change management controls, models can be trained with incorrect data and defective models can be deployed or changed in production, resulting in model failure.

With that, we are familiar with the regulatory landscape around model risk management and some of the common causes of model failure and misuse. Next, let's discuss the ML governance framework.

Understanding the ML governance framework

ML governance is complex as it deals with complex internal and regulatory policies. There are many stakeholders and technology systems involved in the full ML life cycle. Furthermore, the opaque nature of many ML models, data dependencies, ML privacy, and the stochastic behaviors of many ML algorithms make ML governance more challenging.

The governance body in an organization is responsible for establishing policies and the ML governance framework. To operationalize ML risk management, many organizations set up three lines of defense for their organizational structure:

- The first line of defense is owned by the business operations. This line of defense focuses on the development and use of ML models. The business operations are responsible for creating and retaining all data and model assumptions, model behavior, and model performance metrics in structured documents based on model classification and risk exposure. Models are tested and registered, the associated artifacts are persisted, and the results can be reproduced. Once the models have been deployed, system issues, model outputs, model bias, and data and model drift are monitored and addressed according to the established procedures and guidelines.

- The second line of defense is owned by the risk management function, and it focuses on model validation. The risk management function is responsible for independently reviewing and validating the documents that are generated by the first line. This line of defense introduces standards on controls and documentation, makes sure that documents are self-contained, that results are reproducible, and that the limitations of models are well-understood by stakeholders.

- The internal audit owns the third line of defense. The third line of defense mainly focuses on control and processes and less on model artifacts and theories. Specifically, this line of defense is responsible for auditing the first and second lines of defense to ensure all the established processes and guidelines are effectively followed and implemented. This line of defense provides independent validation of internal controls and reviews the documentation, timeliness, frequency, and completeness of the model risk management activities.

As an ML SA, you are normally part of the first line of defense, designing solutions that are compliant with the ML governance framework. In the next section, we will talk about how ML technology fits in the overall governance framework.

Understanding ML bias and explainability

One of the key focus areas for ML governance is bias detection and model explainability. Having ML models exhibiting biased behaviors not only subjects an organization to potential legal consequences but could also result in a public relations nightmare. Specific laws and regulations, such as *Equal Credit Opportunity Act*, prohibit discrimination in business transactions, such as credit transactions based on race, color, religion, sex, nationality origin, marital status, and age. Some other examples of laws against discrimination include the *Civil Rights Act of 1964* and *Age Discrimination in Employment Act of 1967*.

ML bias can result from the underlying prejudice in data. Since ML models are trained using data, if the data contains bias, then the trained model will also exhibit biased behaviors. For example, if you build an ML model to predict a loan default rate as part of the loan application review process, and you use race as one of the features in the training data, then the ML algorithm can potentially pick up race-related patterns and favor certain ethnic groups over others. Bias can be introduced in different stages of the ML life cycle. For example, there could be data selection bias as certain groups might have stronger representation in the data collection stage. There could be labeling bias where a human makes an intentional or unintentional mistake in assigning labels to a dataset. Data sources with disinformation can also be a source of bias that results in biased AI solutions.

The ability to explain the decisions that are made by models helps an organization to satisfy the compliance and audit requirements of the governance bodies. Furthermore, model explainability helps an organization understand the cause-and-effect relationships between the inputs and the ML predictions to make better business decisions. For example, if you can understand the reasons (such as rewards program) behind strong customer interest in a financial product, you can adjust your business strategy, such as doubling down on rewards programs, to increase revenues. Being able to explain model decisions also helps establish trust with domain experts in the ML models. If domain experts agree with how the predictions are made by the models, they are more likely to adopt the models for decision making.

There are various techniques we can use for bias detection and model explainability, and we will take a closer look at some of them in the next section.

Bias detection and mitigation

To detect and mitigate bias, some guiding principles need to be established on what is considered fair. For example, a bank's loan approval process should treat similar people similarly and the process may be considered fair when applicants with similar qualifications are assessed similarly. The bank also needs to ensure different demographic subgroups are treated equally for loan approval and measure metrics, such as the rate for loan rejection to be approximately similar across different demographic subgroups.

Depending on the definition of fairness, bias can be measured using different metrics. Some of these metrics may even contradict with each other. You need to choose the metrics that best support the definition of fairness in terms of the social and legal considerations and inputs from different demographic groups. The following is a list of some of the bias metrics we must consider:

- **Class imbalance**: This metric measures the imbalanced representations of different demographic groups, especially disadvantaged groups, in a dataset.

- **The difference in the positive proportion of observed labels**: This metric measures the differences in positive labels across different demographic groups.

- **Kullback and Leibler (KL) divergence**: This metric compares the probability distribution in features and labels for the different groups, such as advantaged and disadvantaged groups.

- **Conditional demographic disparity in labels**: This metric measures if a group has a bigger proportion of rejected outcomes than accepted outcomes in the same group.

- **Recall difference**: This metric measures if the ML model is finding more true positives for one group (advantaged group) than other groups (disadvantaged groups).

There are several ways we can mitigate bias once it has been detected. The following are some examples that can be applied:

- **Remove features**: This approach helps mitigate bias by removing features that can contribute to the bias, such as gender and age.

- **Rebalance the training data**: This approach corrects bias in different representations for the different groups in the training data.

- **Adjust the labels in the training data**: This approach brings the proportions of labels closer together for the different subgroups.

There are several open source libraries for fairness and bias management, such as the following:

- Fairness (`https://github.com/algofairness/fairness-comparison`)
- Aequitas (`https://github.com/dssg/aequitas`)
- Themis (`https://github.com/LASER-UMASS/Themis`)
- Responsibly (`https://github.com/ResponsiblyAI/responsibly`)
- IBM AI Fairness 360 (`https://aif360.mybluemix.net/`)

There is also a component in SageMaker for bias detection, which we will cover in greater detail later in this chapter.

ML explainability techniques

There are two main concepts when it comes to explaining the behaviors of an ML model:

- **Global explainability**: This is the overall behavior of a model across all data points and is used for model training and/or prediction. This helps us understand how different input features affect the outcome of model predictions. For example, after training an ML model for credit scoring, it is determined that income is the most important feature in predicting high credit scores across the data points for all loan applicants.

- **Local explainability**: This is the behavior of a model for a single data point (instance) and specifies which features had the most influence on the prediction for a single data point. For example, when you try to explain which features influenced the decision the most for a single loan applicant, it might turn out that education was the most important feature, even though income was the most important feature at the global level.

Some ML algorithms, such as linear regression and decision trees, are considered explainable algorithms that have the built-in ability to explain the model. For example, the coefficients of linear regression models directly represent the relative importance of different input features, and the split points in a decision tree represent the rules that are used for decision making.

For black-box models such as neural networks, it is very hard to explain how the decisions are made in part due to non-linearity and model complexity. One technique for solving this is to use a white-box surrogate model to help explain the decisions of a black-box model. For example, you can train a linear regression model in parallel with a black-box neural network model using the same input data. While the linear regression model might not have the same performance as the black-box model, it can be used to explain how the decision was made at a high level.

There are various open source packages, such as **local interpretable model-agnostic explanations (LIME)** and **SHapley Additive exPlanations (SHAP)**, for model explainability. Both LIME and SHAP adopt the surrogate model approach.

LIME

As its name suggests, LIME supports local (instance) explainability. The main idea behind LIME is to perturb the original data points (tweak the data points), feed them into the black-box model, and see the corresponding outputs. The perturbed data points are small changes to the original data point and are weighted based on their proximities to the original data. Then, it fits a surrogate model, such as linear regression, using the perturbed data points and responses. Finally, the trained linear model is used to explain how the decision was made for the original data point.

LIME can be installed as a regular Python package and can be used to explain text classifiers, image classifiers, tabular classifiers, and regression models. The following are the explainers that are available in LIME:

- **Tabular data explainer**: `lime_tabular.LimeTabularExplainer()`
- **Image data explainer**: `lime_image.LimeImageExplainer()`
- **Text data explainer**: `lime_text.LimeTextExplainer()`

LIME has some shortcomings, such as a lack of stability and consistency, since LIME uses random sampling to generate data points for approximation. Also, the linear surrogate might be inaccurate for local data points that cannot be approximated by a linear model.

SHAP

SHAP is a more popular package and addresses some of the shortcomings of LIME. It computes the contribution of each feature regarding the prediction using the coalition game theory concept, where each feature value of each data instance is a player in the coalition.

The basic idea behind the coalition game theory is to form different permutations of coalitions of players when playing a game, then observe the game results from the different permutations, and finally calculate the contribution of each player. For example, if there are three features (*A*, *B*, and *C*) in the training dataset, then there will be eight distinct coalitions (2^3). We train one model for each distinct coalition for a total of eight models. We use all eight models to generate predictions in the dataset, figure out the marginal contribution of each feature, and assign a Shapley value to each feature to indicate the feature importance. For example, if the model that uses a coalition with only features *A* and *B* generates an output of *50*, and the model that uses features *A*, *B*, and *C* generates an output of *60*, then feature *C* has a marginal contribution of *10*. This is just a generalization of the concept; the actual calculation and assignments are more involved.

SHAP can also be installed like a regular Python package. It can be used to explain tree ensemble models, natural language models (such as transformers), and deep learning models. It has the following main explainers:

- **TreeExplainer**: An implementation for computing SHAP values for trees and ensemble of trees algorithms

- **DeepExplainer**: An implementation for computing SHAP values for deep learning models

- **GradientExplainer**: An implementation of the expected gradients to approximate SHAP values for deep learning models

- **LinearExplainer**: Used to explain linear models with independent features

- **KernelExplainer**: A model-agnostic method for estimating SHAP values for any model because it doesn't make assumptions about the model type

SHAP is widely considered the state-of-the-art model explainability algorithm, and it has been implemented in commercial offerings such as SageMaker. It can be used to compute both global feature importance and local explainability for a single instance. It does have some shortcomings as well, such as slow computation associated with KernelExplainer.

Designing an ML platform for governance

ML technology systems are critical in the overall operations of ML governance processes and activities. First, these technology systems need to be designed and built to meet the internal and external policies and guidelines themselves. Second, technology can help with simplifying and automating ML governance activities. The following diagram shows the various ML governance touchpoints in an enterprise ML platform:

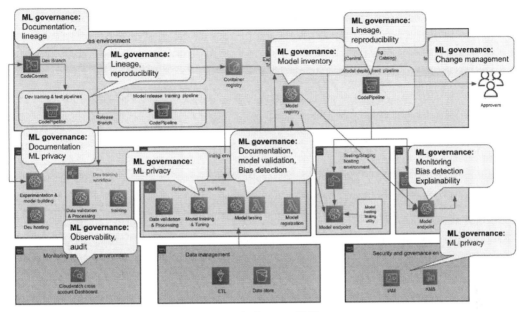

Figure 11.1 – ML platform and ML governance

When an ML platform is built with ML governance in mind, it can capture and supply information to help with the three lines of defense and let you streamline the model risk management workflows. The types of tools that are used for ML governance include online data stores, workflow applications, document sharing systems, and model inventory databases. Now, let's take a closer look at some of the core ML governance components and where an ML platform or technology can fit in.

Data and model documentation

One of the key components of ML governance is documentation. All the models that are used for decision-making should be properly documented. The scope of the documentation may include the following:

- A data overview, including a data quality report on evaluating and assessing the input data

- A model development document, including the methodology and assumptions, model usage instructions, performance and validation results, and other qualitative and quantitative analyses

- A model validation strategy and report by the second and third lines of defense

- Model performance monitoring results and data drift reports

- Model implementation and user acceptance testing reports

The role of the ML platform in ML governance documentation is usually to provide data points that feed into the formal risk management documentations or generate some of the ready-to-use reports. Specifically, an ML platform must be able to track, store, and report the following data points:

- Data quality metrics such as data descriptions, statistics, bias, and errors

- Model metrics and validation results in development and testing

- Model bias and explainability reports

- Model performance monitoring results in production

Amazon SageMaker can produce data and documentation to be included in model risk documentations. Specifically, SageMaker tracks and produces the following information that is relevant for ML governance documentation:

- **Model metrics**: SageMaker Training Service tracks model metrics such as training errors and validation errors.

- **Data and model bias reports**: SageMaker Clarify is the bias detection component in SageMaker. If you enable SageMaker Clarify, you can get data and model bias reports for the training data and trained model. The data and model bias reports provide details such as imbalances in training data and prediction behavior across different age groups and genders.

- **Model explainability reports**: SageMaker Clarify also provides a model explainability feature. It uses SHAP to explain the contribution of each input to the final decision. You can find out more about SHAP at `https://shap.readthedocs.io/en/latest/index.html`.

There are various tools for generating data quality reports. For example, AWS Glue DataBrew can be used to profile input data and generate data quality reports. It reports data statistics such as data distribution, correlation, and missing values.

These data points are available via SageMaker and the DataBrew UI and API and can be manually extracted to meet your needs. However, to operationalize the process, you should implement automated data extraction jobs to extract data points from SageMaker and DataBrew and store them in a purpose-built data store for model risk management. Depending on the business requirements, data from the data science environment, testing environment, or production hosting environment can be extracted for documentation purposes.

Model inventory

The model registry is an essential component in the ML governance framework. It helps provide visibility into the available models and their uses, and it is a key tool for both business operations and risk management to govern the use of ML models. With a model registry, you can keep a catalog of models in different stages, version control the models, and associate metadata, such as training metrics, with the models. You can also manage the approval process for deployment and use this as part of an MLOps pipeline to track lineage and activities against the model training and deployment life cycle.

There are both open source model registry platforms (such as MLFlow model registry) as well as managed model registry services available for model registry management. As we mentioned in *Chapter 9, Building an Enterprise ML Architecture with AWS ML Services*, SageMaker has a managed model registry offering. The SageMaker model registry provides the following key capabilities to support ML governance activities and processes:

- **Model inventory**: All the versions of the different models belong to a respective model group in the SageMaker registry. You can view all the model groups and different versions of a model in the registry. Metadata such as model metrics, training job details, hyperparameters used for training, and training data sources are important data points for the model review and model audit processes. Depending on specific business requirements, you can set up a central model registry for a single enterprise view, or even distributed model registries if that can meet your governance and audit requirements.

- **Model approval and life cycle tracking**: You can track the approval of models and model stages directly inside the SageMaker model registry. This helps the business operations and audits ensure the proper processes are followed.

SageMaker's model registry can be part of an automated MLOps pipeline to help ensure the consistency and repeatability of model management and model updates.

Model monitoring

Post-deployment model monitoring helps detect model failures so that the appropriate remediation actions can be taken to limit risk exposure. Models need to be monitored for system availability and errors, as well as data and model drift and prediction failure.

As we mentioned in *Chapter 9, Building an Enterprise ML Architecture with AWS ML Services*, SageMaker provides a model monitoring feature for both data drift and model drift. Specifically, SageMaker Model Monitor supports the following:

- **Data drift**: With SageMaker Model Monitor, you can monitor data quality issues and data distribution skews (also known as data drift) in production. To use this feature, you must create a baseline using a baseline dataset, such as a model training dataset, to gather data statistics, data types, and suggest constraints for monitoring. SageMaker Model Monitor can capture live inference traffic, calculate data statistics, examine data types, and verify them against the constraints and trigger alerts. For example, if a feature's mean and standard deviation changes significantly from the baseline, an alert can be triggered.

- **Model performance drift**: You can use Model Monitor to detect model performance changes in production. To use this feature, you can create a model performance baseline job using a baseline dataset that contains both the inputs and labels. The baseline job will suggest constraints, which are the metrics thresholds that Model Monitor will monitor against the metrics to be calculated with the ground truth data that was collected in production. These metrics can be optionally sent to CloudWatch for visualization.

- **Feature attribution drift**: When enabled with SageMaker Clarify, SageMaker Model Monitor can report feature attribution drift. Feature attributions are indicators of feature importance for the prediction output. Similar to data and model drift, you can create a SHAP baseline job using baseline data to generate constraint suggestions. The separate monitoring job is then scheduled to monitor predictions in production against the baseline.

SageMaker Model Monitoring can be integrated with automated alerting and response systems to streamline the remediation of model and data issues.

Change management control

To ensure model deployment process consistency to reduce operational risk, as well as to support auditing, the appropriate change management control needs to be put in place. This might include documentation about the nature of the change and its impact, change review and approval, change ticketing, access and activity monitoring, and backout procedures.

There are purpose-built change management tools for workflows and ticketing management. The underlying ML infrastructure needs to integrate with the change management workflow to ensure all the data points are collected and auditable.

SageMaker provides features that can support change management control, such as model approval status change tracking, model deployment logging, and fine-grained activity logging, such as for the IAM roles that were used for model deployment.

Lineage and reproducibility

One of the key requirements in many ML governance frameworks is to establish lineage across data and models so that a model can be reproduced when required. The data that's needed to establish lineage includes training data sources, the algorithm that was used, hyperparameter configuration, and the model training script. SageMaker provides several features to help establish lineage:

- SageMaker training jobs keep lineage data such as training data sources, training job containers (contains algorithm and training script), hyperparameter configuration, and model artifact locations. Historical training job data is immutable in the SageMaker environment for record retention purposes.

- SageMaker Experiment and ML Lineage can contain additional component details, such as data processing, for more complete lineage tracking.

- SageMaker Hosting provides information on the location of the original model artifact and the inference container to trace the lineage from model to endpoint.

These data points are available by calling the SageMaker API. An external application can call the SageMaker API directly to extract this data for review purposes. Alternatively, a data extraction job can be developed to extract these data points and load them into a purpose-built risk management store for analysis.

Observability and auditing

Auditing mostly focuses on process verification and artifact collection in support of audit activities. The underlying platform normally serves as an information source for collecting artifacts. For example, if there is a model risk management policy that requires approval before a model is deployed into production, then the audit will need to access the system of record to ensure such data is collected and retained.

SageMaker and other related services can be data sources in support of the overall audit process. Specifically, it provides the following information that can be relevant for auditing purposes:

- **Activity and access audit trail**: SageMaker sends all audit trail data to CloudWatch logs, which can be retained and analyzed for audit purposes.

- **Model approval tracking**: Model deployment approvals are tracked in SageMaker's model registry. This can be provided to an auditor as evidence that the required approval processes have been followed.

- **Lineage tracking**: SageMaker Experiment and ML Lineage tracking components can track and retain model lineages such as data processing, model training, and model deployment. Lineage tracking information helps the auditor verify that the model can be reproduced using its original data and configuration dependencies.

- **Configuration changes**: System configuration data is captured in AWS CloudTrail as change events. For example, when a SageMaker endpoint is deleted, there will be an entry in CloudTrail indicating this change.

Similarly, automated jobs can be implemented to extract this information and feed it into purpose-built data stores for risk management. An audit is a complex process that can involve many business functions and technology systems. To support the full audit process, you will need the support of multiple technology platforms and human processes to supply the required data.

Security and privacy-preserving ML

ML privacy is becoming increasingly important in ML implementation. To ensure compliance with data privacy regulations or even internal data privacy controls, ML systems need to provide foundational infrastructure security features such as data encryption, network isolation, compute isolation, and private connectivity. With a SageMaker-based ML platform, you can enable the following key security controls:

- **Private networking**: As SageMaker is a fully managed service, it runs in an AWS-owned account. By default, the resources in your AWS account communicate with SageMaker APIs via the public internet. To enable private connectivity to SageMaker components from your own AWS environment, you can attach them to a subnet in your **virtual private cloud** (**VPC**).

- **Storage encryption**: Data-at-rest encryption can be enabled by providing an encryption key when you create a SageMaker notebook, a training job, a processing job, or a hosting endpoint.

- **Disabling internet access**: By default, your SageMaker notebook, training job, and hosting service have access to the internet. This internet access can be disabled via configuration.

In addition to infrastructure security, you also need to think about data privacy and model privacy to protect sensitive information from adversarial attacks, such as reverse engineering sensitive data from anonymized data. There are three main techniques for data privacy protection in ML:

- **Differential privacy**: Differential privacy allows you to share datasets while withholding information about individuals within the dataset. This method works by adding random noises to the computation so that it is hard to reverse engineer the original data (if it is not impossible). For example, you can add noise to the training data or model training gradients to obfuscate the sensitive data.

- **Homomorphic encryption (HE)**: HE is a form of encryption that allows users to perform computations on encrypted data without decrypting it first. This leaves the computation output in an encrypted form that, when decrypted, is equivalent to the output as if the computation were performed on the unencrypted data. With this approach, the data can be encrypted before it is used for model training. The training algorithm will train the model with the encrypted data, and the output can only be decrypted by the data owner with the secret key.

- **Federated learning**: Federated learning allows model training to take place on edge devices while keeping data locally on the device, instead of sending the data to a central training cluster. This protects individual data as it is not shared in a central location, while the global model can still benefit from individual data.

Each of these topics warrants a separate book, so we will not dive into the details of all three. We will only provide an introduction to differential privacy in this book to explain the main intuition and concept behind this method.

Differential privacy

To understand the problem that differential privacy solves, let's take a look at the real-world privacy breach that happened with Netflix. In 2006, Netflix provided 100 million movie ratings, submitted by 480K users, as data for the Netflix price competition. Netflix anonymized usernames with unique subscribers' IDs in the dataset, thinking that this would protect subscribers' identities. Just 16 days later, two university researchers were able to identify some subscribers' true identities by matching their reviews with data from IMDb. This type of attack is called a **linkage attack**, and this exposes the fact that anonymization is not enough in protecting sensitive data. You can find more information about this at `https://en.wikipedia.org/wiki/Netflix_Prize`.

Differential privacy solves this problem by adding noise to the dataset that's used to compute the dataset, so the original data cannot easily be reverse-engineered. In addition to protection against linkage attacks, differential privacy also helps quantify privacy loss as a result of someone running processing against the data. To help understand what this means, let's look at an example.

Suppose your organization is a regional bank and your customer data repository contains sensitive data about your customers, including name, social security number, ZIP code, income, gender, and education. To ensure data privacy, this data cannot be freely shared by all departments, such as the marketing department. However, the aggregate analysis of the customer data, such as the number of customers with income over a certain threshold, can be shared. To enable access to the aggregated data, a data query tool was built to return only the aggregate data (such as count, sum, average, min, and max) to the marketing department. Separately, another database contains customer churn data with unique customer IDs, and a customer support database contains customer names and unique customer IDs. Both the churn database and customer support database are accessible to the marketing department. An ill-intentioned analyst wanted to find the names of customers whose incomes are above a certain threshold for some personal purpose. This analyst queried the database one day and found out that out of 4,000 total customers, there were 30 customers with incomes over $1 million in a particular ZIP code. A couple of days later, they queried the customer data again and found out there were only 29 customers with incomes over $1 million, out of a total of 3,999 customers. Since they had access to the churn database and customer support database, they were able to identify the name of the customer who churned and figured out that this customer had an income of over $1 million.

To prevent this from happening, the query tool was changed to add a little noise (such as adding or removing records) to the result without losing meaningful information about the original data. For example, instead of returning the actual result of 30 customers out of 4,000 customers in the first query, the result of 31 customers out of 4,001 customers was returned. And the second query returns 28 out of 3,997 instead of the actual 29 out of 3,999 figures. This added noise does not significantly change the overall magnitude of the summary result, but it makes reverse-engineering the original data much more difficult as you can't pinpoint a specific record. This is the intuition behind how differential privacy works.

The following diagram shows the concept of differential privacy, where computation is performed on two databases, and noise is added to one of the databases. The goal is to ensure that **Result 1** and **Result 2** are as close as possible as that's where it becomes harder and harder to tell the difference in distribution between **Result 1** and **Result 2**, even though the two databases are slightly different. Here, the Epsilon (ε) value is the privacy loss budget, which is the ceiling of how much probability an output distribution can change when adding/removing a record. The smaller the Epsilon value, the lower the privacy loss:

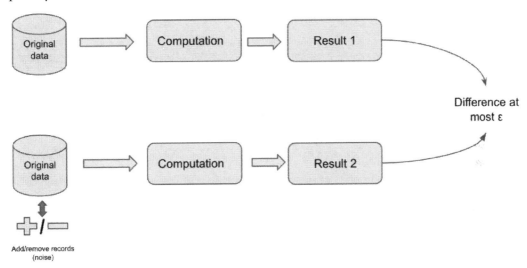

Figure 11.2 – Differential privacy concept

ML models are susceptible to privacy attacks. For example, it is possible to extract information from trained models that directly map to the original training data as deep learning models may have unintentionally memorized the training data. Also, overfitted models are more likely to memorize training data. Differential privacy is one of the techniques that can help minimize the effect of unintended memorization. Since differential privacy can make the computational outputs of two input datasets (one with sensitive data, one with sensitive data removed) almost indistinguishable from a query perspective, the hacker cannot confidently infer whether a piece of sensitive data is in the original dataset or not.

There are different ways to apply differential privacy to ML model training, such as adding noise to the underlying training data or adding noise to the model parameters. Also, it is important to know that differential privacy does not come for free. The higher the privacy protection (smaller epsilon), the lower the model accuracy.

Differential privacy is implemented in TensorFlow Privacy. TensorFlow Privacy provides a differentially private optimizer for model training and requires minimum code changes. The following code sample shows the syntax of using the `DPKerasSGDOptimizer` object for differential privacy training. The main steps are as follows:

1. Install the `tensorflow_privacy` library package.

2. Import `tensorflow_privacy`. Select your differentially private optimizer:

```
optimizer = tensorflow_privacy.DPKerasSGDOptimizer(
    l2_norm_clip=l2_norm_clip,
    noise_multiplier=noise_multiplier,
    num_microbatches=num_microbatches,
    learning_rate=learning_rate)
```

3. Select your loss function:

```
loss = tf.keras.losses.CategoricalCrossentropy(
    from_logits=True,
    reduction=tf.losses.Reduction.NONE)
```

4. Compile your model:

```
model.compile(optimizer=optimizer, loss=loss,
              metrics=['accuracy'])
```

PyTorch supports differential privacy with its `opacus` package. It is also fairly straightforward to use the `opacus` package to enable differential privacy training. The following code sample shows how to wrap an optimizer in the `PrivacyEngine` object, and just use the optimizer the same way in a PyTorch training loop:

```
from opacus import PrivacyEngine
optimizer= torch.optim.SGD(model.parameters(),
                           lr=learning_rate)
privacy_engine = PrivacyEngine(
    model,
    sample_rate=sample_rate,
    max_grad_norm=max_per_sample_grad_norm,
    noise_multiplier = noise_multiplier
)
privacy_engine.attach(optimizer)
```

We have covered several governance and security concepts in this chapter. As we mentioned at the beginning of this chapter, an ML solution architect is normally not responsible for establishing an ML governance framework or implementing a privacy-preserving modeling training architecture. However, an ML SA would be called upon to provide technical guidance on how to support ML governance using the different ML tools. So, knowing about these tools and how they can be used in the overall ML governance framework is quite important.

Next, let's get some hands-on experience with using some of the tools we have talked about.

Hands-on lab – detecting bias, model explainability, and training privacy-preserving models

Building a comprehensive system for ML governance is a complex task. In this hands-on lab, you will learn how to use some of SageMaker's built-in functionality to support certain aspects of ML governance.

Overview of the scenario

As an ML SA, you have been asked to identify technology solutions that support a project that has regulatory implications. Specifically, you need to determine the technical approaches for data bias detection, model explainability, and privacy-preserving model training. Follow these steps to get started.

Detecting bias in the training dataset

Let's start the hands-on lesson:

1. Launch the SageMaker Studio environment:

    A. Launch the same SageMaker Studio environment that you have been using.

    B. Create a new folder called `chapter11`. This will be our working directory for this lab. Create a new Jupyter notebook and name it `bias_explainability.ipynb`. Choose the `Python 3 (data science)` kernel when prompted.

    C. Create a new folder called `data` under the `chapter11` folder. We will use this folder to store our training and testing data.

2. Upload the training data:

   A. We will use the customer churn data (`churn.csv`) that we used in earlier chapters. If you don't have it, you can access it from here: `https://github.com/PacktPublishing/The-Machine-Learning-Solutions-Architect-Handbook/tree/main/Chapter11/data`.

   B. Download the data to your local directory and then upload both files to the newly created `data` directory.

3. Initialize the `sagemaker` environment using the following code block:

```
from sagemaker import Session
session = Session()
bucket = session.default_bucket()
prefix = "sagemaker/bias_explain"
region = session.boto_region_name
# Define IAM role
from sagemaker import get_execution_role
import pandas as pd
import numpy as np
import os
import boto3
role = get_execution_role()
s3_client = boto3.client("s3")
```

4. Load the data from the data directory and display the first few rows. The `Exited` column is the target:

```
training_data = pd.read_csv("data/churn.csv").dropna()
training_data.head()
```

5. Split the data into train and test sets (80/20 split):

```
from sklearn.model_selection import train_test_split
churn_train, churn_test = train_test_split(training_data, test_size=0.2)
```

Create an encoding function to encode the categorical features as numeric:

```
from sklearn import preprocessing
def number_encode_features(df):
    result = df.copy()
```

```
        encoders = {}
    for column in result.columns:
        if result.dtypes[column] == np.object:
            encoders[column] = preprocessing.
LabelEncoder()
            result[column] = encoders[column].fit_
transform(result[column].fillna("None"))
    return result, encoders
```

Process the data for the SageMaker xgboost model, which needs the target to be in the first column. Then, save the files to the data directory:

```
churn_train = pd.concat([churn_train["Exited"], churn_
train.drop(["Exited"], axis=1)], axis=1)
churn_train, _ = number_encode_features(churn_train)
churn_train.to_csv("data/train_churn.csv",
                index=False, header=False)


churn_test, _ = number_encode_features(churn_test)
churn_features = churn_test.drop(["Exited"], axis=1)
churn_target = churn_test["Exited"]
churn_features.to_csv("data/test_churn.csv",
                index=False, header=False)
```

Upload the newly created training and test files to S3 to prepare for model training:

```
from sagemaker.s3 import S3Uploader
from sagemaker.inputs import TrainingInput
train_uri = S3Uploader.upload("data/train_churn.csv",
"s3://{}/{}".format(bucket, prefix))
train_input = TrainingInput(train_uri, content_
type="csv")
test_uri = S3Uploader.upload("data/test_churn.csv",
"s3://{}/{}".format(bucket, prefix))
```

6. Kick off model training using the SageMaker xgboost container:

```
from sagemaker.image_uris import retrieve
from sagemaker.estimator import Estimator
container = retrieve("xgboost", region, version="1.2-1")
xgb = Estimator(container,role, instance_count=1,
```

```
                  instance_type="ml.m5.xlarge",
                  disable_profiler=True,
                  sagemaker_session=session,)
xgb.set_hyperparameters(max_depth=5, eta=0.2, gamma=4,
                        min_child_weight=6,
                        subsample=0.8,
                        objective="binary:logistic",
                        num_round=800,)
xgb.fit({"train": train_input}, logs=False)
```

7. Create a model from the training job to be used with SageMaker Clarify later:

```
model_name = "churn-clarify-model"
model = xgb.create_model(name=model_name)
container_def = model.prepare_container_def()
session.create_model(model_name, role, container_def)
```

8. Instantiate the Clarify processor for running bias detection and explainability:

```
from sagemaker import clarify
clarify_processor = clarify.SageMakerClarifyProcessor(
    role=role, instance_count=1,
    instance_type="ml.m5.xlarge",
    sagemaker_session=session)
```

9. Specify the data configuration. Here, we are using the training data and indicating the target column for the analysis:

```
bias_report_output_path = "s3://{}/{}/clarify-bias".
format(bucket, prefix)
bias_data_config = clarify.DataConfig(
    s3_data_input_path=train_uri,
    s3_output_path=bias_report_output_path,
    label="Exited",
    headers=churn_train.columns.to_list(),
    dataset_type="text/csv")
```

10. Specify the model configuration. A shadow endpoint will be created temporarily for the Clarify processing job:

```
model_config = clarify.ModelConfig(
    model_name=model_name,
    instance_type="ml.m5.xlarge",
    instance_count=1, accept_type="text/csv",
    content_type="text/csv",)
```

11. Specify the threshold. This is the threshold for labeling the prediction. Here, we are specifying that the label is 1 if the probability is 0.8. The default value is 0.5:

```
predictions_config = clarify.
ModelPredictedLabelConfig(probability_threshold=0.8)
```

12. Specify which feature we want to detect bias for using the `BiasConfig` object:

```
bias_config = clarify.BiasConfig(
    label_values_or_threshold=[1],
    facet_name="Gender",
    facet_values_or_threshold=[0])
```

13. Now, we are ready to run the Clarify bias detection job. You should see the job's status and bias analysis details in the output of the cell. The report provides various bias metrics for the `Gender` feature column against the `Exited` prediction target:

```
clarify_processor.run_bias(
    data_config=bias_data_config,
    bias_config=bias_config,
    model_config=model_config,
    model_predicted_label_config=predictions_config,
    pre_training_methods="all",
    post_training_methods="all")
```

This report is also available in the Studio console. You can navigate to the report by going to **SageMaker Components and Registries | Experiments and trials | Unassigned trial components**. Then, right-click on the latest **clarify-bias-XXXX** job and select **Open in trial details**. Finally, click on the **Bias report** tab to see the report.

Explaining feature importance for the trained model

Next, we will use SageMaker Clarify to help explain the model using feature importance. Specifically, SageMaker Clarify uses SHAP to explain the predictions. SHAP works by computing the contribution of each feature to the prediction.

We will continue to use the notebook we have created for bias detection:

1. Specify the SHAP configuration. Here, `number_samples` is the number of synthetic data points to be generated for computing the SHAP value, while `baseline` is the list of rows in the dataset for baseline calculation:

```
shap_config = clarify.SHAPConfig(
    baseline=[churn_features.iloc[0].values.tolist()],
    num_samples=15,
    agg_method="mean_abs",
    save_local_shap_values=True,)
```

2. Specify data configuration for the explainability job. Here, we must provide details such as the input training data and the output path for the report:

```
explainability_output_path = "s3://{}/{}/clarify-
explainability".format(bucket, prefix)
explainability_data_config = clarify.DataConfig(
    s3_data_input_path=train_uri,
    s3_output_path=explainability_output_path,
    label="Exited",
    headers=churn_train.columns.to_list(),
    dataset_type="text/csv")
```

3. Finally, we must run the job to generate the report. You will set the job's status and final report directly inside the notebook output cell. Here, Clarify computes the global feature importance, which means it takes all the inputs and their predictions into account to calculate the contribution for each feature:

```
clarify_processor.run_explainability(
    data_config=explainability_data_config,
    model_config=model_config,
    explainability_config=shap_config,)
```

The model explainability report is also directly accessible inside Studio UI. You can navigate to the report by going to **SageMaker Components and Registries | Experiments and trials | Unassigned trial components**. Then, right-click on the latest **clarify-explainability-XXXX** job and select **Open in trial details**. Finally, click on the **Model explainability** tab. In this example, you will see that age is the most important feature that influences predictions.

Training privacy-preserving models

In this last part of the hands-on lab, you will learn how to use differential privacy for privacy-preserving model training:

1. Create a new folder called `differential privacy` under the `chapter 11` folder. Download the notebook at `https://github.com/PacktPublishing/The-Machine-Learning-Solutions-Architect-Handbook/blob/main/Chapter11/churn_privacy.ipynb` and upload it to the newly created `differential privacy` folder.

2. Run all the cells in the notebook and take note of the training losses at the end. We are not going to explain all the details in this notebook as this notebook simply trains the simple neural network using the same churn dataset we have been using.

3. Now, we must modify this notebook to implement differential privacy model training using the PyTorch `opacus` package. You can also download the modified notebook from `https://github.com/PacktPublishing/The-Machine-Learning-Solutions-Architect-Handbook/blob/main/Chapter11/churn_privacy-modified.ipynb`.

4. Specify the parameters for the `opacus` package's `PrivacyEngine` object. Here, `noise_multiplier` is the ratio of the standard deviation of Gaussian noise to the sensitivity of the function to add noise to, while `max_per_sample_grad_norm` is the maximum norm value for gradients. Any value greater than this norm value will be clipped. The `sample_rate` value is used for figuring out how to build batches for training:

```
max_per_sample_grad_norm = 1.5
sample_rate = batch_size/len(train_ds)
noise_multiplier = 0.8
```

5. Next, we must wrap the privacy engine around the model and optimizer and kick off the training process:

```
from opacus import PrivacyEngine
net = get_CHURN_model()
optimizer = optim.Adam(net.parameters(),
                       weight_decay=0.0001, lr=0.003)
privacy_engine = PrivacyEngine(
    net,
    max_grad_norm=max_per_sample_grad_norm,
    noise_multiplier = noise_multiplier,
    sample_rate = sample_rate,
)
privacy_engine.attach(optimizer)
model = train(trainloader, net, optimizer, batch_size)
```

If you compare the training loss with the training losses you observed earlier without the privacy engine, you will notice some small degradations in the losses across all epochs.

6. Now, let's measure the potential privacy loss with this model:

```
epsilon, best_alpha = privacy_engine.get_privacy_spent()
epsilon, best_alpha = privacy_engine.get_privacy_spent()
print(f" ε={epsilon:.2f}, δ= {privacy_engine.target_
delta}")
```

You should see values for ε and δ. As we discussed earlier, ε is the privacy loss budget, which measures the probability that output can change by adding or removing one record from the training data. δ is the probability of failure that information is accidentally leaked.

Congratulations! You have successfully used SageMaker to detect data and model bias, explain feature importance for a model, and trained a model using differential privacy. All these capabilities are highly relevant for ML governance.

Summary

In this chapter, we covered the ML governance framework and some of its core components. Now, you should have a fundamental understanding of the model risk management framework and its processes and be able to describe the core requirements for implementing ML governance. You should also be able to identify some of the technology capabilities in AWS that support model risk management processes, such as bias detection and model drift detection. The lab section should have provided you with hands-on experience of using SageMaker to implement bias detection, model explainability, and privacy-preserving model training. In the next chapter, we are going to change gear a bit and talk about AI services, including how AI services should be used in combination with ML platforms to support different ML solutions.

12
Building ML Solutions with AWS AI Services

You have come a long way and we are getting close to the finishing line. Up to this point, we have mainly focused on the skills and technologies required to build and deploy ML models using open source technologies and managed ML platforms. To solve business problems with machine learning, however, you don't always have to build, train, and deploy your ML models from scratch. An alternative option is to use fully managed AI services. AI services are fully managed APIs or applications with pre-trained models that perform specific ML tasks, such as object detection or sentiment analysis. Some AI services also allow you to train custom models with your data for a defined ML task, such as document classification. AI services promise to enable organizations to build ML-enabled solutions without requiring strong ML competencies.

In this final chapter, we are going to switch gears and talk about several AWS AI services and where they can be used in business applications. Please note that the focus of this chapter will not be to deep dive into individual AI services, as that warrants dedicated books. Instead, we will focus on ML use cases that can be powered by AI services, and the architecture patterns that you can use to deploy these AI services. After reading this chapter, you should be able to identify some use cases where AI services can be a good fit and know where to find the additional resources to get a deeper understanding of these services. Specifically, we are going to cover the following topics:

- What are AI services?
- Overview of the AWS AI services
- Building intelligent solutions using AI services
- Designing an MLOps architecture for AI services
- Hands-on lab – running ML tasks with AI services

Technical requirements

You will continue to use our AWS environment for the hands-on portion of this book. The associated code samples can be found at `https://github.com/PacktPublishing/The-Machine-Learning-Solutions-Architect-Handbook/tree/main/Chapter12`.

What are AI services?

AI services are pre-built fully managed services that perform a particular set of ML tasks out of the box, such as facial analysis or text analysis. The primary target users for AI services are application developers who want to build AI applications without the need to build ML models from scratch. In contrast, the target audiences for ML platforms are data scientists and ML engineers, who need to go through the full ML life cycle to build and deploy ML models. For an organization, AI services mainly solve the following key challenges:

- **Lack of high-quality training data for ML model development**: To train high-quality models, you need a large amount of high-quality curated data. For many organizations, data poses many challenges in data sourcing, data engineering, and data labeling.

- **Lack of data science skills for building and deploying custom ML models**: Data science and ML engineering skills are scarce in the market and expensive to acquire.

- **Slow product time-to-market**: Building and deploying custom models and engineering infrastructure is time-consuming. This can be a hurdle for a quick time-to-market product delivery goal.

- **Undifferentiated ML capabilities**: Many ML problems can be solved using commodity ML capabilities that do not provide unique competitive advantages. Spending resources on building undifferentiated ML capabilities can be a waste of scarce resources.

- **System scalability challenge**: Managing scalable infrastructure to meet the dynamic market demands and growth is an engineering challenge.

While AI services can provide a cost-effective way for building ML-enabled products quickly, they do come with limitations. The main limitations are the lack of customization flexibility for specific functional and technical requirements. AI services usually focus on specific ML tasks with a predefined set of algorithms, so you usually don't have the flexibility to alter the functionality of the AI services. With AI services, you normally do not have access to the underlying models, thus limiting your ability to deploy the model elsewhere.

The number of offerings in AI services has grown extensively in recent years, and we expect this trend to continue at an accelerated pace. Next, we will talk about several AWS AI services.

Overview of AWS AI services

AWS provides AI services in multiple machine learning domains such as text and vision, as well as AI services for industrial use cases such as manufacturing anomaly detection and predictive maintenance. In this section, we will cover a subset of AWS AI services. The objective of this section will not be to deep dive into individual services, but rather make you aware of the fundamental capabilities offered by these AI services. This will let you know where and how these services can be integrated into your applications.

Amazon Comprehend

NLP has gained significant interest across different industries in solving a range of business problems, such as automatic document processing, text summarization, document understanding, and document management and retrieval. **Amazon Comprehend** is an AI service that can perform NLP analysis on unstructured text documents. At its core, Amazon Comprehend provides the following main capabilities:

- **Entity recognition**: Entities are the who, what, where, and when of text analytics. Entities can be the most important parts of a sentence as they identify the key components in a text. Examples of entities are proper nouns such as a person, place, or product. Entities can be used to create document search indexes and identify key information or relationships across documents.

  Comprehend provides APIs (for example, `DetectEntities`) for detecting entities with its built-in entity recognition models. It can detect entities such as people, places, organizations, and dates from the input text.

  You can also use Comprehend to train a custom entity recognizer for your custom entities if the built-in models do not meet your requirements. To train a custom entity recognizer, you can use the `CreateEntityRecognizer` API with your training data in the following two formats:

  - **Annotation**: You provide the locations of entities (beginning and end offsets of target characters) in a large number of documents, along with the entity type for each pair of offsets. This helps Comprehend train on both the entities and the context they are in.

  - **Entity list**: You provide a list of entities and their entity types in plaintext and Comprehend will train to detect these specific entities.

  You can evaluate the custom model using the metrics emitted by a Comprehend custom model training job. Example evaluation metrics include precision, recall, and F1 scores. Additional details on the evaluation metrics for Comprehend can be found at `https://docs.aws.amazon.com/comprehend/latest/dg/cer-metrics.html`.

  Once the model has been trained, you have the option to deploy the model behind a private prediction endpoint to serve predictions.

- **Sentiment analysis**: Comprehend can detect sentiment in text with its `DetectSentiment` API. Sentiment analysis is widely used in many business use cases, such as analyzing customers' sentiment in customer support calls or understanding customers' perceptions toward products and services in reviews.

- **Topic modeling**: Topic modeling has a wide range of uses, including document understanding, document categorization and organization, information retrieval, and content recommendation. Comprehend can discover common topics among documents with its `StartTopicsDetectionJob` API.

- **Language detection**: Comprehend can detect the dominant language that's used in the text with its `DetectDominantLanguage` API. This feature can help with use cases such as routing incoming customer support call to the right channel based on the language or classifying documents by different languages.

- **Syntax analysis**: Comprehend can perform **part-of-speech** (**POS**) analysis of sentences using its `DetectSyntax` API. Example POSes include nouns, pronouns, verbs, adverbs, conjunctions, and adjectives in a sentence. POS analysis can help with use cases such as checking for the correctness of syntax and grammar in written text.

- **Event detection**: Comprehend can detect a predefined list of financial events such as IPO, stock split, and bankruptcy. It also detects augments associated with events such as the person or company filing for bankruptcy. This relationship helps build a knowledge graph to help us understand the who-did-what for the different events. You can find a full list of event and augment types at `https://docs.aws.amazon.com/comprehend/latest/dg/cer-doc-class.html`.

- **Text classification**: You can train a custom text classifier using your training data with Comprehend. Comprehend lets you train multi-class and multi-label classifiers through its `CreateDocumentClassifier` API. Multi-class assigns a single label to a text, whereas multi-label assigns multiple labels to a text. To evaluate the performance of the custom classifier, Comprehend provides a list of metrics that includes accuracy, recall, and F1 score. You can find the full list of metrics at `https://docs.aws.amazon.com/comprehend/latest/dg/cer-doc-class.html`.

Comprehend APIs can be invoked using the `boto3` library and AWS **command-line interface** (**CLI**). You can find a full list of supported `boto3` methods for Comprehend at `https://boto3.amazonaws.com/v1/documentation/api/latest/reference/services/comprehend.html`. The following shows the Python syntax for invoking Comprehend's entity detection functionality:

```
import boto3client = boto3.client('comprehend')
response = client.detect_entities(Text='<input text>')
```

Amazon Comprehend can be a good fit for building intelligent document processing solutions and other NLP products. It can also serve as a good baseline tool that can be compared with custom NLP models.

Amazon Textract

Many business processes, such as loan application processing, expense processing, and medical claim processing, require extracting text and numbers from images and documents. Currently, many organizations largely handle these processes manually and the process can be highly time-consuming and slow.

Amazon Textract is an **optical character recognition** (**OCR**) AI service that's primarily used for extracting printed text, handwritten text, and numbers from images and PDF documents. Textract is normally used as a processing step for downstream tasks such as document analysis and data entries. The core Textract functionalities are as follows:

- **OCR**: OCR is a computer vision task that detects and extracts text data from PDF documents and images. The OCR component in Textract extracts raw text from the input documents and provides additional structural information about the documents. For example, the Textract output contains hierarchical structural relationships for the different objects in a document such as pages, paragraphs, sentences, and words. Textract also captures the positional information of the different objects in the input document. The hierarchical structural information and object positional data are useful when you're extracting specific information from different locations in the documents. The OCR APIs are `DetectDocumentText` for detecting text synchronously and `StartDocumentTextDetection` for detecting text asynchronously.

- **Table extraction**: Many documents contain tabular data structures and need to be processed as a table. For example, you might have an insurance claim document that contains a list of claim items and their details in different columns, and you may want to enter these claim items into a system. The table extraction component in Textract can extract tables and cells in the tables from a document. To use the table extraction feature, you can use the `AnalyzeDocument` API for synchronous operations and `StartDocumentAnalysis` for asynchronous operations.

- **Form extraction**: Documents such as paystubs and loan application forms contain many name-value pairs whose relationships need to be preserved when they're processed automatically. The form extraction component in Textract can detect these name-value pairs and their relationships for downstream processing, such as entering the names in those documents into a system. The form extraction component shares the same `AnalyzeDocument` and `StartDocumentAnalysis` APIs as the table extraction component.

The Textract APIs are supported in the `boto3` library. The following code sample shows how to detect text using the `boto3` library. The full list of Textract APIs for `boto3` can be found at `https://boto3.amazonaws.com/v1/documentation/api/latest/reference/services/textract.html`.

```
import boto3
client = boto3.client('textract')
response = client.detect_document_text(
        Document={
            'Bytes': b'bytes',
            'S3Object': {
                'Bucket': '<S3 bucket name>',
                'Name': '<name of the file>'}
})
```

Textract also integrates with the **Amazon Augmented AI (A2I)** service to enable human-in-the-loop workflow integration for reviewing low-confidence prediction results from Textract. You can find more information about the A2I service at `https://aws.amazon.com/augmented-ai`.

Amazon Rekognition

Amazon Rekognition is a video and image analysis AI service. It supports a range of use cases, such as metadata extraction from images and videos, content moderation, and security and surveillance. The core capabilities of Rekognition are as follows:

- **Label detection**: Label detection can be applied to use cases such as media metadata extraction for search and discovery, item identification and counting for insurance claim processing, and brand and logo detection.

   Rekognition can detect different objects, scenes, and activities in images and videos, and assign labels to them such as `soccer`, `outdoor`, and `playing soccer`. For the common objects that are detected, it also provides bounding boxes for the objects to indicate their specific positions in the image or videos. To use Rekognition for label detection, you can call the `DetectLabels` API.

   If Rekognition cannot detect specific objects in your images, you can also train a custom label detector with your training data using the `CreateProject` API. Once the model has been trained, you have the option to deploy a private prediction endpoint using the `StartProjectVersion` API.

- **Facial analysis and recognition**: Facial analysis and recognition are useful for use cases such as video surveillance and security, automatic people labeling in images and video for content search, and understanding demographics.

  Rekognition can identify and analyze faces in images and videos. For example, you can perform analysis on faces to detect gender, age, and sentiment. You can also build an index of faces and assign names to them. Rekognition can map a detected face to a face in the index if a match is found.

  The main APIs for facial analysis and recognition are `DetectFaces`, `SearchFaces`, `IndexFaces`, and `CompareFaces`.

- **Content moderation**: Rekognition has APIs (`StartContentModeration`) for detecting images and videos with explicit content and scenes, such as violence. Organizations can use this feature to filter out inappropriate and offensive content before making the content available to consumers.

- **Short text detection**: Rekognition can detect short text in images and provide the bounding boxes around the detected text using its `DetectText` and `StartTextDetection` APIs. This feature can be used to detect street names, the names of stores, and license plate numbers.

- **Personal protection equipment (PPE) detection**: Rekognition provides a built-in feature for detecting PPE in images and videos using the `DetectProtectiveEquipment` API. This feature can be used for automated PPE compliance monitoring.

- **Celebrity identification**: Rekognition also maintains a celebrity database that can be used for identifying known celebrities in images and videos. It has a list of APIs for this feature, including `RecognizeCelebrities` and `GetCelebrityInfo`.

You can use the `boto3` library to access the APIs. The following code snippet shows the syntax of using the label detection feature. The full list of supported `boto3` APIs for Rekognition can be found at `https://boto3.amazonaws.com/v1/documentation/api/latest/reference/services/rekognition.html`:

```
import boto3
client = boto3.client('rekognition')
response = client.detect_labels(
    Image={
        'Bytes': b'bytes',
        'S3Object': {
            'Bucket': '<S3 bucket name>',
```

```
                 'Name': '<file name>'
        }
    })
```

Rekognition also has native integration with Amazon Kinesis Video, a video stream service from AWS. You can build solutions to detect faces in real-time video streams.

Amazon Transcribe

Amazon Transcribe (Transcribe) is a speech-to-text AI service. It can be used to transcribe video and audio files and streams to text for a range of use cases, such as media content and meeting subtitling, call analytics, and converting medical conversations into electronic health records.

Amazon Transcribe supports both real-time transcription and batch transcription and has the following key capabilities:

- **Media transcription**: Transcribe has pre-trained models for converting media files or streams into text in different languages, such as English, Chinese, and Spanish. It also adds punctuation and capitalization to make the transcribed text more readable. To kick off transcription, you can use the `StartTranscriptionJob` and `StartMedicalTranscriptionJob` APIs for batch transcription, the `StartStreamingTranscription` API for streaming transcription, and the `StartMedicalStreamTranscription` API for streaming medical input.

- **Custom models**: You can provide your training data to train custom language models to increase the accuracy of the transcription for industry-specific terms or acronyms. The API for creating custom models is `CreateLanguageModel`.

- **Call analytics**: Transcribe provides building analytics capabilities for calls. The transcripts for calls are displayed in a turn-by-turn format. Some examples of supported analytics include sentiment analysis, call categorization, issue detection (the reason behind the call), and call characteristics (talk time, non-talk time, loudness, interruption). The API for starting a call analytics job is `StartCallAnalyticsJob`.

- **Redaction**: Transcribe can automatically mask or remove sensitive **personally identifiable information (PII)** data from the transcripts to preserve privacy. When transcribing with redaction, Transcribe replaces PII information with **[PII]** in the transcript. To enable redaction, you can configure the `ContentRedaction` parameter in the batch transcription jobs.

- **Subtitle**: Transcribe can generate out-of-the-box subtitle files in WebVTT and SubRip format to use as video subtitles. To enable subtitle file generation, you can configure the `Subtitles` parameter for the transcription job.

Transcribe has a set of APIs for these different operations. The following code sample shows how to use the `boto3` library to kick off a transcription job:

```
import boto3
transcribe_client = boto3.client('transcribe')
transcribe_job = transcribe_client.start_transcription_job(**job_args)
```

You can find the full list of `boto3` APIs for Transcribe at `https://boto3.amazonaws.com/v1/documentation/api/latest/reference/services/transcribe.html`.

Amazon Personalize

Personalized recommendations can help you optimize user engagement and revenues for many businesses such as e-commerce, financial product recommendation, and media content delivery. **Amazon Personalize** allows you to build personalized recommendation models using your data. You can use Personalize as the recommendation engine to power product and content recommendations based on individual tastes and behaviors. At a high level, the Personalize service provides the following three core functionalities:

- **User personalization**: Predicts the items a user will interact with or explore
- **Similar items**: Computes similar items based on the co-occurrence of items and item metadata
- **Personalized re-ranking**: Re-ranks the input list of items for a given user

Amazon Personalize does not provide pre-trained models for recommendations. Instead, you need to train custom models using your data with the built-in algorithms provided by Personalize. To train a personalized model, you need to provide three datasets:

- **Item dataset**: The item dataset contains the attributes of the items you want to recommend. This dataset helps Personalize learn about the contextual information about the items for better recommendations. This dataset is optional.

- **User dataset**: The user dataset contains attributes about the users. This allows Personalize to have a better representation of each user to provide highly personalized recommendations. This dataset is also optional.

- **User-item interaction dataset**: This is a required dataset, and it provides the historical interaction between users and items, such as viewing a movie or purchasing a product. Personalize uses this data to learn the behaviors of individual users toward different items to generate highly personalized recommendations.

To help understand how Personalize works, let's review some of the main Personalize concepts:

- **Dataset group**: Dataset group contains the related datasets (item, user, and interaction dataset) for model training.

- **Recipe**: A recipe is the ML algorithm that's used for model training. Personalize provides multiple recipes for the three main functionalities.

- **Solution**: A solution represents a trained Personalize model.

- **Campaign**: A Personalize campaign is a hosted endpoint for a trained Personalize model to handle recommendation and ranking requests.

To train and deploy a custom model using Personalize, you must follow these steps:

1. **Prepare and ingest the dataset**: In this step, you prepare the dataset in the required format, store it in S3, and then load the dataset into Personalize. There are three main API actions involved in this step – `CreateDatasetGroup`, `CreateDataset`, and `CreateDatasetImportJob`. `CreateDatasetGroup` creates an empty dataset group. `CreateDataset` adds datasets (for example, item dataset, user dataset, and interaction dataset) to a dataset group, and `CreateDatasetImportJob` kicks a data ingestion job to load data from S3 to the Personalize data repository for subsequent model training.

2. **Pick a recipe for model training**: In this step, you choose a recipe (ML algorithm) to use for the different model training processes. There are multiple recipe options available for user personalization, related items, and personalized ranking. You can use the `ListRecipes` API to get the full list of recipes.

3. **Create a solution**: In this step, you configure a solution with the dataset group and recipe for the model training job using the `CreateSolution` API. Then, you use the `CreateSolutionVersion` API to kick off the training job.

4. **Evaluate the model**: In this step, you evaluate the model metrics and determine if they meet the performance target. If they do not, then consider retraining the model using higher-quality and/or more data. Personalize outputs several evaluation metrics for the trained models, such as coverage, mean reciprocal rank, precision, and normalized discounted accumulative gain. You can find more details about these metrics at `https://docs.aws.amazon.com/personalize/latest/dg/working-with-training-metrics.html`. The performance metrics are available in the Personalize management console. You can also get the metrics programmatically using the `GetSolutionMetrics` API.

5. **Create a campaign**: In this final step, you deploy a solution (trained model) into the prediction endpoint so that you can use it in your applications. To do this, you can use the `CreateCampaign` API. You can provide additional configurations such as the **minimum provisioned transaction per second (minProvisionedTPS)** throughput, as well as item exploration configuration. Item exploration configuration allows Personalize to show a percentage of random items to users that are not based on user personalization. The idea is to let users explore items that they have not interacted with before to gauge interest. The item exploration configuration is only applicable for user personalization.

You can use the Personalize management console to build Personalize solutions and campaigns. Alternatively, you can use `boto3` to access the `personalize` API. The following code sample shows the Python syntax for creating a campaign. You can find the full list of `boto3` APIs for Personalize at `https://boto3.amazonaws.com/v1/documentation/api/latest/reference/services/personalize.html`:

```python
import boto3
client = boto3.client('personalize')
response = client.create_campaign(
    name='<name of the campaign>',
    solutionVersionArn='<AWS Arn to the solution>',
    minProvisionedTPS=<provisioned TPS>,
    campaignConfig={
        'itemExplorationConfig': {
            '<name of configuration>': '<value of
configuration>'
        }})
```

Personalize also provides several advanced functionalities, such as filters, which allow you to remove items from your list of items based on rules. You can also optimize the model training using a business objective such as customer loyalty. This feature allows you to give recommendations that optimize a certain business outcome.

Amazon Lex

Conversational agents have been broadly adopted across many different industries to improve the user engagement experience, such as self-service customer support and automating IT functions.

Amazon Lex (Lex) is a service for building conversational interfaces using voice and text. You can use Lex to build a virtual conversational agent to handle customer inquiries, automate IT functions through voice or text commands, or provide general information.

To help understand how Lex works, let's review some of the core Lex concepts:

- **Intent**: Intents are the desired actions, such as booking-a-hotel or get-banking-information.

- **Utterance**: Utterances are user inputs such as *I want to order a small coffee* or *I like to book a flight from New York to Beijing.*

- **Prompt**: A prompt is a mechanism to get users to provide the required information, such as *can you tell me which size of coffee you would like?*

- **Slots**: Slots are required inputs to complete a fulfillment. For example, to fulfill a coffee order, we will need the coffee's type and the size of the coffee.

- **Fulfillment**: Fulfillment is the mechanism to complete the action, such as getting the banking information a customer requested.

To use Amazon Lex, you must use the Amazon Lex management console or APIs to build a Lex bot. The building process involves the following main steps:

1. **Create an intent for the action to take**: The intent represents the main functionality of the Lex bot.

2. **Create several sample utterances for the intent**: The Lex bot will understand these utterances in spoken or text format to kick off an interactive session with the bot.

3. **Create slots**: This specifies the required information to collect from the users before the action can be completed.

4. **Provide a fulfillment hook**: This step connects an intent to a fulfillment function, such as a Lambda function, that performs custom logic or a built-in connector to an external service.

5. **Build the bot**: Build and test if the bot is working as expected using voice and text inputs.

6. **Deploy the bot**: Deploy the bot to a channel such as Slack or Facebook messenger. It also provides an API for programmatic integration.

Lex provides APIs for building and running these bots. You can find the full list of APIs at `https://boto3.amazonaws.com/v1/documentation/api/latest/reference/services/lexv2-models.html` and `https://boto3.amazonaws.com/v1/documentation/api/latest/reference/services/lexv2-runtime.html`.

Lex has a built-in monitoring functionality that you can use to monitor the status and health of the bot. Example monitoring metrics include request latency, missed utterances, and request counts.

Amazon Kendra

Amazon Kendra is a fully managed intelligent search service. It uses machine learning to understand your natural language requests and perform **natural language understanding** (NLU) on the target data sources to return the relevant information. Instead of searching for answers using keywords such as IT desk location and getting a list of documents containing these keywords, you can ask natural language questions such as *Where is the IT desk?* and get the location of the IT desk, such as *3rd floor, room 301.*

You can use Amazon Kendra to solve several use cases. For example, you can use it as part of a contact center workflow where customer agents can quickly find the most relevant information for customer requests. You can also use it within an enterprise for information discovery across different data sources to improve productivity. At a high level, Kendra has the following key functionalities:

- **Document reading understanding**: Kendra performs reading comprehension on the source document and returns the specific information requested by the user in their questions.

- **Frequently asked question (FAQ) matching**: If you provide a list of FAQs, Kendra can automatically match the questions to the answers in the list.

- **Document ranking**: Kendra can return a list of documents that contain the relevant information for the questions asked. To return the list in the order of semantic relevancies, Kendra uses ML to understand the semantic meaning of the documents.

To understand how Kendra works, let's review some of the key technical Amazon Kendra concepts:

- **Index**: An index provides search results for the documents and FAQ lists that it has indexed. Kendra generates indexes for documents and FAQ lists that allow them to be searched.

- **Documents**: Documents can be structured (FAQs) and unstructured (HTML, PDFs) and can be indexed by the Kendra index engine.

- **Data sources**: Data sources are locations where the documents are located. These can be S3 locations, Amazon RDS databases, and Google Workspaces drives, among others. Kendra has a list of built-in connectors for connecting to different data sources.

- **Queries**: Queries are used for getting results from indexes. Queries can be natural language containing criteria and filters.

- **Tags**: Tags are metadata that can be assigned to indexes, data sources, and FAQs.

There are two main steps in setting up Kendra to perform an intelligent search against your documents:

1. **Generate index**: The first step is to set up an index for your documents.

2. **Add documents to index**: Once the index has been created, you can add document sources to the index to be indexed.

Once the index has been created, you use the Kendra `query()` API to get responses for your index with queries. The following code snippet shows the Python syntax for querying an index:

```
kendra = boto3.client('kendra')
query = '${searchString}'
index_id = '${indexID}'
response=kendra.query(
QueryText = query, IndexId = index_id)
```

Kendra has built-in connectors for a range of data sources, so you don't have to build custom code to extract data from those sources. It also has native application integration with Amazon Lex, which allows Lex to send user queries directly to a Kendra index for fulfillment.

Evaluating AWS AI services for ML use cases

To determine if an AI service is a good fit for your use cases, you need to evaluate it across multiple dimensions:

- **Functional requirements**: Identify the functional requirements for your ML use cases and test whether the target AI services provide the features you are looking for. For example, Rekognition is a computer vision service, but it does not support all computer vision tasks. If you have an instance segmentation computer vision use case, you will have to build a model using an algorithm that supports it, such as Mask-RCNN.

- **Model performance against your data**: AWS AI services are trained with data sources to solve common use cases. To ensure the models perform well against your data, use your test dataset to evaluate the model metrics for your specific needs. If the pre-built models do not meet your performance target, then try the custom model building options if the services support it. If neither option works, then consider building custom models with your data.

- **API latency and throughput requirements**: Determine your latency and throughput requirements for your application and test the target AI service's API against your requirement. In general, AWS AI services are designed for low latency and high throughput. However, you might have use cases that require extremely low latency, such as computer vision tasks at the edge. If the AI services cannot meet your requirements, then consider building models and hosting them in the dedicated hosting infrastructure.

- **Security and integration requirements**: Determine your security and integration requirements and validate whether the AI services meet your requirements. For example, you might have custom requirements around authentication and might need to develop a custom integration architecture to enable support.

- **Model reproducibility requirements**: Since AI services manage the pre-trained models and machine learning algorithms for custom models, those models and algorithms can change over time. If you have strict reproducibility requirements, such as training a custom model using an old version of an algorithm for compliance reasons, then verify if the AI service provides such support before using it.

- **Cost**: Understand your usage pattern requirements and evaluate the cost of using the AI services. If the cost of developing and hosting a custom model is more cost-effective, and the operational overhead does not outweigh the cost benefits of a custom model, then consider the build-your-own option.

There are other considerations when it comes to adopting AI services, such as monitoring metrics, versioning the control of APIs for audit requirements, and data types and volume requirements.

Building intelligent solutions with AI services

AI services can be used for building different intelligent solutions. To determine if you can use an AI service for your use case, you must identify the business and ML requirements, then evaluate if an AI service offers the functional and non-functional capabilities you are looking for. In this section, we will present several business use cases and architecture patterns that incorporate AI services.

Automating loan document verification and data extraction

When we apply for a loan from a bank, we need to provide the bank with physical copies of documentation such as tax returns, pay stubs, bank statements, and photo IDs. Upon receiving those documents, the bank needs to verify these documents and enter the information from these documents into loan application systems for further processing. At the time of writing, many banks still perform this verification and data extraction process manually, which is time-consuming and error-prone.

To determine if you can use any AI services to solve your problem, you need to identify the ML problems to be solved. In this particular business workflow, we can identify the following ML problems:

- **Document classification**: Documentation classification is an ML task where the documents are classified into different types, such as driver's license, pay stubs, and bank statements. This process identifies the document types and ensures the required documents are received and can be further processed based on their types.

- **Data extraction**: Data extraction is the task of identifying the relevant information from the documents and extracting it. Examples of such information include customer names and addresses, income information, data of birth details, and bank balances.

As we have learned, these two tasks can be performed by the Comprehend and Textract AI services. The following diagram shows the architecture flow that incorporates these two services:

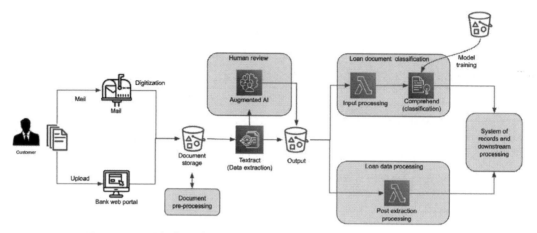

Figure 12.1 – The loan document verification and data extraction process

In this architecture, we use a combination of Textract, Comprehend, and Amazon Augmented AI services to support loan document classification and loan data processing flow.

Loan document classification workflow

First, we need to train a custom text classification model for classifying the text that appears in each type of document. Here, we will train a custom classification model using Comprehend. The training data for Comprehend's custom classifier consists of the necessary input text and labels. Note that Comprehend has limits on the input text size and the maximum number of classes, and this limit can change. Check out the official documentation for the latest limitation details. Once the model has been trained, you get a private API endpoint for the classifier.

Once the custom model has been trained and deployed, the main flow of the architecture is as follows:

1. **Data extraction**: Once the documents have been received and digitized as images or PDFs, Textract can be used to extract text, tabular data, and forms data from the documents. The output will be in JSON format and stored as files in S3.

2. **Human review**: To ensure the high accuracy of the extracted data by Textract, a human-in-the-loop process can be implemented to verify low confidence predictions and manually correct them. This human-in-the-loop workflow can be implemented using the Amazon Augmented AI service.

3. **Document classification**: The JSON outputs are processed to generate classification prediction using the custom Comprehend model that has been trained.

4. **Update downstream systems**: The prediction outputs are passed to downstream systems for further processing.

There are alternative architecture options available. For example, you can also treat documents as images and perform image classification using the Rekognition service. Another option is to train a custom model using your algorithms, such as LayoutLM, and prepare a training dataset with the output of Textract. It is prudent to validate multiple options to achieve the optimal price/performance trade-off when deciding on the right technology.

Loan data processing flow

The loan data processing flow is concerned with processing the JSON outputs from the data extraction process. The JSON document contains raw text and structure details for the entire document, and only a subset of text is needed for downstream processing and storage. The processing scripts can parse the documents using the structures in the JSON file to identify and extract the specific data points required. Then, it can input those data points into the downstream databases or systems.

Media processing and analysis workflow

The media and entertainment industry has accumulated a huge number of digital media assets over the years, and the growth of these new digital assets is accelerating. One key capability in digital assets management is search and discovery. This capability not only impacts the user experience but also the effective monetization of media content. To quickly surface the most relevant content, media companies need to enrich the content with metadata for indexing and searching.

In this particular business challenge, we can identify the following ML problems:

- **Speech-to-text transcription**: The audio portion of videos and audio files need to be transcribed into text transcripts. The transcripts can then be further analyzed for additional information.

- **Text NLP analysis**: NLP analysis such as entity extraction, sentiment analysis, and topic modeling can be performed on the transcripts.

- **Object/people/scene/activity detection**: Compute vision tasks can be performed on video frames and images to extract objects, people, scenes, and activities.

The following diagram shows an architecture that uses Transcribe, Comprehend, and Rekognition to perform the identified ML tasks:

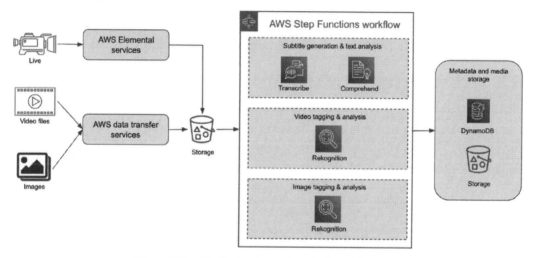

Figure 12.2 – Media tagging and analysis architecture

In this architecture, we build a pipeline for subtitle and text analysis of video content, video tagging and analysis, and image tagging and analysis.

For live video sources such as broadcasting, the AWS Elemental services can take live broadcasting streams, process them, and store them in S3. You can find more details about the Elemental services at https://aws.amazon.com/elemental-live/. Images and video file data sources can be ingested into S3 using a variety of different capabilities, including S3 APIs or higher-level services such as AWS Transfer for **Secure File Transfer Protocol (SFTP)**.

As there are multiple parallel processing streams in the pipeline, we can use AWS Step Functions to orchestrate the parallel execution of different streams. These can generate the following output streams:

- **Subtitle and text analysis stream**: This stream primarily uses the Amazon Transcribe and Amazon Comprehend AI services. Transcribe transcribes the audio portion of the videos and generates both subtitle files and regular transcripts. The regular transcripts are then used by Comprehend to run text analysis. Some example metadata that's extracted from this stream can include the entities of people and places, the language used, and sentiment for different sections of the transcripts.

- **Video tagging and analysis stream**: This stream identifies objects, scenes, activities, people, celebrities, and text with timestamps in the different video frames.

- **Image tagging and analysis stream**: This stream identifies objects, scenes, activities, celebrities, and text in different images.

The outputs from the media processing streams can be further processed and organized as useful metadata for the different media assets. Once this has been done, they are stored in a media metadata repository to support content search and discovery.

E-commerce product recommendation

Product recommendation is an important capability in e-commerce. It is a key enabler for increasing sales, improving engagement experience, and retaining customer loyalty.

In e-commerce product recommendation, multiple functional requirements can be framed as ML problems:

- **Recommendations based on customer behaviors and profiles**: ML algorithms can learn the intrinsic characteristics and purchasing patterns of customers from their past e-commerce interactions to predict the products they will like.

- **Ability to address recommendations of cold items (items without history)**: ML algorithms can explore customers' reactions toward cold items and adjust their recommendations to balance explore (recommending new items) and exploit (recommending known items).

- **Ability to recommend similar items**: ML algorithms can learn the intrinsic characteristics of products based on product attributes and collective interaction patterns from a group of customers to determine product similarity.

With these functional requirements in mind, the following architecture diagram illustrates an e-commerce architecture that uses Amazon Personalize as the recommendation engine:

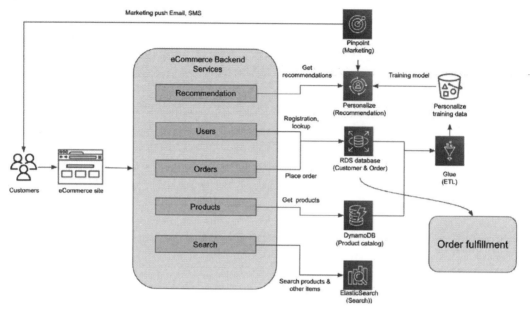

Figure 12.3 – e-commerce site and recommendation architecture

In this architecture, we use Personalize as the recommendation engine to power both the user online experience as well as the user target marketing experience.

The RDS database, DynamoDB, and ElasticSearch are the main data sources for item, user, and interaction data. Glue ETL jobs are used to transform the source data into the datasets required for Personalize solution building.

Once a Personalize solution has been evaluated to meet the desired criteria, it is deployed as a Personalize campaign to serve recommendation requests from customers visiting the e-commerce website.

Amazon Pinpoint is a managed target marketing service. You can use Pinpoint to manage user segmentation and send email and SMS marketing campaigns. In this architecture, the Pinpoint service gets a list of recommended products for a group of target customers and sends out email or SMS campaigns to these users with personalized recommendations.

Customer self-service automation with intelligent search

Good customer service boosts customer satisfaction and builds long-term customer loyalty. However, customer support is very labor-intensive and can result in poor customer satisfaction due to long waiting times and unknowledgeable support agents. The customer self-service capability has been widely adopted by organizations in different industries to deflect customer support call volumes and improve customer satisfaction.

In a customer self-service scenario, we can identify the following ML problems:

- **Automatic speech recognition** (**ASR**): This ML task recognizes human speech and converts it into text, and then uses NLU to understand the meaning of the text.

- **Natural language understanding** (**NLU**): NLU is a subfield of NLP, and it deals with intent understanding and reading comprehension. NLU focuses on the meaning and intent of the text. For example, if the text is *Can I get the cash balance in my savings account?*, then the intent here is *get account balance*. Another example of NLU is understanding the text and extracting specific information from it based on the semantic meaning of the question and the text.

- **Text to speech**: This ML task converts text into natural human voices.

The following diagram shows a sample architecture for implementing a self-service chat functionality for customers to look up customer-related details, as well as general information and FAQs:

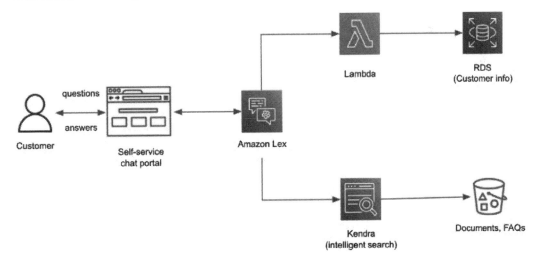

Figure 12.4 – Self-service chat portal with an intelligent virtual assistant

In this architecture, an Amazon Lex bot is used to provide the text-based conversational interface for customer engagement. The customer uses the self-service chat portal to initiate the conversation and the chat portal integrates with the Lex bots via the Lex API.

Lex bots support several different intents, such as *looking up account info*, *update customer profile*, and *How do I return a purchase?*.

Depending on the intent, the Lex bot will route the fulfillment requests to a different backend. For customer account-related inquiries, it will use a Lambda function for fulfillment. For information search-related questions, the Lex bot will send the query to a Kendra index for fulfillment.

Designing an MLOps architecture for AI services

Implementing custom AI service models requires a data engineering, model training, and model deployment pipeline. This process is similar to the process of building, training, and deploying models using an ML platform. As such, we can also adopt MLOps practice for AI services when running them at scale.

Fundamentally, MLOps for AI services intends to deliver similar benefits as MLOps for the ML platform, including process consistency, tooling reusability, reproducibility, delivery scalability, and auditability. Architecturally, we can implement a similar MLOps pattern for AI services.

AWS account setup strategy for AI services and MLOps

To isolate the different environments, we can adopt a multi-account strategy for configuring the MLOps environment for AI services. The following diagram illustrates a design pattern for a multi-account AWS environment. Depending on your organizational requirement for separation of duty and control, you may also consider consolidating these into fewer environments:

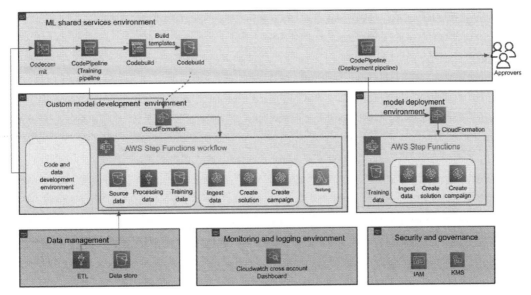

Figure 12.5 – MLOps architecture for AI services on AWS

In this multi-account AWS environment, developers use the custom model development environment to build and test the pipelines for data engineering, model training, and model deployment. When ready, the pipelines are promoted for formal model building and testing using production training data in the model development environment. Since trained AI services models cannot normally be exported, we will need to replicate the model training workflow in the production environment for model deployment.

The shared services environment hosts CI/CD tools such as AWS CodePipeline and AWS CodeBuild. You use the CI/CD tools to build different pipelines for data engineering, model building, and model deployment running in different environments. For example, a pipeline for the UAT environment could have the following components and steps:

- **CodePipeline definition**: This definition would have a CodeBuild step, a CloudFormation execution step, and a Step Functions workflow execution step.

- **CodeBuild step**: The CodeBuild step enriches the CloudFormation template with additional inputs needed to create a Step Functions workflow that orchestrates data engineering, dataset creation, data ingestion, model training, and model deployment.

- **CloudFormation execution step**: This step executes the CloudFormation template to create the Step Functions workflow.

- **Step Function workflow execution step**: This step kicks off the Step Function workflow to run the various steps, such as data engineering and model training, in the workflow. For example, if we build a Step Functions workflow for Personalize model training and deployment, the workflow will consist of six steps: create dataset group, create dataset, import dataset, create solution, create solution version, and create campaign.

In a multi-account environment, there could also be other purpose-built accounts for data management, monitoring, and security.

Code promotion across environments

Similar to the pattern we use for the ML platform, we can use a code repository as the mechanism to promote code to different environments. For example, during code development, a developer creates code artifacts such as data engineering scripts for Glue ETL jobs, CloudFormation template skeletons, and builds specification files for CodeBuild to run different commands. When it is ready to promote them for formal model building and testing, the developer checks the code into a release branch in the code repository. The code check-in event can trigger a CodePipeline job to run the CodeBuild step in the shared services and then run a Step Functions workflow step in the model development environment. When it is ready for production release, a deployment CodePipeline job can be triggered in the shared services environment to execute a CloudFormation template to deploy the model in the production environment.

Monitoring operational metrics for AI services

AI services emit operational statuses to CloudWatch. For example, Amazon Personalize sends metrics such as the number of successful recommendation calls or training job errors. Rekognition sends metrics such as successful request counts and response time. Alarms can be configured to send alerts when specified metrics meet a defined threshold. The following diagram shows a sample monitoring architecture for Amazon Personalize:

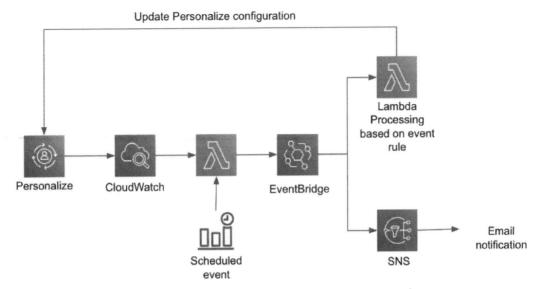

Figure 12.6 – Monitoring architecture for Amazon Personalize

With this monitoring architecture, CloudWatch collects metrics from the Personalize service. A scheduled CloudWatch event triggers a lambda function, which pulls a set of CloudWatch metrics and sends events to the EventBridge service. EventBridge rules can be configured to trigger lambda functions to update Personalize configuration, such as update `minProvisionedTPS` configuration for Personalize when throttling is detected or send an email notification when certain errors occur.

You can also adopt similar monitoring architecture patterns to other AI services, such as Comprehend and Rekognition.

Hands-on lab – running ML tasks using AI services

In this hands-on lab, you will perform a list of ML tasks using Rekognition, Comprehend, Textract, and Transcribe. Follow these steps to get started:

1. Launch the SageMaker Studio profile you created in *Chapter 8, Building a Data Science Environment Using AWS ML Services*. You will create and run new notebooks in this profile.

2. We need to provide the new notebooks with permission to access AI services. To do this, find the Studio execution role for the Studio environment and attach the `AdministratorAccess` IAM policy to it. We will use this policy for simplicity here. In a controlled environment, you would need to design a policy to provide the specific permissions needed to access different services.

3. Clone `https://github.com/PacktPublishing/The-Machine-Learning-Solutions-Architect-Handbook` into your Studio environment using the `git clone https://github.com/PacktPublishing/The-Machine-Learning-Solutions-Architect-Handbook` command if you have not already done so.

4. Run NLP tasks using Comprehend:

   A. Open the `comprehend.ipynb` notebook in the `Chapter12` directory. This notebook performs a list of ML tasks using Comprehend, including language detection, entities detection, sentiment detection, PII detection, key phrases detection, and syntax analysis.

   B. Create some sample text you would like to run NLP analysis on and save it as `comprehend_sample.txt` in the data directory.

   C. Run the following code in the notebook to import the library and set up the `boto3` client for Comprehend:

   ```
   from pprint import pprint
   import boto3 items_to_show = 10
   with open('data/comprehend_sample.txt') as sample_file:
       sample_text = sample_file.read()
   comprehend_client = boto3.client('comprehend')
   ```

   D. Run the following code in the notebook to detect the dominant language in the text:

   ```
   print("detecting dominant language")
   languages = comprehend_client.detect_dominant_language(
                   Text=sample_text)
   lang_code = languages['Languages'][0]['LanguageCode']
   pprint(lang_code)
   ```

   E. Run the following code in the notebook to detect entities:

   ```
   print("Detecting entities using the pre-trained model.")
   entities = comprehend_client.detect_entities(
   ```

```
                    Text=sample_text, LanguageCode=lang_code)
print(f"The first {items_to_show} are:")
pprint(entities['Entities'][:items_to_show])
```

F. Run the following code in the notebook to detect sentiment:

```
print("Detecting sentiment in text")
sentiment = comprehend_client.detect_sentiment(
                    Text=sample_text, LanguageCode=lang_code)
pprint(sentiment['Sentiment'])
pprint(sentiment['SentimentScore'])
```

G. Run the following code in the notebook to detect PII entities:

```
print("Detecting pii entities in text")
pii = comprehend_client.detect_pii_entities(
              Text=sample_text, LanguageCode=lang_code)
pprint(pii['Entities'][:items_to_show])
```

H. Run the following code in the notebook to detect key phrases:

```
print('Dectecting key phrases')
key_phrases = comprehend_client.detect_key_phrases(
                    Text=sample_text, LanguageCode=lang_code)
pprint(key_phrases['KeyPhrases'][:items_to_show])
```

I. Run the following code in the notebook to detect syntax:

```
print('Detecting syntax')
syntax = comprehend_client.detect_syntax(
                    Text=sample_text, LanguageCode=lang_code)
pprint(syntax['SyntaxTokens'][:items_to_show])
```

5. Run an audio transcription job using Transcribe:

A. Open the `transcribe.ipynb` notebook in the `Chapter12` directory. This notebook runs a transcription job using a sample audio file in the data directory.

B. Find a sample MP3 audio file that you would like to run transcription on and save it as `transcribe_sample.mp3` in the data directory.

C. Run the following code in the notebook to set up a `boto3` client for Transcribe:

```
from pprint import pprint
import boto3
import time
transcribe_client = boto3.client('transcribe')
s3_resource = boto3.resource('s3')
```

D. Run the following code in the notebook to create an S3 bucket for storing the audio file:

```
bucket_name = f'transcribe-bucket-{time.time_ns()}'
bucket = s3_resource.create_bucket(
        Bucket=bucket_name,
        CreateBucketConfiguration={
            'LocationConstraint': transcribe_client.meta.
region_name})
media_file_name = 'data/transcribe_sample.mp3'
media_object_key = 'transcribe_sample.mp3'
bucket.upload_file(media_file_name, media_object_key)
media_uri = f's3://{bucket.name}/{media_object_key}'
```

E. Run the following code in the notebook to kick off the transcription job:

```
job_name = f'transcribe_job_{time.time_ns()}'
media_format = 'mp3'
language_code = 'en-US'
job_args = {
            'TranscriptionJobName': job_name,
            'Media': {'MediaFileUri': media_uri},
            'MediaFormat': media_format,
            'LanguageCode': language_code}
transcribe_job = transcribe_client.start_transcription_
job(**job_args)
```

F. Navigate to the **Transcribe** console. Under the **Transcription Jobs** section, you will see the newly created transcription job.

G. Wait until the status changes to **Complete** and click on the job link; you will see the transcripts under the **Text** tab in the **transcription preview** section.

6. Run computer vision with Rekognition:

A. Open the `rekognition.ipynb` notebook in the `Chapter12` directory. This notebook runs a list of text extraction tasks, including text extraction, table extraction, and form extraction.

B. Save a sample image for analysis as `textract_sample.jpeg` in the `data` directory. Try to use a sample image with text, tables, and forms in it.

C. Run the following code in the notebook to set up a `boto3` client for Textract:

```
from pprint import pprint
import boto3
textract_client = boto3.client('textract')
```

D. Run the following code in the notebook to load the image:

```
document_file_name = 'data/textract_sample.png'
with open(document_file_name, 'rb') as document_file:
            document_bytes = document_file.read()
```

E. Run the following code in the notebook to detect tables and forms:

```
print('Detecting tables and forms')
feature_types = ['TABLES', 'FORMS']
tables_forms = textract_client.analyze_document(
        Document={'Bytes': document_bytes},
        FeatureTypes=feature_types)
blocks_to_show = 10
pprint(tables_forms['Blocks'][:blocks_to_show])
```

F. Run the following code in the notebook to detect text:

```
print('Detect text')
text = textract_client.detect_document_text(
        Document={'Bytes': document_bytes})
blocks_to_show = 20
pprint(text['Blocks'][:blocks_to_show])
```

7. Train a recommendation model using Personalize:

    A. Open the `personalize.ipynb` notebook in the `Chapter12` directory. This notebook trains a Personalize model for movie review recommendations using the movie lens dataset. It goes through the process of creating a dataset group/dataset, importing the data, building the solution, and creating a Personalize campaign.

    B. Follow the instructions in the notebook and run all the cells in sequence to complete all the steps.

Congratulations! You have successfully used several AWS AI services and their APIs. As you can see, it is quite straightforward to use AI services with pre-trained models to perform different ML tasks. Training a custom model using AI services involves some additional steps, but the underlying infrastructure and data science details are abstracted away to make it easy for non-data scientists to use these services as well.

Summary

In this chapter, we covered topics surrounding AI services. We went over a list of AWS AI services and where they can be used to build ML solutions. We also talked about adopting MLOps for AI services deployment. Now, you should have a good understanding of what AI services are and know that you don't need to always build custom models to solve ML problems. AI services provide you with a quick way to build AI-enabled applications when they are a good fit.

Hopefully, this book has provided you with a good view of what the ML solutions architecture is and how to apply the various data science knowledge and ML skills to the different ML tasks at hand, such as building an ML platform. It is exciting to be an ML solutions architect now, as you have a broad view of the ML landscape to help different organizations drive digital and business transformation across different industries.

So, what's next? AI/ML is a broad field with many sub-domains, so developing technical depth in all sub-domains would be challenging. If ML solutions architecture sounds interesting to you, you can focus on a couple of areas for your future learning while maintaining a broad understanding of the ML landscape. AI/ML is moving at an accelerated pace, so expect new and fast innovations and constant changes across the different disciplines.

Index

B

Packt.com

Subscribe to our online digital library for full access to over 7,000 books and videos, as well as industry leading tools to help you plan your personal development and advance your career. For more information, please visit our website.

Why subscribe?

- Spend less time learning and more time coding with practical eBooks and Videos from over 4,000 industry professionals

- Improve your learning with Skill Plans built especially for you

- Get a free eBook or video every month

- Fully searchable for easy access to vital information

- Copy and paste, print, and bookmark content

Did you know that Packt offers eBook versions of every book published, with PDF and ePub files available? You can upgrade to the eBook version at packt.com and as a print book customer, you are entitled to a discount on the eBook copy. Get in touch with us at customercare@packtpub.com for more details.

At www.packt.com, you can also read a collection of free technical articles, sign up for a range of free newsletters, and receive exclusive discounts and offers on Packt books and eBooks.

Other Books You May Enjoy

If you enjoyed this book, you may be interested in these other books by Packt:

Machine Learning with Amazon SageMaker Cookbook

Joshua Arvin Lat

ISBN: 9781800567030

- Train and deploy NLP, time series forecasting, and computer vision models to solve different business problems
- Push the limits of customization in SageMaker using custom container images
- Use AutoML capabilities with SageMaker Autopilot to create high-quality models
- Work with effective data analysis and preparation techniques
- Explore solutions for debugging and managing ML experiments and deployments

- Deal with bias detection and ML explainability requirements using SageMaker Clarify

- Automate intermediate and complex deployments and workflows using a variety of solutions

Amazon SageMaker Best Practices

Sireesha Muppala, Randy DeFauw, Shelbee Eigenbrode

ISBN: 9781801070522

- Perform data bias detection with AWS Data Wrangler and SageMaker Clarify

- Speed up data processing with SageMaker Feature Store

- Overcome labeling bias with SageMaker Ground Truth

- Improve training time with the monitoring and profiling capabilities of SageMaker Debugger

- Address the challenge of model deployment automation with CI/CD using the SageMaker model registry

- Explore SageMaker Neo for model optimization

- Implement data and model quality monitoring with Amazon Model Monitor

- Improve training time and reduce costs with SageMaker data and model parallelism

Packt is searching for authors like you

If you're interested in becoming an author for Packt, please visit `authors.packtpub.com` and apply today. We have worked with thousands of developers and tech professionals, just like you, to help them share their insight with the global tech community. You can make a general application, apply for a specific hot topic that we are recruiting an author for, or submit your own idea.

Share Your Thoughts

Now you've finished *The Machine Learning Solutions Architect Handbook*, we'd love to hear your thoughts! Scan the QR code below to go straight to the Amazon review page for this book and share your feedback or leave a review on the site that you purchased it from.

https://packt.link/r/1-801-07216-7

Your review is important to us and the tech community and will help us make sure we're delivering excellent quality content.

Made in the USA
Las Vegas, NV
30 March 2022

46553668R00243